Coloratura

Coloratura

By

MICHAEL GARADY

MIKO MIRACOLOSO LTD

167-169 Great Portland Street

London

Published by Miko Miracoloso LTD
Copyright © Michael Garady 2016
All rights reserved.

ISBN-13: 978-1533534033

Cover design by Michael Garady

ISBN-10: 1533534039

Dedication

This book is dedicated to the songstresses of yesterday, today and tomorrow, whose voices gave and shall continue to give such unalloyed pleasure with their singing. Here are some of them.

Ada, Adelaide, Adelina, Adina, Agnes, Aino, Alda, Alfreda, Alma, Aloysia, Amalia, Amelie, Amelita, Amy, Anetta, Angiolina, Anita, Anja, Anna, Anneliese, Anny, Astra, Astrid, Audrey, Augusta, Aurora, Ava, Barbara, Benedetta, Bernadette, Berta, Bettina, Beverly, Bianca, Bidu, Birgit, Blanche, Brigitte, Bronislava, Bruna, Carla, Carmen, Carolina, Carrie, Caterina, Cecilia, Celestina, Cesira, Cheryl, Christelis, Claire, Clara, Claudia, Cloe, Conchita, Constance, Cora, Core, Dela, Delia, Dora, Doris, Dorothy, Dusolina, Ebe, Edda, Edita, Edith, Editha, Edna, Eide, Eileen, Ekaterina, Eleanor, Eleanora, Elenor, Elfriede, Elisa, Elizabeth, Ellabelle, Ellen, Elly, Elsa, Elvira, Emma, Emmy, Erika, Erna, Ernestine, Essie, Estha, Esther, Etelka, Eugenia, Eva, Evelyn, Fanny, Fedora, Felice, Fiorenza, Florence, Frances, Francisca, Fritzi, Georgette, Geraldine, Germaine, Gertrude, Ghena, Gianna, Gina, Gita, Giuseppina, Gota, Grace, Graziella, Guidita, Guilietta, Gundula, Gwen, Gwyneth, Heather, Hedwig, Helen, Hermione, Herta, Hilde, Hulde, Huni, Idit, Ileana, Ilma, Ilonka, Ilse, Ina, Inez, Irene, Iris, Irmgard, Irra, Isobel, Janet, Janina, Janine, Jarmila, Jean, Jeanette, Jennie, Jennifer, Jenny, Jessica, Jessie, Jessye, Jo, Joan, Johanna, Josepha, Josephine, Joyce, Judith, Juilia, June, Karin, Katharina, Katherina, Katherine, Kathleen, Katia, Kerstin, Kiri,Kirsten, Lea, Lena, Leonie, Leonora, Leontyne, Lesley, Leyla, Licia, Lili, Lilian, Lily, Lina, Lisa, Ljuba, Lois, Lorna, Lotte, Lucette, Lucia, Lucianna, Lucine, Lucrezia, Lucy, Luisa, Lyuba, Mabel, Mado, Magda, Magdalena, Maggie, Malvina, Marcella, Margaret, Margareta, Marguerite, Maria, Marian, Marie, Marietta, Marilyn, Marion, Marjorie, Marta, Martha, Marthe, Martina, Mary, Maryetta, Mathilde, Mattiwilda, Medea, Melanie, Melitta, Mercedes, Meta, Michel, Mildred, Miliza, Milka, Mimi, Mina, Minnie, Mirella, Miriam, Mona, Montserrat, Muriel, Nadine, Nanny, Nell, Nellie, Nina, Ninon, Norma, Oda, Olive, Olympia, Onelia, Oralia, Orelia, Ottilie, Paola, Patrice, Patricia, Pauline, Pierrette, Pilar, Rae, Regina, Regine, Renata, Renate, Rene, Ria, Rina, Rise, Rita, Rosa, Rosalind, Rose, Roseanna, Rosetta, Rosina, Sabine, Salomea, Sara, Sari, Selma, Sena, Sigrid, Sofia, Solange, Stella, Susanna, Suzanne, Sybil, Sylvia, Tanya, Tatiana, Teresa, Thelma, Tiana, Toti, Una, Ursula, Vera, Victoria, Vina, Viorica, Vivienne, Wilhelmine, Wilma, Yma, Yvonne, Zara, Zelia, Zinka

Contents

Introduction

Allegro Con Spirito

It is not surprising that the writer shows such an incisive knowledge of singing, since by all accounts he himself possessed a prodigious boy soprano voice capable of the most unbelievable vocal feats of coloratura singing with an effortless range of over four octaves reaching to the highest note on the piano! Thus he shares with the boy in this book the trauma of his voice breaking, singing being at the centre of their lives.

Although woven around the singing voice, this story is related in such a way as to be easily understood by those who feign would know nothing about vocal art, but nonetheless may wish to know more, by way of examples, in this instance, just several musical works taken up by the female voice. Here the word 'woven' is a useful word in the context of the story since mention is made of a home-grown tapestry given the title of "Journey of the Spirit" by its amateur creator: The work, inspired by a series of celebrated paintings from 'the 16th century' implements real life characters, whilst seeking to ignore and omit the original all important centre piece, a crucifixion, as if in this section there exists no valid area for the subjects to inhabit. Within the actual story many of the characters are brought together by a mutual love of music. Amongst the examples are works by Bach, Purcell, Handel, Schubert, Mozart, Janacek and Mahler against a backdrop of nostalgia and a longing for the past. As such, emotions are shared and divided. Sometimes hopes dashed, despair and elation promoted, lives left in limbo till the final transfiguration; when 'all is fulfilled' and "everything is born anew forever and ever"'.

Peter Feuchtwanger

This book is published to coincide with the commemorative concert held at Leighton House Museum, Holland Park, London, 28th September 2016, to celebrate the life and work of the legendary composer, writer and teacher Peter Feuchtwanger, who's knowledge of singers and bel canto was a revelation.

Chapter One

COLORATURA

The Audition

At the turn of the century, the natural setting for the Conservatorium of Music had been chosen for its magnificent location in the Botanical Gardens, an expansive reserve positioned on a promontory with spectacular views overlooking and sweeping down to the harbour. The building lay nestled back amongst luxuriant variegated trees and shrubs, practically hidden from view as if prying eyes might disturb the music being created from within the hallowed walls. Many a student had entered its sacred portals to study and left after having accomplished their aims, some more successfully than others.

Four decades later, one of the two most highly esteemed voice teachers ensconced in the Conservatorium happened to be a petite German woman, Rosa Oppenheimer, who on special occasions, also made provision for piano tuition. A refugee from pre-war Germany, in her prime she had sung at the Berlin State Opera for a number of seasons until her singing career had been abruptly curtailed in the 30's when the Nazi's stormed to power.

One morning, from her studio window on the first floor of the Conservatorium, Rosa Oppenheimer gazes out at the immense oak standing in the grounds. Ever since she had arrived to teach at the Conservatorium, the ancient tree had held the woman in thrall and on countless occasions she noted the impressive trunk with its brass plaque fastened securely across its girth, bearing the inscription While I live I grow. Meticulous in every detail, mercurial of nature and sound of judgement, punctuality had served 'Madame O', the name she had become referred to at the Conservatorium over the years.

Having lost her entire family and almost every personal possession, she had made a singularly successful bid for freedom, never to return to the place of her birth, but this did not thwart her from yearning for those glorious days when each performance she took part in at the Berlin Staatsoper filled her with inspiration bordering upon ecstasy. Her recollections of the time were as yesterday, lodged in her sharply alert brain. Thus in a form of retrieval she conveniently swapped over the present for the past in order to journey back to the heady days of her teens when first she'd discovered that music was about to play the most significant role in her life.

The Oppenheimer clan had descended from a long line of journeymen, craftsmen, artists and musicians, so it had not been by mere chance that the girl entered into a sacrosanct artistic domain, earning for herself a reputation as a prodigious pianist even though her inclination at the time had been to become a veterinary surgeon. However, music gradually overtook that youthful desire, and finally, on discovering her singing voice, she had been admitted to the opera school, and soon afterwards was allotted some comprimario roles in leading performances at the State Opera House and accordingly went on to sing leading roles.

Throughout those early years, she possessed a fine serviceable soprano voice that could be wholly relied upon to give an above average professional performance. In this respect, she had achieved considerable renown in a variety of roles, more so probably due to her innate musicianship rather than for the actual quality of her clear, attractive voice. All this came to pass in 1938, when she became parted from her parents forever. The impact upon Rosa almost devoured her sanity. Not only did she temporarily lose her voice, but her hands became paralysed and it took a painful period of time before doctors could restore her health and even a modicum of well-being. For this, she had largely to thank Dr Alfred Hertz, who had travelled with her to the new land, both refugees in a foreign country. At last she found solace once more in music. Shortly after her arrival, in a tiny room overlooking the harbour, she accompanied herself on the piano and sang Mendelssohn's On Wings of Song, her hymn of thanks to the ever-present Alfred Hertz. At the same time, she set about writing, and later on had two books published (deservedly winning much acclaim), with the result the Conservatorium engaged her as Professor Emeritus of singing.

Today, Alfred Hertz is no more. World War Two had killed his spirit, and some say that he died of a broken heart. Rosa is again on her own but her students help to fractionally make up for past losses incurred. They are her family. The year is 1942 – as she browses through her lessons' appointments book laid before her on the windowsill she reflects upon this year's new batch of students, none of whom, she regrets have made any lasting impression upon her, so that at the back of her mind, somewhat guiltily, she harbours a secret penchant for that magical something that goes by no known name. The indescribable force, the ineffable that fills a vacant space with utmost grandeur. Nowadays she still retains an infallible musical ear, which in her past singing career personally had won for her much esteem over less musical singers with bigger and better voices. However, much of the spirit of that voice she had so carefully cultivated from her early years had 'stayed behind' in Europe, the desire to further vocalize dissipated, due to the hardships sustained and endured in times of loss and deprivation throughout the war years. Fortunately, with her vast musical knowledge and reputation, and her erudite publications on the singing voice, it had not posed a problem to gain her present highly prestigious key position at the Conservatorium. Notwithstanding, it came as a welcome reward to Rosa to know that she is wholeheartedly accepted and held in such respect and admiration by those of her newly found colleagues. After all, from Europe she had brought with her a valuable golden-age tradition of past splendours which she is more than willing to pass onto the other teachers at the Conservatorium, and, of course, to her students, some of whom could not always understand Madame O, especially when she demands they sing straightforwardly and withhold their passions to let the composer speak, rather than superimpose themselves in his place!

Somewhat fretfully this morning, Rosa Oppenheimer consults her wristwatch and for the third time in a few minutes, glances out through the open studio window.

"Two minutes late!" she notes with a twinge.

This morning she had made provision to arrive one hour ahead of schedule, in order to make ready to hear a boy who is being brought by his father. Madame O having pre-arranged with Austin, the caretaker, to expect both and open the entrance door an hour ahead of official opening time to let them in.

"It seems the more allowances one makes the less seriously one is taken." Rosa laments disdainfully, whilst nervously dusting and repetitively tidying up a shelf full of scores in her exaggeratedly fastidious atelier. Probably of all the studios in the conservatorium, hers is the best located, situated on the harbour side with the added advantage of northern light. Madame Oppenheimer stops short. The mind strays…

It is 1942, Midsummer Day. A breathless hush, buzzing with life and expectation, permeates the summer air. The sky a cloudless, clear azure blue. The air heavy, laden with the scent of Wisteria, Mimosa, Magnolia, Frangipani, Gardenia and Jasmine. From her first floor window, Rosealina feasts her eyes upon and celebrates the extravagant lush vegetation, alight with Flame and Jacaranda trees.

So completely different, this Southern Hemisphere, from the less exotic European flora and fauna she has experienced a few years back. In the distance, the near silence is invaded by a slender chorus of cicadas announcing their affilial preoccupation with shrill song, rapidly to be joined by more of their number increasing in volume, echoing forth to provide a deafening chorus to the bleating of offshore seagulls and numerous songbirds. To Madame O, this is a form of sheer rapture assailing her ears. Already an early sun relentlessly beats down upon the earth and promises to provide another swelteringly hot day, as usual with only the merest hint of a breeze. This is to be Madame O's fourth summer in succession in the new land. To her mind, a land where each season is both emphatic and demonstrative in its arrival, not slow and languorous, but sudden and dramatic. Whilst she feels the warmth of the outside air brush against her, for some unknown reason, a cold shudder momentarily overtakes her body and settles on her bare arms. She regards the calendar and makes a note of her daily schedule, starting each morning at sunrise, when she wakes, and proceeds to read the quotation under the date Tis Midsummer moon with you, you are stark mad. The calendar wording decries Madness is suffered by moon and summer heat. This then is the time when madness is at its height! True, she feels pleasantly delirious, she recalls Dryden's Amphitryon IV.

"What's this, Midsummer-moon? Is all the world gone a-madding?" she narrates.

A wonderful madness, after all, she is exhilarated with the heat of early morning. It is delightful to play the fool occasionally – Horace IV, Odes XII 28. Seize upon the pleasures of the present.

She sighs: Am I really 62? Where has the time flown? Self-convinced over the years that I had stopped ageing at 18 years old! It cannot be, this inexorable aging process. To think that one-day all this will be no more.

She gazes out from the open window, spellbound by nature's ability to mix colours in total harmony.

"Live while you live – Give to God each moment as it flies", she says and hums the words to her own dexterously improvised little tune. Her mother's doctrine on arising each morning to the newborn day. Aloysia Alice Oppenheimer, whose first love had been music, husband, daughter and animals, in that order.fffff

This morning, Madame O again reads the letter received from a Mr Gorrick, informing her that his son's voice is a miracle! She muses: Famous last words. It seems everyone has a unique son. Nevertheless, she remains intrigued. Out of curiosity, she intends to give the man the benefit of the doubt and has forfeited her one morning off to hear the 'miracle' and discuss, if necessary, the boy's future, if any. Next, she skims through the pages of her illustrated diary, a gift from a student. Stops at the St John the Baptist's Day, which the diary notes, describes his as the forerunner of Jesus, the Saint who had been sent to prepare the way of the Lord. Again, that odd cold shudder plays over her bare arms. Alone, she might be tempted to turn on the heater. In mid-summer? Madness indeed! Maybe she considers these cold shudders are due to her miniscule diet, which has remained unchanged since the beginning of the Second World War.

Often she promises herself: "I must attempt to stoke the body furnace." Yet, try as she may, over the years, rarely had she succeeded to gain body weight, nor, for that matter, increase her bodily intake of food. The trouble being, that gradually food, the least of her worries, held little or no interest for her, thus she continued to sustain herself on a microscopic vegetarian diet, alluding cynically to her personal frail, lightweight appearance as that of a "matchstick-thin veteran of past burdensome times."

Presently her mind wavers, her ears alerted outside to the crunch of gravel underfoot. Emerging through the foliage she sees a man and a boy, walking up the winding driveway.

"Ah! This must be they!" Madame O exhales another of her habitual fitful sighs, simultaneously patting into place her mousy brown hair, parted a little off centre and worn in a neat roll. As to her dress sense, this might best be described as a touch retrograde, still pre-war, in fact, orderly to the point of excess, similar to her overly tidy studio. Matching colour schemes and combinations chosen with a discerning artist's elaborate eye to perfection. Never one for discord, Rosa Oppenheimer prefers subtle shades of soft hued colours to primary ones, which she has never been tempted to choose.

From her window ledge, she observes the man, of all things, wears spats. In midsummer. Heaven forbid! A trifle eccentric, to say the least, but she had never had any truck with eccentricity. In fact, on second thoughts, she rather liked odd characteristics in an individual, especially when genuine. She wonders what else she may expect as she watches him waywardly veer from one side of the drive to the other, behaving as one might in the throes of vertigo. Next, caught in the glare of the sun, he stops to shade his eyes and regard the impressive old building looming before him. Behind the man, straggling a short distance away, the boy starts to slowly retreat in a manoeuvre calculated to take him back down the driveway, but the man, quick to notice, catches a firm hold of the boy's wrist, and proceeds to steer him towards the building, where, together, they disappear into the main entrance beneath Madame O's window.

Up on the first floor, Madame O purposely leaves her door slightly ajar, so that she might hear the two approaching and ascending the stone stairs leading to her studio. When she listens she hears the man's comments.

"This old place is deserted, Mark. We must be the only ones here at this time of the morning, except for the caretaker."

At that moment, they must have stopped on the stairs. Their footsteps on the stone no longer audible.

"Now remember, be warned, Marky, these people here are famous teachers, no doubt they want to hear you just as much as you want them to hear you sing, and if you disappoint them, you'll only disappoint yourself. Try not to be shy. I don't mean to say not to be yourself. That's commonsense, isn't it? I'll just take a peek at the minute hand on my watch. We are still a couple of minutes early according to my watch."

Madame O's brow crinkles. She too looks at her wristwatch and compares it to the wall clock. The same. That's why they are late, she thinks; the man's watch is slow. She is about to walk out onto the landing just as the man begins speaking again. Instead, she stops herself, conveniently satisfied that they and she are mutually preparing in advance for the other's arrival. Judging from the conversation, she surmises, it may prove quite a job to gain this adolescent's confidence, and precious time will be wasted. Again, she looks at the time – already five minutes late! Her eyes direct towards the framed motto on the studio wall - Punctuality is the Courtesy of Kings. She now turns the plaque so it conveniently faces the door they would walk through.

While she waits, Madame O reflects on the fact that rarely had she encountered the type of punctuality demanded of its resident artists by the despotic personnel of the Berlin State Opera. One simply had to arrive on the appointed stroke. Not a fraction before, or after. A difficult regime to follow! However, on these southern shores, where the sun melted the seasons so ravishingly into each other, one did not adhere regimentally to hard and fast rules. Although she herself had never quite accustomed herself to this somewhat casual attitude more in keeping with a tropical climate, just as she had never quite felt at ease swimming in the surf, allowing churning breakers to relentlessly crash over your body and toss you, helpless, headfirst into the foaming waves to send you with flaying arms and legs down upon the shingle. One thing in the new country she soon realised – is that hot climates produced an abundance of good, strong, healthy singing voices, as clear as crystal!

For a moment, she remains with her back to the window as she faces the door, adjusting her spectacles, having turned the tape recorder on in the ante room behind the curtain in readiness to record the audition for the purpose of her usual post-analysis of the singer's voice. An invaluable routine, which she had pursued throughout her teaching career.

As the man gives a slight cough in order to announce himself, Madame O, with customary goodwill and displaying a certain ambivalent charm, greets father and son, feigning not to reveal a frisson of indignation at their keeping the wrong time and noticing at once the young boy's extreme nervousness.

"Won't you both come in?" she requests cordially, a formal smile playing across her face. Immediately, her attention is drawn to the man, who exhibits a near pious air of humility: expectation permeating his whole being, as he bends slightly forward to extend a clumsy, strong hand, whose wrist reveals his shirt cuffs caught up under his well-worn coat sleeves, which appear ill-fittingly short. Real-life Millet rustics, Madame O decides impulsively, regarding the boy close on the heels of his father; an apprentice about to follow in the man's footsteps. Either to become a gardener, or a farmer perhaps.

The two stand at the door, not daring to move as if they hadn't heard a word of what Madame O had said. She waiting, then repeated "Do come in, sit down, won't you both? That's right," she beckons to the boy. "Just here." She motions towards two chairs so that neither could fail to notice her 'Punctuality' motto facing them, but any hope of them doing so is forestalled as they feel themselves plunged into an alien world that possibly only existed in the outer spheres of their imagination.

"It is very generous of you, Madame, to give the boy a whole morning, specially as you advised us it's your one free morning off during the week."

Madame O replies with little conviction in her voice.

"Oh, that's all right, Mr Gorrick. How could I resist? After all, your letter is not exactly the run of the mill type of thing one receives every day. Let's say your description sold me on the idea", she adds a little whimsically, with less formality.

Man and boy both appear positively overwhelmed by Madame O's amiable presence, whilst remaining wholly in awe of the interior décor, where numerous photos adorn every conceivable space. The boy gulps almost audibly in recognition as he sets about familiarising himself with photographs of famous singers.

"Madame Melba, Dad!" he gestures towards the portrait of the imperious Australian singer, nodding at another photo whilst brushing the back of his father's hand with his own to draw attention to more pictures.

"Did I hear rightly?" Madame O asks in a surprised tone of voice. "Fancy your young son knowing Marcella Sembrich!"

"I believe he knows every singer under the sun, Madame," he boasts, "Myself! I heard Melba in person, and saw Pavlova dance when I visited the city."

"Oh! You did? How I wish I had heard Melba, Mr Gorrick."

"Straight as a dye!" he comments. "Very memorable because the voice just flowed as though from a stone urn. Also heard Galli-Curci," he adds proudly.

Madame O appears entranced with the man's comments. As the boy's eyes, mesmerised, move around the gallery of celebrated faces, unawares, he automatically silently mouths the names of each and every singer and stops short at the charming black and white silhouettes with the singers' names and dates captioned underneath.

Josefa Hofer, later Weber, Luisa Aloysia Weber, Teresa Saporiti, Elizabeth Auguste Wendling, Katharina Cavalieri..."

"So this is our budding young singer. Has Marco prepared a song for me to hear?"

Mr Gorrick does not bother to correct her. He himself often refers to Mark by a number of names. Marco, Marcy, Marcus – just however the sentiment took him.

"Yes, this is my son," he declares, "but he hasn't prepared anything in particular. We didn't realise." he apologises. The boy turns his head completely away and feigns interest in the door behind him, biting his lip as he does so and clenching his finger nails deeply into the palms of his hands, all the while, not uttering a syllable!

"He hasn't prepared anything at all? Oh dear me!" she remarks fraughtly. "Well, he certainly recognises my gallery of singers. Very commendable! And I'll say this in his favour, none of my young adult students do," Madame O offers in a lack lustre tone of voice, evidently deployed to reveal her disappointment at her own students' indifference.

Gorrick makes no comment as he looks back at the boy whose face still remains turned away, while his father cranes his head to discern the effect on the boy at Madame O's comments, whilst happily noting an infinitesimal slight smile play over the young profile.

"It's usual when auditioning a singer that they come prepared," Madame O remarks stiffly. "But anyhow, Mr Gorrick, out of interest, tell me if I may be so presumptuous to ask, you mentioned you visited the city on occasion..."

"Miss... Mrs... Madame..." the man hesitates, suddenly not knowing quite how best to address the authoritative little woman with her very special, graceful air of refinement and appealing old world cultivation, not to mention a certain type grandeur, which he now foresees to be of a kind quite unfamiliar to him.

"My wife and I have only recently returned to live in the city where I was born. These last years we lived 'up the line' when Mark was born. It's very different here to the way of life we've been familiar with in the country, seeing our next door neighbours were stationed a couple of hundred miles away..." he pauses and grins boyishly, adding as an afterthought, "... as the crow flies," quietly stifling his smile and lowering his tone of voice embarrassingly at the same time as if he has second thoughts, has inadvertently spoken out of place, or has sounded too forward on first meeting.

Uncomfortably, he looks down at his manual worker's hands, hoping his hat gripped in them would help make them vanish. But, by then, Madame O, whose sharp powers of observation no one escapes, has noticed his hands and has already come to her own conclusions, just as she has done about the man himself. Such persons she refers to as 'rarities', 'artisan workers', whom she places on a very high pedestal indeed since, at a glance, she sees these types could neither be manoeuvred nor drawn into any form of bigotry or web of dishonesty. As honest as the day is long, she discerns, as she regards the man's humble and forthright demeanour.

"And do you miss the country?" she continues, no longer giving so much thought to the time of day or to the time expended on conversation of non-musical matters.

"In one way, yes. The landscape, the quietness. In another way, no. Everything circles around Marco. We've adapted to his needs. After all, he's the star of the 'County down' and his needs are ours. The city offers more in the way of what he is drawn to. You see, after school, he haunts the record shops. Nicholsons, Palings, J Stanley Johnsons, Edels, etc. He stands on the steps of the Town Hall on the off chance of catching even a glimpse of a visiting artist. So far, we've only dared take him to one major concert, owing to a slight mishap on the evening. Unfortunately, when the orchestra began to play Mendelssohn's Calm Sea and a Prosperous Voyage, the boy passed out and we had to carry him to the exit in front of everyone, and finally get him home by taxi. Very disturbing indeed. Emotionally, the music simply proved too much for him. He's been complaining to us ever since, how he missed the concert, haven't you, Mark?"

The boy squirms and suddenly turns and belligerently faces his father for an instant and offers him a disdainful, piercing glance for divulging his 'personal secrets'. Madame O notices.

"He's all right," his father adds fondly to help assuage the situation, looking from the boy to the woman, shaking the boy's shoulder a little too confidently so that the boy pulls away, evidently annoyed at his father's overly paternal show of affection.

Madame O looks on, remarking that she has not heard of such a thing because, quite beguiled by the story of Mark's impressionable reaction to the music and the concert, she has momentarily begun to recollect many personal musical events in her own life over the years which had remained stored away. For instance, the first time she had experienced the tragedy of Madame Butterfly in the Opera House and how, as a result, felt herself living the role for weeks after. As she remembers, she foresees only too clearly how father and son dutifully reflect upon and respond to each other's every move and finds herself increasingly appreciating their silently understood interaction with each other, noting from time to time too, how refreshing and unassuming appears the man's total dedication in regards to his son's voice at this first meeting with her. If only more people, in the presence of each other, answered to these two persons mode of mutual understanding, Madame O believes there'd be less worldly problems to deal with and everyone could get on with whatsoever they chose. War and political intrigues might well become things of the past. Creativity and Art, a source of universal rejoicing and sublimation.

As the man observes the dainty bird-like featured woman, he feels increasingly won over to her gracious manner. He cannot but admire the way she conducts herself. Similar, he imagines, to the way Royalty behaves. Come to think of it, Madame O exudes a quality not unlike that of Anna Pavlov, who, when he was a young man of twenty, he had chauffeured to and from her performances. In the back of her limousine, he had been expected to place her feet upon a small dais. His recollection of her sitting there surrounded by floral tributes from admirers was not one easily forgotten, and when she offered him tickets for her appearances, he had been completely won over, especially after seeing her dance the Dying Swan and the Butterfly, and other short pieces. These were eternal moments in his growing up period, which he believes influenced his general attitude to everything around him, and had resulted in an increasing sensitivity, which unknowingly he had passed down to his son.

This morning, Madame O has put Charles Gorrick at his ease by simply appearing to ignore the man's bewilderment. Instead, she evinces a genuinely keen interest in everything he says and that helps to divert his attention from his self-consciousness. She has also been swift to detect his youthful, guileless charm. Another facet of his personality she likes, has been due to the fact that he has not taken anything for granted. She approves of his quiet manners. A little carried away for a moment, she may even have forgotten what father and son were here for.

"But can you briefly tell me a little more about Mark?" she asks, glancing tactfully at the boy standing behind his father, reminding her of a young colt protecting itself from intrusive view.

"Well of course, Madame," Mr Gorrick came to the point. "Above all, he insists that he shall be a singer! Full stop!"

Again, Madame O gives a winning, though slightly enigmatic smile that somehow suits her ever-gracious mien. She looks towards the boy, this time a little more furtively, noting a flushed, fresh face, set off against the tousled, sun-bleached, blond hair and she perceives again the inordinately somewhat withdrawn, nervous manner that she half-suspects encapsulates a quite substantial, volatile temperament, even in one so young.

"Well, that's very nice!" she remarks, not meaning to sound condescending, "but is he not a little young to entertain such ambitions?"

"He is twelve," the father quickly retorts, as he feels the boy half-hidden behind him tug at his coat and whisper to him, and he quickly corrects himself, "Twelve and a half, actually!"

"Oh, I stand corrected. That was presumptuous of me." Madame O remarks: "Yes, of course, I can see. I thought he was younger. Twelve and a half is probably old enough to entertain such ideas. To my mind, youngsters always appear younger that their years. I remember at sixteen being taken for a ten year old."

The boy shuffles uneasily and stands that much closer to his father's side. He turns his head away from Madame O's view, glances quickly up at his father in order to display his irritation and impatience in view of the way the course of the conversation has taken, over the top of his head. His father, sensing the boy's displeasure with him, places a firm hand on his son's shoulder, perhaps to relax him a little and restore his confidence, but the boy winces and pulls tetchily away. However, in moments a graceful and serious expression rides over his immature features as he begins to hum softly on one note. His father thinks; not unlike an ill-tempered cat that has been over-patted and is marking time moments before it intends to vent its fury and let the unwary patter know its true feeling with a nasty scratch and a hiss. Next, the boy once more shyly turns from the woman's gaze and scans the other wall, whilst endeavouring to identify more singers he may have missed.

Madame O continues. "Yes. Should I care to think seriously upon the problem, Mr Gorrick, it may be a somewhat difficult proposition, and even rather meaningless at this early stage of Mark's life, to correctly ascertain his voice or, for that matter, decide where the voice eventually will go."

"I see," the man replies, slightly lost at the idea of the true value of any assessment made before the opportunity arose to pass viable judgement.

"Least of all myself," Madame O cajoles, interrupting the man's thoughts. "No one can predict what happens to the tender young voice after the onset of adolescence."

"Oh yes, I would agree. Well, more or less, that is," the man answers without projecting much conviction in his voice. By now, the boy's whole rigidly upheld body appears to contort and shiver, the same way one does when a sinister maverick thought overtakes the senses and for a moment fills one with ominous forebodings. His bare arms coming out in goose pimples in the overheated room, where the sun had infiltrated. Madame O takes a step closer and imagines that his teeth are chattering. Again, Gorrick firmly places a hand on the boy's shoulder. Madame O, stuck for words, begins to realise how difficult this prolonged experience is proving for the young boy. Truth to tell, an ordeal. So much more difficult for a twelve year old than for adults. Not that a highly nervous disposition cannot be a great asset, she reminds herself, but equally, she sees the boy has become progressively overwrought and excited. Now she wonders, after hearing about his dramatic experience at his first concert, had she not better see them another day when he and his father had time to reconcile more to the reality of what the future held in store for the boy's voice.

"So you see, Mr Gorrick, do you still wish to entertain ideas of a career before his voice has broken? Is that not putting the cart before the horse?"

"Madame, I mean, we just want you to hear him, come rain or shine," Gorrick begs. "The future may hold fears. We can cope with that. It's the present that means so much to us."

"Very well then, shall we make a start? I am afraid I am asking too many questions."

Mr Gorrick overlooks this last remark. "Yes. We'd be ever so grateful, Madame."

"Too much talking and not enough music. After all, that is what we are here for. Never mind anything else! In any case, I'm convinced Mark has a lovely voice," she acquiesces.

By now, Mark has given himself enough respite to breathe and dwell upon the magical surroundings of Madame O's studio, dedicated to singers and singing, not to mention the fact that he fully reckons himself to be in the presence of a famous singer herself. Rosa Oppenheimer, whose name increasingly spells out magic in his child's mind and fills him with rapture. The first 'great' singer he has ever met for any length of time and here he stands only a stone's throw away alongside her in the same room.

At this very moment, Mark's fantasy has passed beyond its peak, but first and foremost he must control his shaking, that presently begins to play and exert its power upon his whole equilibrium. He feels dizzy with elation that this 'famous singer' will actually consent to hear him! Here, in the Conservatorium! It's not possible. Only half an hour ago, he walked up the gravel driveway and wanted to run away, and now he stands amidst rare autographed photographs and the 'exciting woman' standing before him is none other, he presumes, than what is referred to as 'a pocket-sized prima donna'! She, who holds the key to everything. The mere mention of the Berlin State Opera earlier this morning sent him into paroxysms of excitement, made his head spin and float, his stomach heave. But Madame Oppenheimer will never be allowed to know this. The father still holds onto the boy's hand in a detached matter-of-fact way, failing to give a thought to the turmoil raging throughout his son's mind; not realising, that no matter what he did, he cannot control the boy's excitement. Charles Gorrick is tempted to elaborate, almost excuse the boy, by what next he says.

"It's like this, Madame. It's an impossibility for Mark to stop singing with his great gift. All day long, into the night if he could."

Madame O winces slightly and raises her eyebrows querulously at the mention of 'great gift'.

"Sometimes he imitates and accompanies a record of a great singer or sings, often as not, by himself. Whichever. His voice sounds... like..." Gorrick, stuck for words, hesitates. "Well, I might be... I could be wrong, but I know I'm not... Amazing. There! I've said it. But then you are the expert, Madame, and we are in your hands."

"Well, I must confess to being intrigued by your letter when you described Mark's voice as..."

Before she finishes, Gorrick coughs and splutters and assumes an almost accusing tone of voice as Madame O listens.

"Miraculous?"

She looks over at the callow youth, estimating him to be a healthy, nice looking boy with particularly beautiful eyes she perceives, but her expression remains quizzical since she finds it perplexing to imagine the 'great gift' supposedly harbouring inside that slight framework, especially since the possessor of this so-called 'great gift' is still just a mere fledgling. Having never been a parent, Madame opines, this exaggerated comment of his son's voice is, to be sure, no more than blind parental pride.

I suspect every parent probably thinks his offspring is the best, she secretly avows to herself.

"Yes, I'd best leave that decision to you, Madame," Gorrick adds tentatively.

Madame O doesn't hear this last remark, she being of a stubborn nature that invariably could not be swayed. To herself she teased, "A voice is a voice is a voice. Good, bad, indifferent. Can be compared to the human figure. They too come in all different sizes and depths, some excelling, some affecting, rarely both." She believes only in what she hears, not what others tell her. In fact, in the past she had frequently been disappointed by hearsay. With her expert ears, she usually can immediately detect a minor flaw in any voice, and likewise a talent, the singing voice being second nature to her. Indeed, her life's blood. Still, she is not entirely averse to boy's voices, she tries to convince herself, but some are husky and that she does not like. From the corner of his eye, Gorrick watches Madame O, who, as he notes, now appears in a thoughtful mood. He wonders if he has said something wrong to upset her.

No, truth to tell, she is contemplating at length upon boys' voices in general. Above all, if good enough, a boy's voice can work quite well, especially in certain religious works that do not demand too high a tessitura, some works of Bach, for example, Handel, Mozart's Ave Verum; these works suited novice voices where purity of tone is required. In this respect, Madame O can be won over to a particularly angelic quality, a characteristic of the "white" voice of pre-pubescence, sometimes referred to as the voix blanche. Normally though, she retains foremost preference for the fully-fledged mature adult voice. Especially that of the female voice, being her specialty.

"So now what is it to be?" Madame asks in a suitably business-like fashion. "In other words, what is our Mark going to sing?" she brusquely asks a second time, her German accent sending delicious shivers down Mark's spine. Silence. The boy looks to his father expectantly waiting for some form of affirmation, but in his mind, only thinking that before him stood a genuine pocket sized prima donna, just like those described in his collection of music magazines dealing with famous singers. He is thinking of the diminutive French coloratura Lily Pons.

Madame O waits and begins to vaguely wonder if there is any real sense or logic in today's audition, based on an over-enthusiastic father's letter. The fact is that Madame O is a descendant of a very different generation. Rampant emotions and sentiment were not for display purposes. Personal feelings were to be disciplined and kept within the bounds of reason and Madame O, being a strict adherent to reason, invariably does not permit her better-self to betray her innermost feelings, no matter how demanding or self-restricting. In her opinion, self-discipline is an essential requirement of her day-to-day existence, where temperaments are apt to fly amok and where it is preferable to lend a singer a shoulder to cry on.

Madame O regards the boy, who in his extreme shyness still feels hard pressed to acknowledge this dynamic little woman, whom he holds so much in awe. Madame O has not been accustomed to dealing with children.

"Do you read music, Marco?"

The father replies for him. "No, but he sings anything exactly after one hearing."

Madame O's face registers a touch of incredulity.

"Is that rare, Madame Oppenheimer?"

"Of course, very rare."

"Just about every operatic aria imaginable."

"Really! A natural musicality," she comments, yet inside she is thinking this whole scenario is not advancing far. A boy singing on hearsay? Operatic arias? She is not impressed, nor that convinced one way or another, rather, vaguely bemused if anything.

"Yes!" the father continues, determined to get his point across to Madame O, simultaneously experiencing a certain unreasonable futility. "Mark's taught himself."

"Yes of course!" Madame O ventures half-heartedly. Still, she concedes: "That is admirable, Mr Gorrick," adding surreptitiously with a sigh, "especially since he does not read music. Well, we shall endeavour to estimate his musicianship, shan't we?"

For a time, she ponders to herself on aspects of intonation and then returns to the leading question of arias. By such time, the boy appears extremely embarrassed and equally disparaged and vulnerable – a child marooned on an island of self-doubt. In other words, crestfallen. With two adults hovering over him, he directs another menacing look towards his father, whom he resents again, this time for divulging fast held secretive truths that only parents were entitled to know about their children. Madame O wonders whether the boy ever intended to speak for himself, let alone sing, or whether Mr Gorrick preferred always to speak for his son. If that were to be a problem, she anticipates, she would simply decide to cancel further appointments and thank them, and hope to see them perhaps in a year or two. Mark, disturbed now by what he saw as growing indifference to his personal plight, plucks up courage and briefly braces himself, showing the first signs of more level-headed determination; starts by clearing his throat, which rapidly develops into a violent coughing fit, that leaves him spluttering convulsively.

"What next?" Madame O thinks. "Midsummer's appropriate madness – St John, with his book showing the hallowed lamb, but that had been a week ago. My how the time flies. We live and learn."

"Here, wait, I shall fetch a tumbler of water." She disappears behind a curtain while Gorrick quietly counsels the boy.

33

"Mark, whatever is the matter? It's one thing after the other. I've never seen you quite like this. Get a hold of yourself and please loosen that tongue of yours."

The boy, near defeated, wipes a tear of frustration from his cheek, having learned in Madame O's absence to partly control the unnerving coughing fit. Madame O returns with water.

"Here, Mark!" She offers him the water. Eyes downwards, the boy swallows the draft in one gulp as Madame watches him unexpectedly afterwards open his mouth so wide, animal like, locking his jaw as if he were yawning which, in fact, he is not! Some sort of nervous boyish reflex action, Madame presumed, as she deduces 'a very large mouth on what she now deems to be a very strange boy indeed', as she becomes increasingly interested in all these mounting overtures to a non-singing event, and begins to attune herself to this morning's singularly peculiar circumstances. Just as she convinces herself they were getting nowhere fast, the boy blurts out in his high clear child's voice, as though uttering a cry for help, "Lucia!" Charles Gorrick intervenes demonstrably.

"What is that, Mark? Lucia?" and then announces proudly, "Ah, that's it, the boy wants to sing 'Lucia'."

"Lucia Luci. De Capua or De Curtiss. I can't remember which," Madame remarks.

"No. Donizetti's Lucia di Lammermoor, but he also knows the Italian song well from Beniamino Gigli's record."

"Yes, quite, the Gigli recording," Madame agrees unconvincingly, trying to recall in her mind when or where she'd last heard the song.

"I see," she answers, slightly disturbed by this outburst. "Lucia di Lammermoor." Mild shock is registering in the air around her. "Who of us would not have dearly loved to have sung such a rewarding role?" she romanticises. "Unfortunately I could not, much to my regret." She pauses. "The role didn't lay in the fat of the voice for me. But the boy would like to? I see, I see," as if her mind were elsewhere, her voice tapers off into a whisper as, without the aid of a music score, from memory Madame O sets about on the piano executing the magisterial orchestral introduction for harp and strings as she plays the opening bars of Lucia's first aria.

"Do you know, if one considers hugely gifted geniuses, such as Donizetti, already dead at fifty-one, having written sixty-seven or so operas, overtaken by mental illness like his heroine Lucia. It scarcely bears thinking of, don't you agree, Mr Gorrick?"

'Hugely gifted geniuses'; the phrases leap through Charles Gorrick's thoughts. Immediately, Mark comes to mind, and how after a single hearing the boy could sing anything he heard as though he were a re-incarnation, recollecting the past into the present.

"No, Madame!" Gorrick concurs, "It doesn't bear thinking about." Simultaneously, he addresses his son. "Does it Mark?" The boy patiently nods in agreement.

Madame O stops playing. Still thinking of Donizetti's early demise. Madame O shakes her head in disbelief, as if she had told herself something that she had never known before and proceeds to retrieve half-heartedly from a glass cabinet, the score of Lucia di Lammermoor, wondering just what she'd let herself in for today, opens it, and places it on the piano, cautiously muttering from time to time in German "Ungewöhnlich – Unusual."

She leafs through the pages until she arrives at Lucia's first aria in question. It is some time since she perused these same pages and tentatively she begins to play, simultaneously recalling her experience of the opera in Berlin. Her wonderfully pliable fingers barely brushing the keys, the sounds she produces, exquisite in the extreme. Not one harsh tone amongst them. The way she plays, the music may well have been composed by her favourite composer Mendelssohn, just as much as Donizetti – soft and languorous.

Madame O recollects how in her experience, many an excellent singer had gone towards their doom in this role, not least vocally in this daunting opening aria, which demands a quite exceptional carrying voice, and certainly not that of a boy. The boy, now deathly still, appears awestruck, and listens attentively as Madame progresses to the harp solo section so that the piano now indeed emulates the harp and string sections pizzicato, and when it comes to the turn of the voices of Lucia and her maid to enter, the boy declines to open his mouth. Madame stops and repeats the orchestral introduction and again the harp passage, waits, looks at him coaxingly – attempting to conceal her disappointment.

"Well, Marco!" and she endeavours to lead him with her voice at the opening recitative "Ancor non giunse" – Hath he forgotten me, this last phrase with its impending hint alluding to Mark.

"There, I've played the opening section, and now it's your turn. This is where you mean to sing, Marco", as she allows the music to unfold, herself becoming increasingly involved with the melody and perhaps a little less with Mark so that she does not pay so much attention to him.

"What a lovely invention!" she exclaims as she rediscovers new musical points of interest in the lilting music. "Won't you join me, my dear?" she suggests temptingly.

As best he can, Charles Gorrick sits, willing his son to begin, but the boy remains mute, helplessly tongue-tied, longing and exasperation registering in his bright blue eyes.

Madame O calls, "If you can't sing the words, Mark, I won't mind at all if you prefer to make up the sounds best-suited to your voice!"

Soon, Madame O may be forgiven for believing the whole situation has taken on 'farcical' proportions, as she reflects upon a boy planning to sing one of opera's most difficult coloratura parts.

"Very well, Mr Asquith, we shall wait and see!" she tells herself, sardonically. How much longer the boy would remain voiceless, Madame O theorises, shall be down to an act of providence. Still, she thinks such events have their good side, tend to bring one back to one's senses, in fact, prove we are not always riding on the crest of the wave, duped by hearsay. Sometimes we are dumped headlong into the surf breakers and as such, must seek to regain our composure through other different means available at the time. It goes without saying we have little choice but to carry on persevering!

From time to time, the only element to remind her of the boy's presence is his intermittent coughing. A difficult boy, no doubt, she contends. A very difficult boy. Perhaps she feels herself to blame for being altogether too forthcoming and brusque in manner to deal with his highly-strung constitution. As a last resort, it occurs to her to deploy yet another tactic. She sets about coaxingly, softening her own speaking voice to a mere thread of tone as if she is making a Morendo, a favourite vocal effect.

"Mark," she appeals, "may I at least just once hear the sound of your voice in order to obtain the merest idea for your future singing career so that both your father here, and yourself and myself of course, have a fuller indication of what the future holds in store? A simple ballad perhaps?"

By now, the boy struggles with his anxiety and longing. Regarding the piano ruefully, not once apparently acknowledging Madame O's suggestions, still his mouth refuses to open and obey him, so Madame O refrains from saying more and remains seated, patiently exploring the music score of Lucia, whilst trying to decide an alternative for the boy to sing. She turns the pages back and forth until she returns to the main section of the first recitative and cavatina, Regnava nel silenzio – the silence all lay slumbering, the first part of which she announces "is not so difficult at all", knowing full well in herself it is actually what the aria works up to that finally takes the singer to task.

"Alas, Marco, those days are over when I could have vocally demonstrated to you what I mean."

This last comment suddenly arouses and wins the boy's sympathy so that he imagines how terrible it would be for a singer to lose their voice. Madame O continues. "How about if I try to sing the part of Alisa, Lucia's companion's opening section? Mark? I think I could even tackle a few bars for you" she says as she begins to read out phonetically the words and then sing them to her own accompaniment.

"In-cau-ta! A che mi trag-gi! Av-ven-tu-rar-ti or che il fra-tel qui venne, è fo-lle ar-dir- Imprudent to ask him hither – think of my brother – What if he should discover – thou sought his foe?"

"Sing it for me," Madame O asks the boy. Mark's mind diverts momentarily as her words recall for him Beniamino Gigli singing the Neapolitan song "Cante per me".

"Sing it to me, just to refresh my memory", Madame O again requests the boy in a dissolute tone of voice, but her plea falls on deaf ears. The boy's father pensively looks on, unable to assist, thinking, by Jimminy this is a hard act to follow. He glimpses the clock on the wall ticking away the precious minutes, leaving Madame O to explain to herself why this increasingly curious situation verges towards the absurd. Still, she remains determined to win over the boy's sympathy and deal with the nervous state that so obstructs his ability to properly vocalise.

"I know then!" she confides tactfully. "How about, as an alternative, some simple scales to go on with, Marco? Look here – I think I have the solution.

At once, perceiving the boy's lessening discomfort, she strikes the notes C, d, E, F, G on the piano. The idea works. The boy plucks up courage as if no longer able to resist the temptation and his voice softly begins to follow Madame O on the piano. However, suddenly from his throat ushers the most appalling, errant squawk, enough to scare off a flock of peacocks. Mark's shocked father looks on helplessly whilst Madame stops in her tracks; a pained expression on her already strained features. Notwithstanding, the boy's face registers utter misery. Even so, Madame O, in embarrassment, manages to project a mock smile to soften his anguish. What follows next owes itself to one of those unmitigated events that are apt to occur in times of mental duress, such as funerals and weddings. The boy's father, knowing in advance the embarrassing consequences his own actions are about to make, cannot stifle a loud chuckle, signalling chortles from Madame O herself, until, the small room resounded with laughter.

The boy desperately looks askance, firstly at one, then the other, before realising the effect he has caused, and in no time at all, he too joins in unrestrainedly until his stomach's muscles ache and cramp and tears mingle with frustration well up in his eyes. Just as suddenly, all is silent until Madame O's genius for innovation comes into its own. In her hand, she takes a tuning fork, braces herself, exercising an excessively straight-faced school-marmish attitude, deliberately tapping authoritatively whilst announcing "Time, gentlemen, please!" which causes grins all around. Gorrick can't resist an extra salacious jibe "I didn't know we had a crow in our midst chasing a peacock!" It takes some little time for the three people in the room to regain their composure and Madame O has little or no idea what to expect next.

"Well then, gentlemen, am I to take it we are at last ready to commence after that somewhat unconventional, rather unpropitious false start?"

She directs a knowing glance in Mark's direction, and notes his more relaxed state; a slight grin appearing and remaining on his lightly tanned complexion. Madame O gloats upon the fact that the unpredictable, brief interlude has helped rid the boy of his nervousness. Mark nods back at her, glad to find his nerves increasingly held at bay, signalling Madame O to play the same four ascending notes from middle C, one after the other. Meanwhile, Gorrick briefly interrupts to add, "He does have a slight cold!" Nevertheless, the boy now in all seriousness, obediently follows the piano. The surprising ordinariness of the sounds he produces at this stage are both lacklustre and wholly unmemorable, yet Charles Gorrick can thank his lucky stars that the boy has loosened up and at last made a start.

Madame O looks straight ahead impersonally, her ears attuned to every nuance, then ventures, "Again, Marco?" and the boy sings the same four notes even more lifelessly. Gorrick tries to catch his son's attention but Mark's eyes, flickering strangely, look ceiling-wards, as though glaring arc lights are being shone into them, whilst he wilfully concentrates to centre his voice in an effort to desperately improve upon the shoddy notes already emitted from his throat.

"He's holding back, alright," Charles Gorrick silently and impatiently tells himself. "In fact, it doesn't remotely sound like his voice. The scamp! Woe is me!" he still silently muses. Not unlike Madame O, he also wonders where on earth all this will lead to, before quietly commenting "Why Madame, had I not known Mark's voice back to front, I'd swear it wasn't his," hoping his remark may buck the boy up into remedying the problem, whilst simultaneously thinking, "What am I supposed to do to get him going and shake that stubborn voice out of him!" He smiles frustratedly to himself as Mark steals a cautious glance in his direction. The boy probably takes the smile on his father's face to be a mark of approval, but this time, he wouldn't have guessed that going on in his father's head, the man is willing his unresponsive son to stop playing the ass. After all, they'd come to the Conservatorium to impress this 'great' woman and seek her valuable advice, not exhaust her with nonsensical preliminaries. Ideally, Mark's father would liked to have demanded aloud "Let's have a foretaste of your true voice, get it out of your system, Marco!"

Just then, one or two pleasantly bell-like sounds ring forth, enough for Gorrick to prick up his ears. A recognisable Mark note! Now, at least he anticipates, the boy would slowly come into his own. The fact being today Mark's ultra-sensitivity needs to be coaxed no end before he would finally find his 'wings', so to speak, but so far not nearly enough to make the slightest impact upon the supposedly foremost acute musical ear in the country, who as is well known, could usually within mini-seconds discover the vocal rights and wrongs in a singer.

Still Mark inclines to hold back that little extra, until Madame O enjoins tersely although this time, with more ring and vigour in her voice.

"There's nothing to be embarrassed about, Marco, I'm not here to judge, only to listen," she endorses soothingly in yet another patient endeavour to assuage whatever prevaricating fears the boy upholds.

His father remarks "On one condition, Madame, that he makes no more squawks!"

The boy stifles a grin and manages to further relax. Fully aware, Gorrick realises now that a certain amount of reassurance stands to free his son's voice of inhibitions, and as such, he is ready with any form of encouragement he feels fit to deal forth. Gorrick waits with bated breath. His last remark has succeeded to impulsively provoke the boy into singing an extra, mezza voce, half octave above the last scale. Madame O turns around and comments diffidently,

"Good! Charming sound, Mark! So is that about your range? Middle C to high C? A very pleasing top C indeed!"

The boy twitches but does not reply. Instead, he looks vacantly towards his father for a response to Madame O's question.

"Never!" Gorrick, not one to usually boast, speaks up for him. "Without sounding too over the top, Madame, might I say that's scarcely even the beginning of my son's voice."

Madame O smiles in return to his boast, the type of smile one might predict from a highly knowledgeable professor to put an over-confident student in his place.

"Mr Gorrick, please do not think for one minute I intend to belittle you or the boy. On the contrary, that is about the range one would expect of a good boy's treble."

Gorrick is beginning to lose faith in Madame O's musical acumen and explanations regarding voices. Likewise, she is prematurely convinced there is nothing remotely miraculous about the boy's voice.

"I should like to hear him sing preferably something simple – not too ambitious, not the Lucia aria," she advises tamely.

Charles Gorrick's mind wearily journeys off at a tangent, something difficult would be more in keeping he told himself, nevertheless, he answers "All right, Madame, something simple it shall be. Mark, how about The Last Rose of Summer?"

Madame O motions to the boy. "Perfect choice. Oh yes," she enthuses, "I should dearly love you to sing that song. Of course, you know, it's pure Bel Canto. After all, this lovely old song did not escape the attentions of no less a composer than Friedrich Von Flotow, when he implemented it into his opera Martha, nor Donizetti in Anna Bolenas mad scene, but it shouldn't be too much of a strain on your voice, Mark?"

Although he only has himself to blame, the boy displays an unintentional, sickly, defeated smile, suppressed and peeved that he had not been asked to start with something more stirring, such as the Polacca from I Puritani or La Sonnambula, either of which would set his mind apace, and make him forget himself and carry him to far off lands and places – the Dresden State Opera, La Scala, The Royal Opera House, Covent Garden, allow him to let loose with some vocal fireworks, but Madame O is determined to have her say and hear the song and she makes no bones about it. So, when she begins to play the Thomas Moore masterpiece from memory, Mark enters and sings at exactly the correct moment. Madame O breaths a sigh of pleasure and, at the end of the song, remains with her eyes closed, lost in reverie of a kind.

"What can one say!" Madame O exclaims convincingly. "In fact, sung that way with simplicity, I could hear it over and over again."

She turns to Gorrick, who is agog to hear more compliments. Instead, Madame diverts, "Do you know I have a problem with all my singers on the question of simplicity. It's an ongoing problem. For instance, I recall just yesterday, an impossibly over-laden Mozart aria! Simplicity is by far and above the most difficult attainment in art. The singer either puts too much of themselves into a song or aria or too much of something else, whatever that may be. It's beyond me."

She shakes her head and goes even further, as if addressing herself. "Does Mark know the song well?"

"What a question?" Gorrick reflects, inwardly subduing his frustration at a remark he deems fatuous. "Quite well, Madame," he replies, dejected in one respect – that Madame seems to be going around in circles.

"Mmm!" she concurs. "Very rewarding! Oh, and I must say this, Mr Gorrick, before we continue. His voice has rather unusual clarity, in fact, a near unnatural clarity! Very appealing, especially as boys' voices are often husky."

Charles Gorrick is already fully aware of what are to him, minor, obvious, rather than profound observations of Marks' voice. As for Mark, he is not listening at all. His eyes have settled upon a sepia photograph of Melba as 'Lucia', signed and dated 1910. He bides his time, patiently waiting to be asked to continue. However, his glances at Melba's photo do not miss Madame O's attention as she continues with her assessment of his voice, repeating "A quite unnatural clarity!"

Gorrick toys with the comment, automatically repeating after her somewhat unenthusiastically and mechanically "Yes, Madame, a quite unnatural clarity!" under his breath, thinking to himself, "The most unnatural natural voice ever." If only

Madame cared to pay more attention since above all, he finds the word 'perfection' blatantly absent from her remarks of his son's voice.

"As I was saying only yesterday," Madame O digresses, "a pupil of mine who prides herself on being a Mozartian, attempted a hugely difficult coloratura aria, K419, (Mark's ears prick at the mere mention of 'hugely difficult'), but simplicity eluded her, and for the life of me, I could not convince the poor girl otherwise. Of course, she sang the piece with lashings of fervour and temperament, but that is not enough! In any case, I am not overly given to dramatics, at least where the singing voice is concerned. It can, of course, harm the vocal cords and hence the production of the voice, and eventually lead to utter ruin as was the case of Malibran, dead at 28, and Pasta, whose career lasted only 10 years."

Gorrick, somewhat at a loss for words, stands by mutely listening with mounting frustration, impatient to have Madame's more definite views on Mark's voice and no other singers. Naturally biased, he keeps wondering why Madame O diverts and digresses onto the subject of a pupil of hers who sang a Mozart aria! What has that to do with Mark? Crickey! By now, Mark could have 'strutted his stuff', that is, had the boy helped too and only given himself ample opportunity and not forestalled so much.

Madame O continues. "And why do I tell you his, Mr Gorrick? Because unlike that particular pupil of mine, this boy of yours possesses 'simplicity' in droves, and I dearly hope he won't ever lose it when he grows up."

Charles Gorrick replies in a conciliatory tone of voice. "I am sure he won't Madame," feeling himself and the boy at last slightly redeemed – at least for the time being. "Oh, by the way, Madame, may we enquire the name of the Mozart aria?"

"Of course, the title is No, no, che non ne sei capace, K419. Mozart inserted the aria into Pasquale Anfossi's opera Il Curioso Indiscreto, composed in Paris in 1777."

"And you say the aria is difficult?"

"Extremely so," Madame O replies.

"And where can we hear it for ourselves?"

"Why do you ask, Mr Gorrick?"

"So we can buy a record."

"Oh, no, there is no available recording, though somewhere tucked away I believe I have an old acoustic recording I could let you hear one day, sung by a German colleague of mine and dating back to the early part of the century, Hedwig Francillo Kaufmann. Hedwig, if I remember rightly, was born in 1878. That would make her all of 64 years old today. Two years older than me," Madame O adds wistfully.

"I should like the boy to tackle it."

"Oh, no, it would be quite beyond him."

Mr Gorrick looks at his son, whose eyes are flickering brightly. "We shall see about that," Charles Gorrick thinks wryly.

"Anyhow, Mr Gorrick, he doesn't read music."

"No, but his mother is a good sight reader, and we have an old upright she can accompany him on."

Madame O refrains from further comment and returns to the reasons for their coming, asking with a certain finality whether Mr Gorrick would like a written testament from her.

"I would be only too pleased to – it's always helpful for Eisteddfods, etc. After all, I can wholeheartedly state that Mark has a charming voice of quite substantial range, that is for a boy treble of course. No, I shall only be too pleased, Mr Gorrick."

Gorrick has become increasingly frustrated with what he owns to be the famous teacher's diffidence, somewhat bordering on lack of involvement and foresight. "Whatever. Whichever. Has she only noticed the clarity? And what of the remarkable promise? Well of all the dumb… No! Is that as far as her instincts of detection and knowledge taken her? Inconceivable!" he thinks, regarding the boy with a mixture of indignation and admiration. How in the world can anyone be content to call it a day after only hearing a couple of scales and The Last Rose of Summer, which he thinks did very little to show off Mark's true voice. "Barmy! That's what I call it. Midsummer balminess. That's what it boils down to. No, we've got to take the bull by the horns. I can see Madame needs to be pummelled and agitated into finally recognising what lies below and beyond Mark's throat." For the umpteenth time, he perseveres and protests and hints again silently to himself at Mark's voice.

"Thank you, Madame, but what you've heard is nothing compared to what he can do," Gorrick interrupts.

"Nothing? Oh, I wouldn't have described Mark's voice as nothing," Madame O retorts with an irritatingly ingratiating smile to Gorrick's way of thinking. His eyes expressing bafflement as he looks askance at the boy, who, for the time being, seems reasonably satisfied with the pronouncements that have led to his being at the centre of a drawn out discussion. He smiles back blandly at his father. Gorrick begins to see Madame O's lightweight reaction as indifference, which he finds hard to stomach. Well, she has every right, he supposes. After all, he assumes, she being one of the most distinguished teachers of singing in the world, her days are probably so taken up with teaching, listening and adjudicating it could be that she is not so accurate or interested anymore. Nevertheless, her reaction is maddening to Charles Gorrick's way of thinking, until it occurs to him that she may not have any actual interest in a young boy's voice and, if so, it is likely, such an assessment of his voice might misfire miserably, he convinces himself dejectedly.

As Madame O excuses herself and retires to the annexe, father and son hastily hatch a whispered strategic surprise tactic. Mr Gorrick at an exact moment will give a signal lifting his eyes to the ceiling and Mark will issue forth with a brilliant scale.

Madame O returns and greets them with the customary courtesy she reserves for everyone. She looks at her watch and again seats herself at the piano. Unbeknownst to either father or son, she too has devised a plan that might make a young boy of Mark's temperament rise to the challenge and sing out to his heart's content. She turns to the wedding scene of the opera and plays the rollicking introduction march in F major for the beginning of the duet of Raymondo and Lucia. Those few notes on the piano are to indeed work in the capacity of a magic talisman and bring Mark out of himself.

Before Gorrick has the opportunity to direct a knowing wink at his son, the music overtakes the boy in an almost cataclysmic fashion. Again, with his eyes flickering strangely, his voice, perfectly focussed, leaps forth remarkably to an octave and a 4th to the F in altissimo and then swiftly climbs to the C above high C and to the last C on the piano! And without even a semblance of a breath, then proceeds to embark upon a series of astonishing vocal effects, breaking into a sustained disembodied full-bodied trill, finally dispatches off into an inaudible taper which charges the fraught atmosphere. Finally, the marvellously controlled voice leaps forth once more with renewed vigour to soar aloft with superhuman agility and fly siren-like off into every conceivable space around the small room and finally escape through the window and over the treetops into the Botanical Gardens. A feat of such immense magnitude to man's mind, no one has ever attempted nor succeeded to execute before!

"Heavens," Gorrick thinks to himself, "that's not what we had planned, nor what I had remotely counted upon. That was nothing short of miraculous." Even he, now lost for words, who boasted of knowing his son's voice backwards, has been taken by complete surprise, had never imagined in his wildest dreams to hear the boy sing out so effortlessly in an all risks, no holds barred display of superhuman, dazzling, virtuosity. Now, Gorrick thinks excitedly to himself, as he could scarcely keep a hold on his emotions, if that doesn't set the world afire, nothing will!

He watches as Madame O disbelievingly repeatedly fingers the same note on the top of the piano, but not a word does she utter. Then, after a short time, she pulls down the lid of the piano resolutely and heavily leans both elbows upon the lid, placing her hands to her temples, and remains thus for several minutes with her back to the boy and his father.

Father and son stand quietly, awaiting her decision, knowing full well that the cat has at last been let out of the bag. Gorrick shakes his head from side to side in utter disbelief at the boy's staggering pyrotechnical display and, thunderstruck, looks at him squarely in the eyes to convey to him just what an affect the voice had upon him, although furtive attempts to embrace the boy are met with a friendly rebuff, Mark preferring to stand his ground and wait for the official verdict. Several times, Gorrick looks to Madame O for some form of acknowledgement, but she remains with her back to them. Her hands held up before her, suspended over the closed keyboard. Meanwhile, imperceptibly, she makes to raise herself from the piano and slowly turns around towards them. To father and son's way of thinking, the expression on her face is indescribable as she looks down at the carpet. Averts her eyes from them, and somehow manages to mark with measured tread the few steps over towards the boy and his father, proffering a hand to both as if to support herself. Her breathing short, and still not uttering a word, she moves her lips as if to speak. Her expression says everything. Subsequently, she quietly retires behind the curtain to presumably prepare some tea as Mark and his father intently follow her with their gaze, though neither makes as much as a murmur.

For a moment, Mark appears as though he is tempted to speak, but instead characteristically settles to open his mouth extremely wide and press his fingers against two small muscles either side of his jaws, as if checking to see they were in place and intact, after which he resorts to a becalmed soft half-smile. They wait silently as Madame O returns with three cups and saucers and a filled teapot on a tray, which she half-heartedly places on a small side table and prepares at last to again meet their gaze. The expression on her face, now a mixture of awe, bewilderment and elation. Still silent, she seats herself, pours the tea distractedly and then slowly, trancelike, pushes the tray towards the boy and his father.

"Please," she tells them, as she takes a crisp white lace handkerchief tucked in her belt, firstly wipes her spectacles and then her eyes. Gorrick is the first to speak.

"Are you all right Madame?"

She gulps forth a forced, brave smile. A short gasp in her throat, places her hand over his and strains to regain her voice, "I – I am overcome," she answers in a shaking voice.

Charles Gorrick clasps her hand in his. For some moments, everyone stays silent. Mark edges closer towards her so that she can just sense his breath on her bare arms as he peers up into her face. She looks down at him. "Thank you, Mark, thank you both."

As father and son make their way back down the driveway, Mark begins to chirpily make up for not saying a word throughout the 'hearing' with Madame O and starts talking freely.

"I wish we could have stayed longer."

"Well, it was the best part of the morning, Mark."

"She grew nicer than I imagined she would be when I first saw her," he tells his father. But at the same time he seems concerned with the idea she had been a leading soprano at the Berlin Opera, because it conjures up a vivid picture in his mind of a huge palace-like auditorium that blinds the eye with gold awnings and crimson plush. A place he has never experienced but could well envisage, where an abundance of marvellous voices ricochet in all directions.

"Well, you can understand how worthwhile today has been – especially when she took both our hands in hers and remained unable to say anything. And then that simple phrase she uttered, "I'm overcome", spoke volumes apart, that is, from the expression on her face. No! I'm convinced you couldn't have wished for a better person to hear you. Although I can say, here and now, I had my doubts that you'd make it, and finally open your mouth at all, in the allotted time."

Mark answers detachedly, "But I did, didn't I, Dad?"

"You certainly did, and how!"

Charles Gorrick's voice chokes for a moment. He wants to tell his son how proud he is of him, but thinks better of it when the boy instinctively veers away and meets his eyes, registering one of those characteristic expressions of his, which Mr Gorrick has learned from past experience, refuted any such personal advance.

Gorrick considers the boy for a moment. Always there, usually willing, but the moment you get too close, dog-like he strains to get away. No! For his age the boy is an unusually independent vessel apt to shun compliments unless he solicits them himself. In Mark's outlook, there exists no genuine need to be flattered that is until he sends out his own signals, the moment he feels in need of assurance or appreciation. Again, Mark asks:

"Did I sing all right, Dad?" tugging at his father's coat.

"You know you did. What a question, Mark! I wondered what was happening. Couldn't believe what had come over you. The studio was vibrating." The boy half-turns his face away preparing what next to say. A slight smile of satisfaction gathers over his features.

"I didn't quite do what we had planned," he grins.

"You certainly didn't, Mark, which proves I can always rely on you to frighten the wits out of me!"

"It was that Donizetti March that Madame played which affected me and made me feel dizzy, and I felt my voice leaving my body. The music took me over and I wanted to yell and shout but my voice wouldn't let me. It wanted to sing and escape and, as it did so, I felt it climbing higher and higher and I forgot myself."

"Need I tell you, Mark, your voice sounded completely effortless and so controlled, and shall I tell you something else? I believe what you did today has no parallel, and will never be equalled."

The boy smiles. "It was so easy. I felt I could do anything I wished," he reflects dreamily. Then in an instant his face clouds over. A pall of gloom settles in his eyes. Carried away, Gorrick did not notice and continues.

"It was well worth waiting for, Mark, and do you know, I believe that laughing fit we all shared helped to relieve the nervous tension."

Gorrick looks down on the boy as they walk and notes how he has suddenly become broody and melancholy.

"Are you all right, Mark?" he asks, noting the unexpected mood swing. The boy looks up into his father's eyes.

"When Madame tried she could scarcely sing a note. She said the worst thing that can happen to a singer is to lose their voice."

Charles Gorrick stops. "At her age, 62, that's fairly natural.

Mark remains silent and pensive then somehow finds what he wants to say.

"I'd rather die than lose my voice!"

"Who said you were going to?"

"What, die, Dad?"

"No, lose your voice?"

"I don't know," Mark replies again, not quite knowing how to say what he means to express.

"Mark, don't start eating your heart out about something that is not going to happen. Think of the magical vocal tapestry you wove today. When we see Madame O next she will tell you her reaction, but today she is in no condition to express anything, let alone herself. That's why I knew it best to leave her alone when we did. Let's sit down for a moment in the shade," Gorrick suggests.

The sound of cicadas all around is near deafening; the gardens are in full bloom, the sun blistering.

"Beautiful, isn't it?"

Mark does not reply. His mind is elsewhere.

"I liked her more and more, especially when she seemed stuck in her world."

"How do you mean, Mark?"

"Well, first she scared me. Then she gradually became – I can't explain – friendly and understanding, and when she cried and pretended to wipe her glasses, I wanted to go up to her and let her know that I understood, but I couldn't make myself do it."

"I'm sure she would have appreciated that. Why didn't you? You did actually go up to her though!"

"Yes, I know, that's all. It would have been soppy. She was upset, Dad, because she can't sing anymore!"

"That wasn't the only reason, Mark, nor the true reason." The boy does not need to be told why. He smiles softly to himself.

When they arrive home, a message from Madame O already awaits them. Mrs Gorrick confirms that the woman who had phoned to arrange the next meeting had sounded very quiet and almost apologetic.

"I think the shock had been too great for her," Gorrick remarks. "Mark sang like an angel and when he finally topped it with a vocal cadenza to end all cadenzas, all heaven broke loose."

Chapter Two

The Second Visit

When they next met, Madame O determined not to let go of her emotions and restrained herself from embracing Mark.

"Oh, I couldn't wait to see you both again," she announced enthusiastically.

"There are a number of things I would like to discuss with you Mr Gorrick. Meanwhile I have a suggestion to make; since Mark is so enamoured with my picture gallery perhaps he might like to be left alone downstairs in the Conservatorium's Gallery of musicians where he is bound to find a reference to every famous singer. It is located on the ground floor. Old programmes and posters galore. Some I donated myself from my Berlin Opera days."

The mere mention of this whetted Mark's eagerness.

"Well, if you come with me, I shall take you downstairs and leave you to browse around there, while your father and I have a chat together. Does that appeal to you, Mark?"

The boy nodded his approval. "I shan't be long, Mr Gorrick. Please make yourself at home."

Madame O returned in no time at all.

"Like myself, the boy is blissful and in seventh heaven, Mr Gorrick," she reported. "You should have seen the sense of rapture enveloping him as he made a beeline for the Melba cabinet. She paused. "I must apologise for yesterday. As you may well imagine, the voice – that voice of his – took me by complete surprise, and I suppose I still haven't got over the shock."

"Oh, I'm sorry Madame O, although I must also admit to being quite unprepared for what I heard Mark do."

"Well, I think today, Mr Gorrick, you'll find me in more settled mood seeing I've had the best part of a sleepless night to dwell upon Mark's amazing vocal display which left me speechless. As I've said, in my ignorance yesterday, I described the voice as merely beautiful, that was before the voice launched off into the stratosphere."

"Oh! I shouldn't have called that ignorance, Madame. How were you to know about the rest of the voice?"

"Yes, I suppose so, but you did continuously allude and hint to his voice in a way which should have made me realise there was more to it than I imagined – an octave indeed! I suppose we teachers feel we know everything. Over the years we become somewhat stilted, carried away with our own importance. It takes something like this to bring us to our senses."

At last, Charles Gorrick felt a welcome sense of vindication in Madame O's words. Now all he need do would be to sit back and listen to her advice. Madame O continued heaping praise.

"It dawned on me overnight what a natural wonder that voice of his is. But why am I bothering to tell all this to the one who knows this astonishing instrument better than anyone else? Forgive me, Mr Gorrick, for my over indulgence. Anything I say now must sound rather paltry to your ears."

"No, Madame. On the contrary, this is what we came for, to gain from your great knowledge. Mind you, I did become a little impatient when I saw my son dying to show off his prowess, and not being able to do so.

"I can well imagine, Mr Gorrick, but I had no inkling at the time of his real worth. To be honest, I admit at the beginning I thought, just another voice! Ridiculous of me to say the least!" Gorrick smiled widely.

Madame O continued. "For myself, the discovery of such a voice can be likened to discovering a previously unknown masterpiece, from the hand of a Leonardo or a Mozart. Today I must confess to feeling guilty and uncomfortable at my diffidence in the matter earlier on yesterday. Had events not happened the way they did I may not even have bothered too much to hear Mark again. No! That's not quite true, because I did detect something special when he sang The Last Rose of Summer. Perhaps on second thoughts I might be forgiven."

Now Madame O appeared to be a little less vehement with herself.

"Of course you knew!" Charles Gorrick tried to convince her. "Of course you knew!"

Madame O dabbed thoughtfully at her eyes. "Hayfever at this time of the year," she contrived sheepishly. "How moved Bruno would have been," she commented.

"Your husband, Bruno?"

"No, Bruno Walter, the greatest conductor I ever had the honour to know and work with, but before Mark returns, and I've contemplated what I'm about to say, throughout the night…" she paused inwardly, hand over her heart as if about to take a solemn avowal. "How shall I begin to explain? Mr Gorrick, yesterday has been a revelation of mammoth proportions to me."

She remained with hand on heart. "One which will forever stay indelibly steeped within my memory."

Charles Gorrick's forehead crinkled, his eyebrows raised. He half smiled, stuck for words, a little choked.

Madame O grasped his hand for support. "We so called 'professors', I've heard said, are a splinter group. I can count on my fingers the truly memorable moments when one considers a long career. Not enough. We hear voice upon voice. Some lovely voices I daresay, especially here in the Southern Hemisphere. We often attempt to resurrect, redeem and release those potentially great voices. Yet, rarely do we succeed. Mediocrity is the bane. You release a voice, but the singer's mind simply isn't up to the demand made by the composer or a career. These singers finally expire into the background. Sad but true. We teachers spend much of our time redressing 'the plight of the voice', untethering the poor tortured, inadequate thing from its cage of ribs. But for me, first and foremost, the voice has always been a soul – imprisoned by the body. But, when it is a free spirit we, the teachers, rejoice that it has found itself, and we have in part succeeded with our mission. So you see, we continue like patient dogs waiting to be rewarded with a bone. The rewards are certainly there, but are few and far between. We can become cynical, even when our work is temporarily finished, because there is any number of hopeful aspirants waiting to take the previous student's place after they have matriculated from the Conservatorium. And we are required to launch upon a liberation process all over again!

Invariably most voices suffer from some restriction or another, and as such fall into varying categories and compartments. As I see it, the range of the voice is divided into: The low notes, which are there to soothe away pain and anguish. A unique contralto immediately comes to mind who I shall refer to later. The middle notes are there, closest to the heart. That same unique contralto voice comes to mind. Then we come to the high notes, so placed as to assail and overwhelm the senses, to divert our everyday attention, to touch upon certain sleeping nerve ends – innervating us and lulling us into a sense of escape over and beyond fast held boundaries. However, on that rarest occasion, when all three come together encroaching upon each other in harmonious, effortless fashion, usually unexpectedly, a miracle has evolved - Colcancas!" she muttered under her breath.

Madame O pointed to her throat, "These two slight, delicate little cords, hiding down here, with tiny muscles, are the prime progenitors of such a remarkable, disembodied, life force!" She paused to find words. Madame O smiled, now she released her hand.

"You can be proud of yourself, Mr Gorrick, very proud indeed."

At this remark, Madame O excused herself and stole behind the curtain. Charles Gorrick stood up to his full height, well over six feet, remaining immobile and wondering what to expect next. He knew he sensed in Madame O's words and remarks a two-fold combination of strangely exciting yet unsettling intimations. Miracle! The word spun through his somewhat beleaguered mind and nearly proved too much for him. Madame O had certainly put him at his ease, yet to be the father of Mark is one thing, come to fully understand a famous teacher's comments, another! He began to feel a tingling sensation across his forehead reaching his temples and onto his ears, and in that brief moment, all he wished for was to watch the kitchenette curtains open and to see the radiant expression on Madame O's face as she reappeared and, when she did, Charles Gorrick searched the woman's face, discovered across her fine features, and eyes a look of longing.

For no particular reason she pulled at her cardigan sleeve disconcertingly.

"Mr Gorrick, what I am about to say may startle you. I can assure you though after yesterday – I repeat today – I am more than startled. I am in a state of deep and irretrievable, irrevocable, irreversible, wonderful shock. Since I have to admit after much deliberation, I can honestly say your boy possesses far and above the most astonishing voice I have ever had the great good fortune to encounter."

As she strove to make her remarks more concordant and plausible with the situation, she paused again and looked across the music room at the collection of framed photographs of the most celebrated singers of their time, amongst them Cantors and legendary Castrati.

"I have known any number of great singers, bless them, as you can see," she looked askance at a portrait of Adelina Patti, "but you can imagine," she stated in a mocking tone, "how it must feel for someone like myself to be brought to her senses by a boy and his father, and for me to have nurtured all my life a set, blinkered outlook only to be winched and wrenched suddenly out of the blue towards the end of that life and have that set outlook upturned and refuted in a matter of a few hours."

She stopped, her voice emotional, and began again.

"It is a startling prospect both to the senses and to one's whole way of thinking, I doubt I shall ever be the same person again." She murmured, "What a voice can do."

Charles Gorrick now began to comprehend the significance of Madame O's unbelievable mission.

Madame O continued disjointedly. "Well, it has happened Mr Gorrick, and as God as my judge, you are my sole witness. What happened here in this very room yesterday is beyond my wildest dreams. I shall never forget the way your son looked at me before he left yesterday, but to tell the truth at the time there simply was nothing I could do or say to mitigate my true feelings.

Madame O no longer struggled. Tears welled up in her eyes. "You see, under such circumstances the words 'Totidem verbis' cannot convey the true meaning when one is so profoundly affected. In that moment only silence speaks."

Charles Gorrick looked at the photos on the wall, her words tugging at his own emotions. He had no idea where to look and he found himself silently thanking her without even the barest words to convey his joy and intense gratitude. He wanted to comfort her but, like Mark, didn't know how. Instead, he asked, "Shall I go and tell the boy?"

"Yes, yes, but please just one more moment," Madame O said. "Don't say too much to him yet. However, when you bring him back, I should like to make a blueprint test of the voice. Analyse it by way of some specially devised vocalizations of my own, and find out just what lies under that mysterious veil of tears and laughter. In fact, I can hardly wait. Do I convince you?" She laughed light-heartedly.

Gorrick thought for a moment. "I'm sure you'll understand why he didn't talk, Madame!"

"Of course the poor boy was completely het up and overcome with emotion. She looked into Gorrick's face as if there she had discovered everything she needed to find. Nightingales aren't expected to speak," she added with exaltation in her voice.

Madame O briefly explained the way to the museum to Gorrick. "Very well, Madame, whatever you suggest. I'll go and fetch him."

"Yes, please do. Mark is probably wondering what we've been saying about him behind his back."

"If only he knew. His ears would be tingling," Gorrick quipped good-naturedly.

As Gorrick hastily exited the room, Madame O thought to herself aloud, "When they return I shall be in better command of my absurd rampant emotions!"

Gorrick met his son on the stairs, Mark's face literally aglow. When they returned a half minute later, Madame O, commented, "That was quick, Charles."

"We met halfway," he turned to Madame O and whispered, "Mark's overawed Madame – he couldn't wait to get back."

Mark suppressed a wayward smile as he looked in Madame O's direction. He had immediately observed the overall change in her manner today. To his young alert eyes she appeared subdued and more approachable, the way he liked to imagine an older woman to be and this made him feel increasingly at ease and, as a consequence, more competent to give his utmost vocally during the remainder of the time to be spent in Madame's formidable presence. Upon noticing Mark's obvious pleasure at coming back from the exhibition, Madame O suggested he could go back any time he wished, perhaps again next time with his father.

Evidently, however, according to the expression on the boy's face, her suggestion didn't overly carry too much weight, so that she felt free to retain her genuine enthusiasm for the preceding time she had allotted to hearing Mark. Yet what followed next could be judged as a perverse 'put off by Madame, faced as she was with too exciting a 'face to face' event that was about to follow. In a nutshell, Madame O was in fact putting off the truth because the truth was almost too electrifying to deal with! She knew that in the future she must revise much of what she'd written and had published previous to this encounter with Mark Gorrick.

Presently, at her age, she must endeavour to address the boy directly who, with his natural intuition, she'd found herself suddenly in awe of, to the point of embarrassment. However, in his presence, she managed to affect some semblance of composure and began addressing both father and son in what she believed to be the best chosen appropriate manner she could adopt for the purpose, not unlike the way in which she addressed learned scholars in the lecture rooms of the Conservatorium and other musical establishments when she had been called upon to reveal her teaching methods or give learned pronouncement on the singing voice. As she made to start she took account of how Mark, waited for any word or demand she might instigate. A little off - putting because she was about to demonstrate by way of her own expertise to a mere child whose God given talent far outweighed her own capabilities, or so she thought. She felt herself to be a prisoner or a custodian of old ways and customs. Meanwhile, once she suspected how in awe of her the boy had been, she responded a little more naturally to her own misgivings knowing the boy would remain statue like - allowing nothing to interrupt the intensity of the attention he paid his own conceived notion of this bird like 'pocket sized Prima Donna'.

"So, Mark, it is prudent of me that I should mention…"

She stopped for breath, her concentration momentarily awry, almost moaned as she experienced and attempted to suppress the excitement and inference of the 'discovery' now before her and overtaking her.

She began again, "We teachers refer to the highest of all female voices as the soprano acuto sfogato. Rarely though do few of these type of voices reach the A in altissimo which yesterday you reached and far beyond. Mozart's wife, Constanza, and his sister-in-law, Aloysia Weber both reached the A in alt. Madame said as she pointed to the charming portraits of the two singers dated 1764 hanging over the piano. It is usually only in some of Mozart's concert arias these very high notes are demanded of the soprano and it is considered most desirable if such voices reach the F in alt, for example, Mozart's Queen of the Night in The Magic Flute."

Immediately Mark started humming the aria. Madame stopped, waited, listened and, when he stopped, continued.

"For example Richard Strauss's Zerbinetta in 'Ariadne auf Naxos'. These very high ranges are rare but not a problem for my friend Erna Sack of course who sang the C above high C without any appreciable difficulty, but then Erna was unique, at least till yesterday!" Madame O smiled knowingly. Mark remained the 'steadfast tin soldier', not giving away the least sign of emotion whilst well aware of his father's thoughts on the matter, although never once looking directly at him.

"That's Erna Sack there on the right as 'Lucia' in the Delerium Scene." Mark's eyes roved languorously and settled upon the photo of the celebrated singer, "Die Deutsche Nachitgall" as she is known in the world today.

"Curiously enough the greatest coloraturas could not necessarily boast these altitudinous notes amongst them Christine Nilsonn, Jenny Lind, Etelka Gerster, Tetrazzini, - Melba, Patti, nor did they attempt them even in certain roles requiring them to do so. So what I am declaring is that to sing the C above high C, then ascend on past the D, thence onto E and then onto the next F another octave higher, is a feat virtually impossible – unknown – until –" she paused ruefully, characteristically dabbed at her eyes, and spoke emotionally through her smile "- until yesterday," again looking at Charles Gorrick knowingly.

"Now what puzzles me – coming to Mark's voice, is that the human throat as we have known it is not made that way, and yet," she suddenly expounded without having intended to in Mark's presence, "here we have a boy's voice contradicting every known device or facet of what we have supposedly learned about voices. For strength, security, ease of delivery, total sublime coloratura technique in the highest register with no apparent weakening in either volume or breath control – where,

where has it all come from? I would be reluctant to say whether from any one particular re-incarnation of a single voice or rather an amalgam, a composite of many voices? And yet there is no voice I can compare this extraordinary instrument with. It is indeed thrilling! Tales abound of mythical voices producing prodigious sounds but I dare say 'this voice' has of its innate quality – the divine." Madame continued unaware of speaking directly to father and son.

Even as she spoke, her words began to trail off and be uttered trance-like, as conflicting thought processes now besieged her mind. For a moment she lost track of what she had just said. Since those last notes of the day before, returned to re-echo through her head. Until yesterday, as far as she had been concerned, there they lay concealed in a child's undeveloped throat! And so, having thought and said as much, Madame O, her mind somewhat torn asunder, remained in a daunted state.

"Now where does that leave us?" she questioned.

From one moment to the next, confident in herself and of her vastly acquired musical knowledge, whilst in the next moment she regarded herself faced with the infallible presence of this world 'wunderkind", at once feeling herself deprived of her hard earned status, convinced all is as nothing. Whether it be either her published erudite treatise on the singing voice, or her teaching.

For a short time, she paused to observe the boy at the centre of all this mind arresting upheaval, noting his scant body weight, scarcely taking up sparse little space and yet whose boundless talent and superhuman vocal gifts could not be contained within Madame O's universe of a myriad voices. How? She asked had she found herself, from one day to the next, plunged headlong into an ocean of miraculous notes, cadenzas, cascades, and furthermore, she asked why had a mere stripling of a boy been chosen as the leading player in this mammoth quest for vocal sovereignty?

For a time, Madame O felt at a loss, unable to borrow from her ever reliable ingenuity and logic as she so fruitfully did in her profession when dealing with an unknown quantity. And that is exactly how she stayed throughout the remainder of the time spent in the boy's company that morning.

Now she felt progessively small and humble. She clenched her hands in her lap. "Oh, dear God," silently she muttered obliquely placing a hand to her mouth.

It all seemed a dream. Since yesterday, she speculated, she is no longer one of the two foremost singing teachers at the Conservatorium. Nor is she any longer her own mentor. Instead she has become in that short time no less than committed to a juvenile God given sculptural voice descended down to her from another world, releasing a surfeit of emotions – fear, awe, intimidation, admiration, all rolled into a piece, not to mention an immense overbearing sadness. Long dead emotions rained down upon her, gathered forces, pummelled her.

She exclaimed in a small choked voice, "Please, please, wait here a moment," muttering repeatedly as if everything that had transpired had only just dawned upon her. Stopped in her tracks, she placed her hand somewhat frustratedly on the boy's shoulders to make sure he is real. Peered deeply into his brightly shining eyes. "Just wait here a minute. Stay!" she gushed as if ordering a dog to obey its master, "I have a brainwave. With both your permissions I'll inform De Vries. I'll return in a moment."

Yes, please do, Madame," replied Gorrick mindlessly, as she rather comically made a dash to leave the room by the swiftest means possible. Not stopping to explain, she almost skidded, colliding with an ornamental music stand nearly knocking it to the floor, but quite soberly the boy reached out and managed to save it.

With scarcely a cursory backward glance, Madame O fled from the room as speedily as her slim little legs could carry her, returning for an instant to courteously acknowledge Mark's father whom she had ignored in her pandemonium.

"We've been here two hours already, Dad!"

The moment she had disappeared, father and son were alone together again. Mark's father had time to remonstrate, "Good on you, Mark!"

He almost shook the boy as if to make his son realise his worth. Mr Gorrick could be more himself and congratulate the boy without sounding too proud of him in Madame O's presence. "I knew you wouldn't disappoint." Then, "No one can sing like him," he continued in the third person, beaming to himself. "You heard what the little woman said, didn't you?"

"About altissimo?"

"No, Mark, about your voice?"

"No I don't remember anything else she said." The boy's thoughts were now diverted elsewhere. He had become especially curious about the name 'altissimo' to denote the particular range in which he had produced the last notes. Indeed, he appeared to relish the fact?

"Madame said I sang in 'altissimo', a B flat or something. What is 'altissimo' supposed to mean, Dad?"

"I guess way up in the clouds." his father answered, "Although I'm not sure of the facts. Shall we ask the professor exactly what it means when she returns?"

"Something else. Are you certain, Dad?" I didn't sound like a sissy up there, so high? Boys are supposed to have deep voices.

Gorrick's face registered no surprise, only solicitude, "Course not. What makes you think and say such a foolish thing, Mark?"

"I don't know," the boy replied thoughtfully.

"Wouldn't I tell you if I thought you did, Mark? You never heard me tell you a lie, did you?"

"No," the boy replied reassured.

"To tell the truth, Mark, you did sound like a magic flute."

Mark ignored the last remark. "Dad?"

"Yes, Mark. What is it now?"

"When I sang that last note it didn't feel that high although my head felt strange, as if it were whizzing me around the room!" Again the expression on Mark's face was far away.

"Listen, Mark, don't you go getting any wrong ideas and decide you want to fly, although your voice flies off thrillingly into the clouds. I'd definitely have to ground you," he mocked, "if you started to entertain any such far fetched ideas like that, apart from which poor Madame in her present state would probably have a fit! Heaven knows what you've done to her, Marco. We need you here. Remember that."

"Dad," the boy persisted earnestly, "shall I try to sing again before Madame returns?"

"Go on then, if it makes you happy. You can't get enough can you? But be snappy about it. You never know, she may not take kindly to the idea that you've all but made yourself at home in her studio."

The boy briskly looked around him. A grin on his face mirroring his excitement. His eyes radiant, glassy, yet near expressionless.

"But are you sure I don't sound like a sissy?"

"Stop saying things like that," Gorrick insisted, "No, how many more times must I tell you? You're a magic flute and that's final. Here, I'll go to the piano myself and hit that note again for you. Is that the note Madame played?"

Mark nodded and said, "I think so." He opened his mouth from which poured forth the purest sound. It had become an impossibility for Gorrick ever to cease being amazed at these vocal feats, "Attaboy, Marco!"

Mark started as before, ever so softly - even tentatively, 'whispering endearments to the muses', then increasing the sound, swelling and pouring out the note as if large bellows had been created to fit his small chest cavity.

When he stopped, he said to his father, "Dad, I think you may have hit a note higher on the piano. That was not the B Flat that Madame called it, that was the next note so it must have been a C. I'm certain. I know because it felt different in my throat."

"Yes, come to think of it, Mark, you could be correct. It probably is a higher note because I felt my ears tingling. Look, hadn't you better stop for a while just in case you earn us the sack – the Erna Sack - and are thrown off the premises?"

But the boy had already started singing the Fountain aria from Lucia, then shortly after dutifully complied, to stop, as a tall, slim, elegantly dressed man, with shiny, sleeked back black hair and matching moustache and goatee, entered the room. "I can promise you both that if I have anything to do with it, you certainly won't be thrown off the premises," he said good heartedly, smiling, "and I can assure you that note was indeed the unheard of C above C in alt. To be exact! To my knowledge the highest note ever emitted from a human throat, as far as I know. Quite a triumph for a tiddler to be so technically proficient! And no falsetto at that! And I judge not a fluke? Also I might add it sounded so easy!"

Gorrick smiled knowingly at Mark, a look which inferred that some more shock tactics were about to be embarked upon and encountered en route.

The man had spoken in a softly grained slightly accented voice whilst doing his best to hide his excitement. He introduced himself, "The name is De Vries." He reached a finely manicured strong hand out to Charles Gorrick as Madame O appeared, breathless and in a flurry, a few steps behind him, her spectacles now swinging recklessly from the chain around her neck. An absent-mindedly grasped notebook and pen in her hand.

De Vries turned to Madame O a little pretentiously.

"Quite right, Rosa, we do indeed have a young phenomenon unexpectedly in our midst, and an extremely young one at that."

He stopped to stroke his smooth, pale, elegant forehead now crinkled into furrows of doubt. "However, the leading question is how are we to deal with such a short lived wonder?" he said drawing a chair up to the piano and beckoning his pint sized colleague to come and sit with him.

"Short lived?" Gorrick exclaimed.

De Vries invited the boy to sing anything he felt like. Mark, having grown a shade more confident since his encounter with Madame O, needed no further prompting. Madame O's presence worked wonders. He looked in her direction for confirmation and duly received it. Assured, he executed a few endlessly long sustained trills, followed in hot pursuit by a series of extraordinary staccato notes up and down the scale at rapid breakneck speed without once stopping for breath. De Vries watched incredulously when the boy added again a snippet of the Fountain aria.

De Vries whispered to Madame O. "Do you notice, Rosa, he doesn't bother to breathe? How? What's his secret? That alone requires a mastery which we lesser folk are apt to have worked for years at."

Madame O looked visibly taken aback by this last remark, tactless to her professional status. But she quickly saw the truth in his words.

"Twelve years old did I hear you say?" he asked, thoughtfully stroking his goatee.

Mark continued to pluck unbridled notes in random fashion from nowhere and, as he did so, he stole knowing glances at Madame O, which she acknowledged timidly, as if by now the two shared a secret bond. It is as much as Madame O can do to calm her nerves while she proceeds to pencil around today's date on the wall calendar to remind herself that reality still existed and one wasn't living out a dream. Now De Vries, increasingly less in command of his former sobriety, addressed Gorrick in what could have been interpreted as an almost pompous mien of voice.

"I see now exactly what my esteemed colleague here meant when she wished me to hear your son, Mr Gorrick. Yes! Indeed I believe she has every good reason. For I say this in all humility, we have here a God-given voice in a class of its own. I am in full agreement with Madame. For myself, I have to admit I have never before heard a true vocal phenomenon such as we have here." He stopped short to take a deep breath and regain some vestige of his temporarily lost composure, stroking a finely, elongated manicured hand across his noble forehead to resettle a wayward lock of hair. It's enough to rekindle the faith amongst today's vocal debauchery," he continued, "but I must make a serious admonition if you will bear with me! It is but a matter of weeks, possibly months away at the most, before this wonderful instrument will cease to be".

De Vries's voice darkened and took on the sombre tone of some learned physician announcing a sinister prognosis to his patient.

"Whatever do you mean?" Gorrick asked disbelievingly, again placing a re-assuring hand on the boy's shoulder.

"Dear Mr Gorrick, it is like this – I shall explain. The sole destroyer of such a boy's voice is time. Time will see to the voice's demise. Let us not use the word destruction – but in its place the adult male voice takes over and the boy's voice becomes either tenor or baritone or stentorian basso profundo or, heaven forbid, a non-descript nothing. Each of which, I may tell you, is on the cards. So you see, if the boy is to receive his new voice intact, he will need to hibernate vocally in order to nurture his present voice if the unknown replacement is to survive at all during the difficult transition period. It is my opinion that for this purpose, Mark would be well advised to stop singing, or at the moment he detects the merest change or strain in his voice, otherwise he may suffer unpleasant or disappointing consequences."

Everyone looked hugely despondent. "Stop singing! But he will be unable to stop singing!" Gorrick said, "That would be virtually impossible and unnatural for him! He has never stopped since he was three years old."

"I can well imagine. That then must remain in the hands and the laps of the Gods, Mr Gorrick, unless you yourself are willing to encourage him to stop during this all important period of pubescent change."

No one spoke. Charles Gorrick's grim face registered bewilderment. It had never occurred to him that his son's voice would ever be anywhere but in the present. There, before him, ringing exaltedly in his ears.

Mark smiled wistfully. He had isolated himself from the conversation and had not at all digested De Vries's woebegone inference. Dreamingly he had watched the expression on the man's face as he spoke, had seen his mouth move but thankfully had failed to listen to the sinister outpouring. In his dreamlike state, Mark had only heard the word: 'singing', and he could hardly wait to be asked to vocalise again.

Deadened by De Vries's prediction, Madame O blankly watched the boy, but all too soon the truth dawned on her and she too felt a pang of growing unease and alarm overtaking her. Again she resorted to her mother tongue.

"Whatever is to be done? If only there were a way out. Some solution. A palliative. If only something could be done to cocoon, encapsulate that voice in a protective vacuum for all time."

Having planted the seeds of uncertainty, De Vries thanked everyone and cordially excused himself to prepare for his next pupil. A disconsolate air played upon his fine features and tall graceful figure as he left the room forgetting to close the door behind him.

The moment he had gone, Madame O plucked up, somehow relieved to be rid of reality. Seeing despondency in Gorrick's eyes she tried to ease matters. "Let us try and forget for the moment those pessimistic words of my learned colleague."

"Awful idea isn't it Madame?"

Gorrick remarked in a dejected voice looking first into her eyes for some form of solace before casting a fretful glance at Mark's profile by the windows, glad of the fact that his son, oblivious to the drama, smiled over at the treetops and into the distance. Seeing the contentment on Mark's face, Gorrick thought, 'I'm glad, he didn't register what's in store for him, but I hate to think what it would do to him if he were made to realise. Best he carry on regardless.'

He remembered a time when Mark had voluntarily stopped singing a year or so back, and that being only for a week, had put the boy in a severe state of despair and depression.

Madame O perked up. "Would it be too much to ask to hear him again render The Fountain aria from the beginning of Lucia?" At the mere mention of "Lucia", Mark awoke from his self-induced reverie and now stood on terra ferma. This was the moment he awaited - to be asked to sing again.

The piano sounded the introduction to Regnava nel silenzio as Madame O in between playing pointed to the phonetically printed words on the score. As always, standing with his head held high, mouth wide, Mark started effortlessly to sing in Italian. Madame O excitedly had already transcribed the piece up so that the aria was in F, a key better suited to the boy's bell-like high range. Mark sang the aria with added meaning –

"Hath he forgot me? Imprudent. To ask him hither. Think of thy brother, what if he should discover thou loveth his foe. I'd warn him. I've called him hither that I may tell him what danger lurks around him. Ah wherefore roam thy glances wild and affrighted. 'Tis the fountain. I tremble whenever I behold it. Knowst thou the legend. Upon this spot they say that a Ravenswood slew the maid that loved him in jealous madness. The hapless maiden rests in its water its tide closed over her forever. Her wrath once stood before me. What sayst thou? I'll tell thee. In silence all lay slumbering. Dark was the night, and o'er clouded. No star was gleaming, the palid moon in veils of storm was shrouded when on the air a sigh was borne and then a sorrowing wail, I saw her on the margin of the tide. There stood a shadow, a shadow pale. Ah, she moved her lips as if to speak. But I alas could not hear her. Then as in warning she waved her hand. I did not dare draw near her. And while I watched her motionless, she vanished from my sight, and o'er the streamlets silver tide shone forth a lurid light, presage of sorrow that vision foreboded. Thus do I fear thy future is clouded. Dearest Lucy I pray thee forgo thy fatal love ere grief o'erwhelm thee. Grief dissolveth beneath his glances. Life is rapture when he is near. Were he but here, Oh ecstasy. Naught should I know of sorrow... Bring me a happy morrow. Oh love to thee I pray, to thee I pray. Let my fears be now forgot. One hour of joy. Oh grant me. Let words of love enchant me and trouble now flees me. May heaven all thy wishes grant thee. But oh, mayst now never regret this day. Dearest Lucy, hear I.

In between, Mark stopped. The room had become very warm. The boy appeared slightly faint. His forehead wet. When the window was opened, refreshed he resumed.

As the last top E Flat flew around Madame O's studio and out through the open window and echoed across the Botanical Gardens, Mark spontaneously took upon himself to interpolate one of those highly impassioned improvised cadenzas of his that sent extra shock waves of excitement out through and over the airwaves and again he experienced that whizzing sensation in his head, as if his young body were no longer earthbound but soaring skywards. As the time spent together came to a close, it took some while for Madame O to recuperate and compose herself after the stupendous vocal feat.

"When can we meet again?" Madame asked. Charles Gorrick stood to attention and answered, "Whenever you wish Madame. We are now at your disposal."

"Tomorrow?"

"The sooner, the better," he replied.

Madame O smiled broadly.

Mark sprang in front of his father as they sauntered down the driveway. Just as they were about to disappear from sight, the boy sensed Madame O's eyes behind him and, joined by his father, turned and waved to her.

Chapter Three

Anton De Vries

The boy's voice still rang in the ears of Madame O as her student entered the room. Silently, she reflected on her position at the Conservatorium. 'How gladly I would abandon my profession to launch my undivided attention on that one voice – no matter how short lived it may be.'

She sighed regretfully. Just two more pupils this afternoon and her working day at the Conservatorium would come to an end, and not a moment too soon. Madame O could barely wait to finish with her last pupil, Lorna Budge. Miss Budge, a spinsterish young woman, appeared older than her 25 years and had proven over half a decade with Madame O unable to learn a new piece, with the result that Madame had all but given up hope of hearing Lorna sing anything new. Over the 5 years, Madame had been overly sympathetic and solicitous – that being her nature – and had not had the heart to deter the girl's enjoyment or ambition, for Lorna inscribed each piece she sang from her limited repertoire with profound depth. However, Madame O's head is ringing with 'that other voice'.

Madame O finished punctually on the stroke of 5 o'clock and rushed to an adjoining room to discuss Mark Gorrick's audition that morning with De Vries.

"So Anton?" she asked not needing to restrain her anguish with such a close colleague. De Vries ceremoniously folded his arms.

"My dear Rosealma, you know already my views on the subject. But firstly let me make this quite clear when I say I've never truly nursed a penchant for the coloratura voice. Having stated that, I must add that the boy's voice is no mere coloratura – his is a unique voice and a spectacular one at that. Of great rounded beauty and warmth, not to mention the flute like ethereal effect above the stave it captures so ardently, as heavenwards it climbs."

Madame O had never heard De Vries quite so carried away. It encouraged her zeal even more.

"Not only is it vested with immense power and exceptional, nay unbelievable, range enough to hold any listener in its thrall, but also the boy is such a natural musician that his voice never errs beyond a certain perfection. The more I've dwelt on these facts, the more unaccountable the voice becomes in my mind – leaves virtually nothing to one's imagination."

De Vries leaned forward and looked searchingly into his colleague's eyes. "Neither you nor I, dear Rosa, shall ever be quite the same again after hearing such a wonder."

Madame O digested Anton De Vries's words with utmost seriousness.

"And if I may be permitted to make another observation, Rosa you seem beside yourself. I believe it has been a positively therapeutic tonic for you since I can't recall seeing you like this before and, well, what is there to say, it's marvellous. You've become younger, more alive, you've taken on a new lease of life." De Vries gently took her hand in his, peered even more deeply into her eyes and affirmed, "We have been present at an auspicious occasion, Rosa, the like of which happens rarely if ever. We may consider ourselves very fortunate indeed." He pronounced his words with the solemn air of a wise inveterate counsellor.

Madame O nodded, one hand now resting under her chin as she pensively surveyed the Botanical Gardens. She thought how her colleague had condensed into seemingly few words her own thoughts on the matter. 'Multum in parro' as her father would say, 'Much in little'. However, what De Vries had to say next shocked her back to her senses.

"Having said as much, Rosa, we have to face facts. Just as surely as there on the wall the clock chimes away the daylight hours. It doesn't stop there. Time sees to it that nothing lasts forever, least of all a boy's voice. That amazing voice we heard this morning is already a day older since yesterday and fate decrees that finally, according to the boy's age, his voice too must find its way into the vocal graveyard of adolescence!

Madame O had not been prepared for the last ominous awakening.

"Whatever are you suggesting, Anton?"

"In a nutshell it is this. You must prepare yourself. At the mere tick of a clock, in fact any day now, the boy's voice is due to break. Perhaps shatter unrelentingly and it can never be the same voice ever again! It may break into a 1,000 useless little segments or one perfect vessel."

Madame O felt De Vries's words pierce through her. "I must say, I'd put any such thoughts aside," she confessed.

"Of course you had Rosa. But like myself, you too are totally overcome. However the difference between us is that I am a realist and I am in full realisation of the doom that lies hidden in magnificent and wonderful objects."

Madame O's face drained of all expression. In a forlorn tone of voice, she half questioned, "Then, there's nothing to be done to save the voice? Of course, you are right!"

"Well, you should know, Rosa. You've written a master work on voices. You weren't awarded all those prizes for nothing. You are a genius in your own right with an immense knowledge of the singing voice at your fingertips. With such a wealth of knowledge," he continued, "there's no denying the fact that the boy's voice as we heard it today lays balanced on a precipice. This voice, which thrills and exalts us simply cannot continue in its present unique state for much longer. He is twelve years old and, sad to say, change is inevitable and imminent."

Now all happiness had turned to sadness for the once sprightly little German professor. De Vries had cast a dark mantle of reality over her short lived joy.

"Had we been living a Greek myth, Rosealma, no doubt the Gods would have found a way to deal with the problem – not take a backwards glance to Alceste", he mused. "And the boy's voice would be saved for posterity. End of fairy tale! But here we sit, plunged right in the middle of brash reality! Curiously enough, adolescence for a girl's voice does not pose such a danger. Their young voices frequently make the transition without loss or detriment of quality. One need only refer back to Patti and Lind to realise that fact." De Vries digressed, "By the way, did you think to record Mark for your post analysis?"

"Oh yes, thank glory. Of course, as you know Anton, I never neglect to record an audition from behind the kitchenette curtain. Without the aid of recording it is so easy to overlook a shortcoming in an audition when the teacher may have became carried away by the sheer personality of an artist, or vice versa, heaven forbid."

"Such as the pathetic event some months ago when that poor demented woman brought her talentless, voiceless daughter to us declaring her to be the greatest singer in the world?"

"Oh yes, how best to forget such a travesty?"

"Indeed, a travesty of much tarnished misconception. Still we must not condone such enthusiasm in the name of music, no matter how unfounded the conception."

"Pity then our prodigy was not a girl!" De Vries's voice tapered off into a regretful murmur, soon replaced by a disconcerting dark tone which at once possessed the power to implant itself upon Madame O's doubt ridden mind.

"'Tis a heart-breaking situation, nevertheless these are the sad prospects we singers and teachers are bound to encounter and obliged to face up to throughout our lives," De Vries continued to elaborate, taking a sermon like stance as he imparted his views.

"It is indeed so much worse for the young male upon reaching adolescence, because rather more frequently than is supposed the boy's voice breaks to major change and upheaval so as to perhaps leave behind a much lamented memory, a mere remnant, a threat, a trail of destruction. In tatters the glory that once was – 'one of the ruins that Cromwell knocked about a bit', as Marie Lloyd would have it," De Vries teased mockingly.

"Please, Anton, this is no joking matter!"

"I'm sorry, Rosa, I am just trying to get my point across. Nevertheless," De Vries carried on regardless with his dark speculation, "at best a tenor, or worse, a scant serviceable admixture, neither one voice nor t'other. In any case, whatever one cares to think or say, nothing suffices for the eventual loss of a once cherished untarnished voice after destiny chooses to steal it right from underneath our noses. Fate having past ordained that the precious voice dwelt safely for a short lived period of time in the boy's pre-adolescent throat. And, in this instance, particularly since we are referring to Mark's voice, a vocal rarity if ever, and which given the opportunity one would never tire of and would gladly listen to for a lifetime and forget all others! In today's world, his purity of sound is of an unfathomable quality which promises to be a universal loss once it departs. Whether we shall ever experience that type of purity reborn in another different throat, I doubt very much."

Since De Vries so convincingly drummed home the truth, naturally Madame O had become progressively disparaged by his all too insistent, yet totally honest, assessment. In similar vein he pursued his pessimistic outpouring.

"Divine heritage, in fact, but from where one asks?" De Vries, addressing himself, toyed with the description trippingly on the tongue. "I think we can use that phrase, Rosa, with complete justification."

This elegant man with his princely features ruminated. Constantly drawn to the inevitability of one's own fate as a way of life, De Vries had more or less seeped himself in tragedy of an almost voyeuristic kind which first hand led him to experience another's misery rather than blindly accept his own lonely isolated existence filled with remorse for past loves. Now that he singularly foresaw tragedy looming large in the boy's future, De Vries appeared even more reconciled to dwelling within that sombre world so much of his own creation.

He intoned dryly - "Remember, Rosa, in Mark's case we are speaking in terms of the 'Divine'! If either of us were never to hear another voice one would readily believe, as long as memory serves us, this voice, of a mere child mind you, will outshine and outlive all others."

Madame O reflected upon his words, telling herself she alone must strive to rectify the situation, knowing full well only a miracle could save the day. Yet, lurking somewhere at the back of her thoughts, an inner voice chanted and informed her that ultimately the boy's voice might, at the last moment, be saved for posterity; be preserved from the harsh forces of nature. But how to accomplish this far off possibility for the present remained an unanswerable reality.

Meanwhile Madame O, having construed and acknowledged De Vries's verbal forebodings, sat stony faced as if she were a patient receiving her doctor's sinister prognosis. Unlike De Vries, throughout her life, she had never given up hope in the name of destiny. Nor had she permitted herself to give into pessimism, even under the most dire circumstances. Had she done so all those years back, today she would no longer have been able to carry forth with her marathon task of music. Hers is a combination of resignation and resilience, an adopted stance, now indeed a permanent stand-by. Nor is she about to renege on these very attributes, which have served her stalwartly throughout difficult times. Still, De Vries's voice droned on monotonously in the background.

"I once heard of a boy's voice, said to have been sublime. Personally I should doubt anywhere in the league of your prodigy, Rosa. Anyhow that particular boy's voice, when he came of age, literally overnight, simply dissipated into nothingness and deserted him."

Curiously enough, De Vries's last pronouncement dramatically caught Madame O's ear, spurred her on with an odd sense of hope. "If only there were a way to…" she questioned. And then she came out with it, ""nip the wonder in the bud? Her mind dwelt at length upon the castrati of the 17th century and how, for months on end, she had carried out extensive research in this area, as part result of which her definitive treatise on the human voice had been swiftly taken up for publication to much critical and professional acclaim. The inside sleeve of the book jacket outlined the purpose of the book thus "In this learned and fascinated treatise, the foremost expert on singing, Frau Professor Rosealma Oppenheimer, presents readers with a valuable insight into her chosen subject. Tracing at length the advent of the much vaunted and oft times awe-inspiring castrati of the baroque era, and thence journeying into the latter dayrealm of the legendary reigning coloraturas from the 18th and 19th centuaries (which Prof. Oppenheimer in a footnote is quick to explain stating that all of her chosen examples are exemplary in the field of coloraturas), finishing up with the fascinating survey of renowned cantors such as Jadlowker and Joseph Schmidt, Chagy, Sirota, Hershman, Katz, Waldman, all adept operatic tenors in the field of coloraturas, who sang not only in the synagogues of their home towns, but also went on to become opera singers in their own right. Throughout her book, we meet with many illustrious names, amongst them Caffarelli, Senesino, Bernacchi, Carestini, Farinelli, Ferri, Pauluccio, Sontag, Lind, Gerster, Melba, Tetrazzini, Sirota, Hessleman, Fleishmann, not to mention a seemingly inexhaustible number of singers from past times who also succeeded in making their mark." A critic wrote, "Interesting enough not once throughout her book is the professor able to cite the true singer of her dreams for which she sums up her vocal equations: 1/3 part col, can, cas and for this purpose she coins the phrase "Colcancas", signifying the ideal vocal combination of unattainable ideals all contained in one voice! Hence the title of her book. "

Madame O continued, "Anton, think of all those amazing lost voices, reference and descriptions of which have come down to us from the various periods starting with the baroque."

"Oh, yes," De Vries ventured, "are you suggesting orchiectomy? That of course would be the only possibility and although it scarcely bears thinking about, it would of course unnaturally beget fruit," De Vries responded acrimoniously, "but, can you imagine Rosa, the latter day mayhem involved in such a medical undertaking. The far reaching manifold implications. The outcome if successful! The incomparable boy's voice not only left in its present virginal state, but also given leeway to grow in stature as he matures with the added advantage of the adult's enlarged diaphragm, voice cage and lungs. Inconceivable! Sensational to say the least. Ah, the thought of it sends one off into raptures. A world wonder! A return to the 17th century of vocal daydreams with the added advantage of your learning. But enough, Rosealma! Basta! Basta! Before my thoughts completely run away with my imagination!" But he was tempted to continue, "Of course, castration is, and has been for ages, against the law. No parent would condone such a barbarous act by the knife. Today no medical man be permitted to execute it. No law abiding society would give way. Few would even begin to comprehend the deployment of such a mutilation even for the further promulgation of music."

Madame O interjected, "But what could be more mutilating than nature's crude way of relieving the boy of his most prodigious natural God given gift. His voice?"

"Then you are suggesting…?"

"Oh, please, Anton, must you always jump to conclusions? I'm not suggesting anything of the kind." In her desperation, Madame O now spoke with tears of frustration and irritation welling up in her eyes. "Anton, what then are the prospects? You are the realist as you admit yourself. I the fantasist. In your opinion, at least. Please try and help me find a way before it's too late. After all you've been responsible for sewing the seeds of doubt in my mind, and now it's your turn to right matters!"

"Rosealma," De Vries confided, characteristically taking her small hands in the palms of his own. "I have already told you – it is touch and go as to whether the boy's singing voice survives at all! This of necessity you must first bring yourself to accept, my dear. Remember a voice such as his is only on loan from the gods for a brief expediency of time.   Such a wonder simply flashes across the firmament flickering and coruscating with all the short lived exaltation of a comet."

Madame O remarked resignedly with a deep sigh, " True - I am only too fully aware of everything you mention, Anton. Even as you suggest, should his voice break into the most glorious tenor or baritone, in respect of the present sublime quality of his voice, it would never compensate fully. I doubt if another voice could substitute – deal such an innervating force and effect upon the listener's senses."

"Yes, Rosa. I agree with you fully and wholeheartedly on that count. Yes, you are probably correct. No manner of other voice would compete, let alone compensate for the loss of his present voice." De Vries exhibited an air of fruitless world-weariness, and shortly after, his energies spent, finally he bid his colleague 'good evening'.

That same night, Madame O scarcely slept. No longer had she the same need or desire of her constant habit to return to yesteryear to singularly find solace in the youthful golden days of her short lived operatic career. Since hearing Mark, the present held a wealth of new meaning and interest for her. Even so, the idea of a full day's teaching posed an almost unbearable task for her. Now all she wanted is to be there for the boy and no one else. Her thoughts saturated with those 'mark-iavellian' ethereal sounds she kept reminding herself, how in one day, due to the intervention of 'divine providence', her entire outlook and existence had been dramatically altered. When Madame O switched off the night light, she half hummed, half sang Piave's text to Violetta's ecstatic declamation from "Traviata". E strano – e strano mysterioso.   The words had returned to recall memories of Madame O's first appearance in Verdi's opera. The year 1933. The place, a provincial opera house at Murnau am Stafelsee in Germany. For the best part of tonight she would lie awake thinking over how eventful and curious her life had been. 'We only imagine we know what our thoughts describe. Yet when the reality dawns upon us, we see only too well that we have all but lived under an illusion. Can this be the true way of our thoughts?' Still wide awake in the early hours, Madame O felt an irresistible urge to see the boy, be near him. She must wait, contact the father first thing tomorrow if only to exchange a few words and make contact with the human vessel responsible for the 'wonder', that now promised even more to profoundly affect her whole outlook and existence. Yes, she must by all accounts act swiftly in the matter she repeatedly told herself, until finally sleep overtook her.

Chapter Four

A Portrait of Mark

Next day Madame O telephoned. The boy answered breathlessly. His speaking voice near enough resembling that of a young girl. Madame O perhaps made her first mistake: "Is that Mr Gorrick's daughter?" she asked of the unfamiliar voice. Her question met with silence at the other end of the line. After which came Charles Gorrick's voice.

"I'm ringing to ask if we could arrange for Mark to sing again for me, Charles?"

"Of course, he'd like nothing better, that goes without saying," Gorrick replied enthusiastically to her request. "Actually, Mark is right beside me. Wouldn't you, Marko?" The boy nodded haphazardly towards his father. A characteristic frown settling across his brow his father noted detachedly.

"Want to say a few words?"

The boy shunned the suggestion.

"The trouble is, Madame, the family is rather disturbed about what Maestro De Vries said yesterday. In fact, his realistic remarks took us by surprise. Unsettled the lad to say the least."

The boy edged closer to his father in order to overhear Madame O's reply. "I agree," she hesitated, "It's simply too dreadful to contemplate. I'm truly sorry – De Vries can be very blunt, but he is a realist and let me assure you his concern is genuine. Truth to tell, Charles, time is of the essence, whether we wish to admit it to ourselves or not."

"Are we then to believe Maestro De Vries, that the voice can disappear overnight, Madame? So quickly?"

A pause followed on the other end of the line, "Yes indeed, Charles, the problem is every bit as pressing as that."

Gorrick experienced a sickening sensation in the pit of his stomach. He held the receiver up closer so Mark didn't hear.

"If it is of any consolation, Charles, I am racking my brain for a way out of this conundrum!"

"What's that you say, Madame?"

"This dilemma," she replied, "Look, could we, as agreed, arrange to meet over tea at my private house?"

"Of course, Madame, you say when. Tomorrow? The weekend?"

"The sooner the better."

"Well, I must say how grateful we are for your interest."

"It's more than interest, Charles. As a teacher I feel I have a loyalty to you and Mark."

"Shall we say tomorrow promptly at your house, Madame?" Gorrick emphasised the last word. "Yes, we have the address. Your house is almost next door to the Rifle Range at the bottom of the park."

"Exactly."

"Never mind, we shall find Windermere Cottage."

When Charles Gorrick replaced the phone, he turned to Mark who sat glumly, his hands folded listlessly upon his lap. Gorrick again noted how in the course of his conversation with Madame O the boy's face had gradually drained of all colour.

"What's the matter, Mark? What's gone wrong now?"

The boy refused to answer. Instead he looked past his father sullenly into the distance, despair written in his young eyes. Gorrick need only steal a surreptitious glance at his son to realize a disturbing factor was continuing to beset and dull the boy's senses.

"Whatever it is, I promise you Mark we shall get over this."

But the boy failed to respond. He just rubbed his eyes and continued scowling into the distance as if his father no longer existed.

Next day at the appointed time, father and son duly arrived on Madame O's doorstep and Charles Gorrick presented her with a large bunch of colourful Zinnias freshly picked from their garden by Latilly Gorrick. Madame O thanked them profusely and led them directly into the conservatory, a bright sunny room with numerous pots of sweet smelling winter narcissi permeating the air. In the centre of the room stood a refectory table laid for afternoon tea.

"Please make yourselves at home while I put the flowers in water. I shan't be a moment," she said before disappearing down the adjoining hallway. Gorrick's eyes rested on the wonderful display of narcissi before admiring the meticulously laid table. When Madame O rejoined them, he asked, "How can winter flowers appear in midsummer?"

"I've learned how to force them. It's quite simple once you know how. Of course it's important to get the timing just so, and grow them in a conservatory."

As Madame O placed a teapot and jug of hot water on the table, she couldn't fail to notice the boy's dejection and his pallor. Could he have grown thinner overnight? Naturally she withheld any comment. The boy's silence had created a somewhat tense atmosphere. Even his character had altered, a silvery glint of aggression shone through in his eyes. Where, she asked herself, had she encountered that icy stare before? Hurriedly she endeavoured to thrust the thought aside. She also noticed both father and son acted as though they were no longer on speaking terms. Not the happiest situation for a stranger such as Madame O who, each working day, had more than her share of temperamental singers to contend with.

"Well then! I think we are ready to begin," she uttered slightly nervously, "Shall we make a start?"

Charles Gorrick shot an uneasy glance at his son, "Mmmh – we'd enjoy that wouldn't we. Mark?"

The boy simply glared ahead. His lips determinedly pursed into an unwavering grimace. Suddenly he stood upright, shuffled irritably, and sat himself several feet further away from his father near the end of the table, ignoring the man's question and now remaining with eyes downcast. The most Madame O could attempt under the circumstances; a self-conscious little cough as she set about pouring tea. Gorrick consciously ignored Mark, instead he admired Madame O's artistry – on the table, an assortment of plateaued sandwiches, milk, butter, scones, honey.

"Mark's favourite food," he told Madame O before commenting on the glistening china tea service, which Madame O showered much reverence upon as she offered each of her guests a cup and saucer. Mark ignored her offer whilst both adults feigned not to notice his attitude.

"I have to admit, Madame, I can't ever remember having seen such beautiful china."

"Nymphenburg," she announced. "One of a few surviving family heirlooms. I'm so pleased you like it, Charles." The boy winced at the mention of his father's Christian name.

"It's, well, what can I say, Madame? Worthy of royalty!"

"How nicely put, Charles."

"Goodness, and you've gone to an awful lot of trouble for us."

"That's a pleasure. No trouble at all."

"Don't you agree, Mark?" Gorrick asked his son, a note of impatience tinged with reproach creeping into his voice.

Madame O realised how fruitless the man's efforts were to rescue the odd situation and encourage his son to say a few words; resurrect the boy from his inert gloom, and Mark stubbornly declined to make a move or reply, remaining mute, indifferently directing his attention through the French windows across into the garden, by such time as which Madame O appeared a little 'frayed at the edges'. Now it became her turn to frown, an expression of disappointment on her brow overtaking her previous radiance. She darted an uncomfortable glance towards Charles Gorrick, but the man chose to avert his eyes icily over to the boy in order to make his feelings quite apparent.

"Come on, Mark!" he urged, "for goodness sake, what's going on?"

Madame O guessed herself at fault – referring as she had done on the phone to Mark as his 'sister', whereas Gorrick concurred to himself Mark's impossible behaviour had been due to the fact that he had allowed the boy to eavesdrop on the telephone conversation between Madame O and himself. Whatever the reason, he just wished Mark would put a stop to this nonsense. Nonsense! Mark suddenly, head first to one side and then to the other, peered quizzically into his father's eyes, exactly the way dogs act as they try to comprehend their master's intentions. Gorrick looked aside but already the boy had gained a knowing glimpse into his father's thoughts. 'If only he would let sleeping dogs lie!' The boy is now taking matters into his own hands and at this point there seemed no stopping him. Madame pondered how a child exerted such command over them both. What secret had he nurtured and digested overnight to launch himself into this black mood? Then without warning, he stood his ground, wildly grappling with and pushing his chair backwards on its side to the floor and, with clenched fits, blurted out in a near incoherent sickening cry, the way an animal might being slaughtered.

"It's not nonsense! I'm going to lose my voice and both of you know it. I'm glad it's going to happen," Mark spoke revengefully, vehemently delivering another impassioned outcry, "Then you won't be able to hear me sing. Good!" he threatened.

"And another thing, I'm not a sissy. I don't want to sing anymore in a girl's voice. I hate it. I want to be a fireman, or something, get covered in dirt. Set on fire!" he bleated menacingly in a rasping, unrecognisable voice that tore at his vocal cords as he ranted.

Gorrick looked at the ground not daring to meet the boy's threateningly icy stare. He knew when best to recoil in his son's presence.

Madame O, speechless and not knowing how to deal with this impossible outburst, would gladly have tried to pacify the boy but thought better of it and instead quietly left the room, momentarily forgetting everything she had prepared and looked forward to that afternoon. Now the boy would never sing. Madness had a way of dealing the cruellest blows. Madame O had seen a singer carried away in a mad moment jump into the orchestra pit, but she had never experienced a child become so incensed over what appeared to be almost nothing, but then she had never dealt with a young singing genius before. Perhaps it is best this happened now rather than later? Until now she hadn't realised just how unnerving the sight of a child, acting as if the greater powers had taken a hold of him, plunging him into a dark abyss from which there appeared no return. The boy's unpredictability had overtaken her. In a peculiar manner he had acted the way he sang, impulsively and dangerously, albeit with a slight difference. When he sang, there was no question of harm to his voice so correct had been his natural technique and intuitive judgement, every wondrous note falling perfectly into place whilst still daring himself to further conquer the heights. No, she must not give up. No matter what difficulties she incurred today. It is only natural, with the weight of that incredible gift, that a mere child, fights to deal mentally and physically with what might, she surmised, be interpreted as an artistic burden, a phenomenon of nature.

Slowly, she retraced her steps and returned to the room where a painful silence ensued. Charles Gorrick's face exhibited both embarrassment and bewilderment, unable to find a ready explanation for his son's behaviour. In front of him, Mark paced a few steps, hovered before his father as though he were about to strike him, clenching his fists and, in a frantic gesture, appearing taller than his real height, undid his belt and ripped at it through the loops of his shorts. Next, he placed one hand on his belt as if about to lash out at them and, with his other free hand in a wild form of self-strangulation, clenched tightly at his own neck. Bluish wealds immediately appeared on his now grown pale skin. Madame O, horrified, drew a deep breath. She scarcely dared exhale for fear of inciting the boy further. The merest attention at this stage she felt could send him quite berserk. She sensed her temples raging. Presently the boy made another move, reversing backwards, one arm outstretched towards them, as much as to say 'keep away if you know what's good for you both.'

"Mark, for goodness sake! Stop this," Gorrick demanded.

A pained crazed expression played over the boy's face as he defiantly swaggered with an exaggerated sense of menacing deliberation, aggressively pushing past his father and making his way out through the open French windows and trudging stolidly down the path to the furtherest end of the garden where an ornamental fountain played; furiously whipping the ground with his belt which by this time he had completely unfastened from around his waist. From where Gorrick and a stunned Madame O sat, well within earshot of the weekend rifle practice, a shot rang out into the air as the boy slumped down behind a tree where he lay supine, motionless. Madame O could just make out the back of his blonde tousled head. A shoulder and a leg stretched across a grass verge. In that moment she experienced a surge of compassion for this self-torturing child.

"What was that?" Gorrick asked peering into the woman's face.

"It's the weekend rifle practise. Sometimes sounds as if they are a few feet away," she stammered. "I can't imagine why grown men and women want to play with guns," she added, still unnerved.

"No. There are many things I also find difficult to imagine about adults," Gorrick replied.

Madame O smiled insecurely, acknowledging his comment. "Should I go down there to Mark?"

"Goodness no, Madame! That would only tend to make matters worse. Something's got into him. Mind you, it's an ongoing occurrence, these usually long drawn out extended sulking periods, but today is the worst I've ever seen him."

Madame O tautly settled back in her chair, "Oh?" she replied nervously peering back down in the boy's direction. "I only hope it's not my fault," she nodded apologetically.

"For what, Madame?"

"Upsetting him so badly."

"Oh no, Madame, none of it. As I said, many things are biting away at him. It's an affliction. Why? Why does it have to be Mark?" he complained.

"I must say, Charles, I am very concerned not to be able to help him. It's terrible to see someone so young fighting with invisible demons."

"Thank you, Madame, for your understanding. In effect, you see Mark's making a stand. Let me outline a few facts. In one respect he is drawing attention to himself. At the same time, he also wishes to be ignored, but not before he has let you know that he is both angry and disturbed by some untoward element that has badly unsettled him. You could say he feels wronged!"

"Is it something you or I have promoted in him?"

"I can't say exactly at this stage. When these unpredictable outpourings occur, they can only be guessed at. His mind is at loggerheads with itself. His actions are something else. Now should you approach him that will only give him an opportunity to steer his anger even more positively into action or should I correct myself and say into more negative action. After all, these neurotic reactions of his, on the surface at least often seem negative in the extreme."

Madame O sighed. "How I longed today to hear the boy sing."

Gorrick explained. "It takes some time for him to calm down. Allow the adrenaline to settle. But unlike our canary, to approach him before he has self-revived could be harmful to himself. Only he can get rid of his problem. If anyone intervenes he might go to pieces all over again, injure himself even."

"Injure?"

"Yes, in this moment he is suffering a form of self inflicted mental pain and anguish. He is persecuting himself."

"But, Charles, that is awful."

"True, but only he can ride out the storm."

"How will he be when he becomes an adult?"

"Hopefully it will all be left behind him. It will be wonderful to see him rid of this self-penalization," Gorrick looked fondly in the boy's direction.

Still no sign of bodily movement.

"Although you may not know it, Madame, you and I at this moment are re-enacting the all important process of playing at the passive – non-intrusive audience."

"The Greek chorus?" Madame ventured timidly.

Gorrick seemed not to hear. "In this capacity we also act as catalyst so that eventually, but only in his time, he will revert to normal. Quicker without audience participation and slower with them - because all the while he feels our presence, he fights himself not to give in to us."

As Charles Gorrick looked into the distance he exclaimed, "He has eyes in the back of his head and is fully aware of the intentional upset he has been instrumental in creating. I doubt if he'll sing after this. I should have known better once I saw how he started behaving yesterday," Gorrick admonished himself.

He paused to collect and establish his thoughts, "and what is often frustrating, his father and mother have a devil of a task to ever find out what's eating away at him. Naturally one supposes these upsets can only be initiated by those closest to him, nevertheless these dark moods can happen when least expected, sometimes when we are not around. I don't like to say it, but it's not just a case of being highly strung, it goes much deeper than that. Long ago my wife and I decided he's more grown up than we are! Anyway he's been on the verge all of today. One thing I can say for certain, he has more or less intimated over the last twenty-four hours, the fact he feels and knows he is going to lose his voice, which saddens me no end. But there again, that is only part truth. You have to be a mind reader to guess what else is disturbing him. Perhaps he expects you should know that because he himself is readily capable of doing the same. Reading your thoughts. You simply cannot withhold any secret incoming thought from him. Embarrassing to say the least, it is to be read like a book by your own twelve year old son. My wife has come to deal fairly successfully with these smouldering mood swings. With much difficulty she simply pretends to ignore them and we have come to the conclusion that this is what the boy demands from almost everyone. It's all part of a strange ritualistic strategy he deploys. Put it this way, Madame, I suppose in his child/adult outlook, if you as his witness cannot actually realise at very first meeting by all the hints he strews in your path, then in his eyes you have failed to pass muster! Does that sound far-fetched?"

"That's both remarkable and a difficult proposition to follow," Madame O commented, her face expressing alarm at the prospects.

"Yes, you agree it's both upsetting and frustrating, isn't it, Madame?"

Madame O responded understandingly, shook her head once or twice, "Yes indeed – especially if you have never met him before."

"And this Madame, I've had to learn, comes undeniably from carrying the burden of an enormous talent."

Madame O finished his sentence, "Not just a glorious voice, but the supreme gift of expressing that voice with all the sublime sensitivity and unerring instinct of the mature artist-singer."

"You think that do you, Madame?"

"I know it!" Madame O volunteered, as she felt her eyes blurring at the thought.

"Well, when I tell my wife what you have just said, she will dearly wish to meet you because she has said as much herself but would never say it to anyone else," Gorrick replied modestly, not permitting himself to add his own personal opinion in that moment. Madame O kept glancing uneasily to where the back of the boy's head, not having moved an inch, remained visible.

"I know what you are thinking, Madame," Gorrick spoke as he followed her gaze. "He has scarcely spoken a word since our telephone call yesterday except to mention his voice. Do you know the meaning of apoplexy?"

"Yes I do. You don't mean to tell me he suffers from apoplexy?"

"No, but he can feign it. And that is exactly what he's up to now. It's both a way of replenishing an ache within himself and simultaneously loosening it."

"I'm not sure if I know what you mean."

"Never mind, Madame. Do you know the more I dwell upon it, the more I'm thinking we shouldn't have bothered you today. As if you haven't enough on your plate to deal with!"

Madame O looked hugely disappointed, "Oh, but Charles, that is far from the truth."

"Besides, Mark's behaviour in front of you Madame is a bit much – unforgivable."

"No Charles! Please don't feel bad. With a voice like his, one would forgive him for just about anything! He is only twelve years old after all."

"Old enough," Charles Gorrick replied, "I blame everything on Mark's hyper-sensitivity. It acts as an affliction on his every move."

"But without it there'd be no creativity."

Gorrick nodded vaguely, drew his chair a little closer to Madame O. "I should explain further. Mark tends to work himself up into a highly nervous state at the end of which he all but expires, swoons. Latilly thinks it's the body's means of containing his mind's anguish which all but puts him at his lowest ebb."

"The mind's anguish?" Madame O asked.

"Yes, his body all but gives up on him. He actually becomes limp like a rag doll. This state of torpor has been frightening for us, his parents, although we are reconciled by now. Yes, we've often questioned if it's not some physical form of protection. Let me give you an odd example. Up until recently, he owned a pet canary that sang divinely but on occasion the bird became so emotionally carried away that we had to nurse him back to consciousness."

"A canary?"

"Yes, a canary. It took some time to revive him. We needed to gently place him in the palm of one hand and stroke him with the other until, with a bit of a flutter, he became his lively old self. None the worse for wear! From the beginning, with so many human traits, he reminded us of Mark. In fact he helped us to better understand the boy, and ourselves as well."

"That sounds to me to be a fit. Birds do have fits." Madame O hesitantly suggested.

"Some form of paroxysm, the vet said, " Gorrick replied. "I can't say exactly. We believe over excitement brought on this state to such an extent that the tiny frame somehow could not contain itself emotionally, finally leaving the little creature totally drained."

Madame O sat watching the expression of genuine pain and anguish crossing Charles Gorrick's lean features so that she temporarily forgot about the boy down at the fountain.

"When the canary fainted, he appeared quite dead until, as I said, we began to routinely realise it had been a necessary safety device that more times than not saved it's life," Gorrick continued.

"Did it happen often?"

"No, not often, but recently it proved fatal. We all felt so useless to see that perfect creature bravely fighting with all it's might to please us, which he always did, to revive. We were after all his principal concern. His reason for living. But his super efforts to return defeated him. No longer did he possess the youthful means nor the necessary reserves of strength left to resurrect himself from the fray. A five year old canary is vulnerable in the extreme and his life petered out. He became an emblem of fortitude for us."

Gorrick gave a nervous cough. "Of course, we had no desire to get another although the vet suggested we should, but Mark insisted against it. We soon realised and learned with the bird's passing that there is just the one of everything, and my wife and I have since made it a rule to treat as a rare gift, and with utmost respect, anything – man or beast – that crosses our path. Naturally, his passing, early one morning caught us unawares especially, coming as it did, shortly after an old friend also departed this life. Mark suffered terribly from both events. Not a visible tear mind you, which made it worse. Kept to his room mostly. In fact for weeks on end we couldn't get as much as a word out of him and he had to be kept from attending school. There are just the three of us and none of us could even refer to the bird or our old friend Florrie without being overcome. You could say we all three were suspended in grief. Even now!" he stopped.

Visibly affected by the importance Gorrick attached to these events, Madame O interrupted, "I think it's time to fetch more boiling water, Charles. Shan't be a moment." She excused herself.

When she returned, Gorrick continued, "But here is the crux of the matter, Madame. Bird and boy adopted each other's attributes! Initially, the pet shop owner, despite the bird's handsome and neat appearance, sold him as a 'dud'. A 'non sequitur' as he put it. We didn't mind because the bird was so engaging and after all we knew nothing about birds. That he was supposedly no warbler held no interest for us. Yet it took a very short time under Mark's guidance for the canary to become a true warbler. Marvellous when you think about it. A total transformation. Not in character, mind! That scarcely changed from the outset. We noticed when Mark either whistled or sang a scale, lo and behold, Joseph imitated him to the point of adding embellishments as Mark is so fond of doing. Well I never! In no time the bird could whistle parts of the second aria of the Queen of the Night from Mozart's 'Magic Flute'," Madame O's eyebrows raised. "and the flute or piccolo beginning of Rossini's overture to 'Cenerentola' How can you explain a bird becoming so human? I put it down to bird intelligence encompassing our own type of human emotions. I mean to say, how else does one account for their tiny brain? Anyhow, joy definitely was his main preoccupation. Recalling the day we brought him back in a small cardboard box, he didn't even make a whimper, and when we placed him in his cage, he proved already to be completely tame at only a month or two old. Immediately flew onto your shoulder and stayed put until you placed him back in his cage. What do you make of that, Madame?"

Her emotions drained, painful memories being recalled, Madame O replied quietly, "I wish I'd heard him."

A hint of steel playing in his clear sky blue eyes, Charles Gorrick continued, "At this stage I should take the opportunity to tell you a little more about Mark, that is if you would like me to "Madame."

"Oh please, Charles," Madame O replied, the memory of the boy's voice whirling round in her head.

"To give you some idea of his character, which is complex. As an infant he nursed a frightening habit of holding his breath, hyper-ventilating. This occurred at the first signs of not getting his own way. Music usually at the forefront of the problem. Every time it happened he had to be dunked into a tub of cold water so that he gasped in shock and his lungs filled up with air to make him breathe normally. Later this breathing problem turned to increasingly severe attacks of asthma, so that we were obliged to stay in the city in case he needed hospitalisation. To tell the truth, the years have not improved that side of things," Gorrick hesitated, "however, there is another happier side to the story. Never dark without light! The magic side; the fairy tale side of things. You see, Madame, I've always loved the singing voice. From my youth I managed to put together a collection of gramophone records, which I played on an early wind-up Vocalian gramophone that has become the centrepiece of our household. Otherwise all I've learnt is from listening to old records. I used to be a farmer but now that I've returned to the city, I'm again following a natural bent. I can run up just about anything on my old Singer sewing machine, trousers, shirts, and dresses. Never learned, mind you, I expect you'd put it down to a natural facility somewhat in the manner Mark just opens his mouth and his voice appears."

"So this natural facility runs in the family?"

"I suppose you could say that. The only part I'm not keen on is bicycling from suburb to suburb to secure orders, but I still have time to give vent to another of my 'creative urgencies', Gorrick smiled, "apart from being 'a man of the cloth,'" he quipped, "old cars. Recently I found an old Vauxhall with a Dickie seat for Mark and which I'm in the process of renovating. But to get back to Mark - the fairy tale side of things. I can recall the exact moment of his 'emergence'. One day after a particularly long trek, I bicycled back home with a 78 record found in a junk shop for tuppence ha'penny. The song, Rossini's 'La Danza' sung extravagantly, best way I could describe, by the Polish soprano, Miliza Korjus. Whew! Stunning! As I played it Mark, a five year old, came running out and cried and cried. Began to hold his breath until I was obliged to play the record numerous times over, after which he breathed naturally, whilst I became exhausted under the strain. Still I didn't mind. I was just grateful for his reaction. He demanded to be allowed to play the record himself. His small hands winding away at the gramophone handle. Then to my absolute astonishment, when I'd only left the room a minute or two, 'the voice' in all its pristine glory made its first appearance. An exact replica of the Korjus voice. All the Italian words intact as far as my ears told me. A flawless union. Note perfect he sang a duet with the record. The only time you could tell it was not Korjus singing a duet with herself being when he added his own so called 'obligatory additions' now and then. My wife and myself, were bedazzled, deeply moved, excited beyond belief. As for Mark he just stood there, an ever widening smile reaching across his face!"

"A five year old!" Madame O exclaimed.

"That day taught us how reality disappears and how fantasy can begin to take over your life, and continues to do so ever since. From that time onwards, the child's singing endlessly filled the house. I became obliged to buy more records, which my limited finances just about permitted me to furnish his needs.

"Such a voracious appetite, Charles? In one so young?"

"A good description indeed, Madame. We had to continuously stoke the infant dynamo on new songs and arias, and as quickly as we fed him, it merely whetted his appetite for more."

"But I've never heard anything like this told, Charles. It's the strangest and, at the same time, the most beguiling tale I've heard. In fact I wouldn't believe it had I not already heard what he can do with his voice. Now I'm willing to believe anything. So tell me again, how did you feel about this gift?"

"You mean the gift of the child, or his gift of a voice, or both? Delirious would be putting it mildly. We were the proud possessors of our own private nightingale. Think about it, Madame. Not only that. You might be tempted to consider him part human, part bird, part adult, part child. For a time we didn't quite comprehend this magic combination in one so young. Each day posed a different revelation. What to us became an astonishing feat owes to the fact that after one or two hearings, the song or aria remained steadfastly imprinted upon those prodigious vocal cords of his."

"And his innate musicality never once allowed his ears to err Charles?"

"Yes, so that with or without accompaniment, as you've experienced yourself, his intonation was never even remotely at fault. Apart from which, of course as you might imagine, he also possesses perfect pitch."

Madame O sighed with pleasure tinged with exasperation when she temporarily remembered her own vocal prowess, whilst momentarily forgetting the disturbing events enacted over tea, till she began imagining instead the excitement running throughout the Gorrick household.

"We felt chosen. A wonderful fairy tale installed within our midst. We had never heard of similar events occurring, voice-wise at least, although my wife had been aware the great Adelina Patti, who already sang as a child of eight, but we could not draw a similar parallel whereby a boy's voice had near enough matured at such an early age so that the voice could encompass some of the more difficult pieces written for the human voice. In no time, Mark started effortlessly singing whole stretches of operas written for the most celebrated singers from the past. And all the while those instrumental vocal sounds changed at random to imitate oboe, piccolo, violin, piano or flute. As our city neighbours never grew tired of telling us, 'So gorgeous on the ears'. Whenever we looked out there they were, just sitting, stunned. The older folk, some who remembered a great singer or two, sat overcome with emotion, tears welling, especially the Levy sisters, our close neighbours. Nona Levy made the boy's favourite honey cakes, not only for him but also supplied them to his audience, the old age pensioners sitting outside. The place became something of a song festival. Anyone who wanted being free to listen.

"At that early age what a repertoire he commanded!" Madame O exclaimed.

"Each time I procured a new record, in no time he knew it by heart before I'd even afforded myself the chance of getting him another. For example he actually sang all the versions of Lucia's arias including that of Galli-Curci, Tetrazzini and so on, adding quite often a set of his own show-stopper embellishments and cadenzas. Italian songs featured too – Canta per me, Carnival of Venice, Funiculi Funicula, Il bacio 'Parla waltz, Santa Lucia, Mari Mari, Tiritomba... Just imagine, a five year old singing whole potpourris. Well I was kept at my sewing machine in an attempt to make ends meet, now I had a new situation – to buy more and more gramophone records. I bought all I could afford but even those were not enough. Still Mark did not approve of everything he heard. Wagner, for instance, nurtured a blank spot. To his way of thinking – morbid. No, he has a discerning ear but what we admired most, rarely if ever did he not improve on the chosen work by his artistry. One only had to hear 'Musica Proibita to realise where the child's sentiments lay. 'Non tis scordar' made Nina Levy weep. That is how it was. Everyone had their chosen favourite piece and yet his voice speaks to all. When not playing records, it had to be the radio. So there you have it, Madame, a thumbnail sketch of Mark's origins."

"I have to say it over and over again, Charles, this tale gives food for thought because one cannot estimate too much what lies behind the individual's exterior. How wrong I had been the other day at the Conservatorium. Mark is obviously no run-of-the-mill encounter. Far from it. He most certainly doesn't answer to a set equation, and far be it for me to have foolishly taken him for granted as I did, basing my assumption on conventional reaction."

"It's quite true. You can simply go on discovering certain things about him that you'd never dreamt of before. But, as I have intimated, one has to tread softly in order to bring the very best out in him and proceed to 'distil the essence', as our dear friend Mr Mosely advised."

Madame O nodded cautiously and peered closer through the French windows. "I feel greatly relieved having been able to formulate and dwell upon what you've passed onto me. Although it does seem an eternity that he's spending down at the fountain. Are you certain…," she broke off gesturing towards the still prostrate figure leaning up against the tree. "Had we not better go down there?"

"No, as I said, I promise you, it's best to wait. That is if you don't mind bearing with me a little longer."

"Of course. Anything to abide by the rules," Madame O smiled. "Then he's going to be all right?"

"Of course," Gorrick assured. "There is, I'm glad to say, a very grown up side to Mark and that is what we as his parents have come to rely on in stressful moments when he is under duress, where one emotion fights against the other. Needless to say, the grown up side usually comes out victorious. As to the childlike, well I suppose that simply goes on being the child."

"A supremely gifted child," Madame O added. You know, it's a very understanding way you have of putting things together, quite remarkable really, so that I begin to understand the boy all the more readily."

"Well, concerning my wife and I, we have very little choice. To understand Mark is a demanding, long-term education on its own. As I've said to put it briefly, we learnt quite a few things about ourselves which we never realised before, which brings me to another of Mark's special sides worth mentioning. It is this, as far as strangers go, at the moment you may not believe it, but once he knows you better he will do his utmost to please you. Go to any lengths to help. That is his most endearing quality. Irresistible, or should I say ennobling. A bit of a performing seal until he gets wind of ulterior motives encircling him.

"Cave! Cave!" Madame smilingly remarked.

"Needs appreciation and lots of it. As for criticism, that best be put on hold to the point of fault. He simply cannot deal with it. His mother's fault. Tilly never judges, nor criticises. Has no need of it. I know he only looks like a baby but the mature things he comes out with! Only recently, Florrie – Oh no, I'd better not go into that…," he paused. "It's as though the boy has a sixth sense. How else does one explain knowing of things he previously knew nothing of? Sometimes at night my wife and I just sit up and wonder. Wonder if perhaps there isn't someone else lurking beneath that solitary childlike exterior. That very dear friend, Herbert Mosely, whose name is always on the tip of my tongue, has helped us greatly in our own personal management of the boy. An old bachelor and artist, he says with utmost conviction that the boy is a re-incarnation. Of whom or what we ask him? Naturally he could not say except to agree that the boy possesses a sixth sense. In his own words, 'a prophetic type nature' that both informs and forewarns the young brain of certain coming events! Furthermore, our old friend thinks the boy a genius of a kind. For instance, Herbert finds his drawings very mature for one so young with little of the child in them as, that is, one generally comes to look at children's drawings. You see he can get a likeness in a few swift strokes as though he is looking right through the subject directly into their soul."

Madame O just nodded, absorbing revelation upon revelation.

"Which brings me to another problem. My wife and I are often taken to task to deal correctly with his ultra-hypersensitivity, which of course, his whole existence is firmly built upon. We fully realise we must not wound or destroy it by one wrong move and that particular pressing task, I might add, has nearly cost us dearly. We must always be not only on the defensive but also guard the 'watch tower' in relays. If you understand what I am getting at?"

"Yes, of course. What a responsibility you have set yourselves."

"Yes, if we say something off-guard without thinking of the consequence, one wrong move and we pay the penalty. Mind you, not immediately. Oh no, that would be to escape too easily. No, later on there comes the overall vengeance scenario!"

"Oh!" Madame O murmured through clenched teeth. "Si vendetta tremenda vendetta!" or words to that effect.

"One right word is what Tilly and I forever aim at in respect of Mark's temperament. Likewise, any inadvertent or harmless exclamation taken the wrong way which he might latch onto can easily be sorely misinterpreted. Heaven forbid! It's as dangerous as playing with a fireball and dousing it in petrol to put out the flames."

"As serious as that, Charles?"

"No. I'm slightly exaggerating I suppose. What I mean to say is some situations can be very uneasy. Put it this way, lurking within the child, Tilly and I never underestimate the inner adult seeking refuge behind whatever statement or action Tilly and myself are responsible for, correct or incorrect, Mark slowly digests and processes. In effect, the exact opposite procedure he adopts to his amazingly innovative music processing where the words and notes spontaneously overtake him in one swift swoop. Yes, I can tell you Madame, many's the time we've had to sit back through numerous tense moments and grit our teeth. This 'uncertainty aspect' that Mark promotes, often leads us down a path of indecision because naturally we want what is best for the boy. Sometimes I think if only he could forget his 'hang ups' – bury the hatchet once and for all – life would be so much easier all round. The trouble is he possesses an infallible conscious stricken type of memory. Remembers every detail, meticulously storing away in his mind every observation, good, bad, indifferent. In general most people tend to only absorb what they deem necessary, what they require, and no more. Not so with him. Each and every particle of information is scanned and scrutinized, following which he works on the results, as does a scientist, analytical theorist or physicist. Nothing, it seems, is frittered away.

After which for long periods he is abnormally calm given over to meditation and introspection."

"That too is the method with which he undertakes his singing?"

"Yes, every phrase is allotted its rightful place. Every breath given its due."

"So, Charles, one is speaking here of the mature artist masquerading in juvenile apparel!"

"Precisely, Madame. I know you understand exactly what I've been trying to get at."

As she learned more about Mark, Madame O felt a surprising pang of possessiveness overtake her. Ideally she wanted to keep the boy all to herself. Own him – and his voice.

Charles Gorrick continued with his portrayal of his son. "Concerning the expressions on people's faces and their personal inner voices, Mark's mind acts as a catchment area. He misses nothing. He's a human lie detector. Always looking for the truth. A translator of souls; their pain and anguish. Having stated as much, one is hard put to guess what else is going on in his mind which, I guarantee, is at the time the most closed circuit you'll ever encounter in anyone so that, for example, if he upholds a grievance, feels wrongly done by, then all those especially personal endearing qualities and characteristics he is blessed with disperse in a flash of temperament, become as nothing."

Madame O just had time to remark, "Heaven forbid anyone on the end of his resentment!"

"Too right, Madame! Once wronged his recalcitrant nature knows no bounds. It's as if that opposite side in him simply won't permit him to forgive! Even though on the surface all may appear well while harbouring and festering down within, turmoil is hard and fast at work. And try as he may, he can't for the life of him seem able to shake off these constraints and stubbornly held resolutions. Latilly and I try to treat this 'Mark-iavellian' problem with a pinch of salt. We see it somewhat as a form of extended speculation on his behalf whereby he patiently, or should I say relentlessly, sets about weighing the 'pros and cons' of any situation crossing his path that incessantly bugs and disturbs him!"

"You see mostly everything the boy adjudges to be either wrong or correct, good or bad, essentially depends on his stubborn fast held attitude when he sets out to deal with the gravitas of a given situation in which he becomes rapidly involved. And you would be quite correct in assuming, with his type of volatile nature, these situations are frequent." Gorrick paused to reflect, then commented, "And does he weigh them up? Does he ever!"

"And how exactly would he go about that, Charles?"

"The answer is this. In an anguished and restless mind such as his, where one crisis follows upon another, there are several ways. Long ago, Tilly and I concluded his emotions work in a set pattern that needed to be carefully organised and laid out in a formulated design. As I think I've already said, this particular ritual cannot be hurried along."

"That's a difficult proposition for an outsider such as myself to contend with."

"Yes, and don't I know it from past experience. No one beyond his immediate family circle could even begin to comprehend the complexity of the boy's thoughts and actions. Any outsider, moreover, is bound to be so overwhelmed with his voice when they first hear it that they tend to bypass all else. It simply proves beyond them to enter his secret domain founded and built upon by his exaggerated hypersensitivity, not to mention a touch of venom here and there to provide bite and texture to the very fabric of his highly charged temperament. He reminds me of a fox, difficult to tame and forever stationed at his observation post waiting, perhaps stalking an imaginary quarry. Yet forever on guard keeping his distance because he readily creates an impasse, a road block, so to speak. Should you try to get too close he shies away to take up another equally distant isolated vantage point from where to keep watch."

"But surely, with so much playing on his mind, that must exhaust the mind of such a young fellow?" Madame O suggested.

"Oddly enough, Tilly and me actually think he thrives on this highly charged emotional diet. After all his attitude hasn't shifted that much since his 'official' imminent 'emergence' at age five or so" Gorrick added with a mock twinkle in his eye.

Madame O suddenly remembered the expression on the boy's face earlier on today, and the manner in which he stood up from the tea table. "He is not violent though is he?" she asked.

Gorrick carefully weighed up her question. "No, I wouldn't say so. Mean and moody, yes, when the 'condition' or circumstances warrants, and sullen. A pity because these overbearing emotions get in the way of his singing and singing is the only way he truly wishes to express himself. He scarcely talks, and never to strangers!" For a while, Charles Gorrick pondered Madame O's question. "Come to think of it, now you mention it, Mark did get violent. Just the once let me say to allay your fears. Took it on his own shoulders to let it out on the proverbial school bully, Johnny Boles. Mark let the lad know what he thought of him. Up until that time no one took too much notice of Mark, nor he of anyone else. No one had any idea he sang either. Nor did he wish to give his music teacher the slightest opportunity to know he possessed a voice. Too embarrassed the other children would make a mockery of him. Anyway, that's beside the point. To get back to the school episode. He gave Johnny Boles a bloodied nose after an incident involving a couple of refugee children Mark liked. The children were new to the class and were rather insultingly referred to as 'refos' by the others. After school, Mark pinned his foe down on the ground and set about giving him hell for leather. Caught him up in such a fierce grip around the lad's throat for some time that he became powerless to fight off Mark. However, when he finally escaped Mark's clutches and started punching and kicking out at him, Mark ended up giving him a black eye and knocked out a front tooth for extra good measure. This affray all happened so out of character that it took everyone by surprise and, believe it or not, the outcome of this scrap was the boy's father came round to thank Tilly and myself for being indirectly responsible for knocking some sense into his uncontrollable son. The good side is both boys became the best of friends. In fact, Johnny who has no voice to speak of, after finally hearing Mark is still determined to be a singer. Apart from which, nowadays, he is a nicely behaved friendly lad. Mark had made, what was for him, the correct decision. He and his chosen 'prey' or foe, in this case Johnny, have become as I said the best of friends, but it could easily have resulted differently."

"And today down there in the garden?" Madame O appeared uncertain of herself.

"At the moment, Madame, we can't be too sure. We don't quite know what's going on tucked away in the dark recesses. Not least owing to Mark's unpredictable nature in dealing with overpowering matters that disturb him and which, curiously, I've always qualified makes his singing such a thrilling experience; a dangerous musical escapade!"

Madame O agreed and proclaimed in no uncertain terms, "In any other singer, his unsparing type of spontaneity that goes to frightening lengths to gamble with the voice's natural function, would otherwise prove fatal, spell vocal disaster and ruin. You need a 'true' voice such as his before taking risks and throwing all scruples to the wind."

"And a considerable dash of unpredictability," Gorrick added. "Indeed, Madame, the risks he takes vocally in anyone else, as you say, would court instant danger, spell disaster, but with him you could say it's a 'cinch'".

As the afternoon passed on, Madame O all but forgot the time, so absorbed and intrigued with the conversation had she become. The food remained untouched. The tea lukewarm. The combined personalities of father and temporarily absent son had overtaken and engrossed her.

Charles Gorrick continued, "Still, once you get to know him you will be better qualified to understand the many faceted guises his character takes on. To Tilly and me, he can be near enough unrecognisable on occasion."

"Strange you should mention that, Charles, because when I met him earlier on today, he struck me as being rather different to how I remembered him just 24 hours ago. Paler, older, thinner, even taller! Less focussed if I can put it that way."

"It's true. He's growing up at a frantic rate, both mentally and physically. His progress from one month to the next is unnerving. A month seems more like a year, to us at least, and in that time the 'doting son' runs the full gamut of emotions. So you see, he gives Tilly and me a run for our money! For instance, not so long ago, he upset his mother so much. Well we ought not to go into that!" Gorrick thought better of it and continued, "suffice to say, the aftermath being he couldn't do enough to make amends to Tilly, so guilt-laden had he become. Over the next months he went out of his way to repent. Exaggeratedly so, because in the first place the 'upset' was not so serious. How can I describe his actions without sounding foolish? 'Saintly' would be one way of putting it either acting in his own defence or otherwise. One is hard put to tell. But his actions had unforeseen adverse repercussions. He kept on penalising himself to the point of self-starvation and, this will surprise you Madame, it had been our neighbours, the sisters Ethel and Nona Levy who drew our attention to the facts. How we could be so blind at the time remains for us one of those impenetrable mysteries, and yet it's true. We were either too close to him or, a more likely explanation, we believe our blindness in relation to his condition probably due to Mark's waylaying us with his disembodied singing that acted on us at the time as would a tranquilliser. Those eerie disembodied siren like sounds he daily produced should somehow have forewarned us something rare and wonderful was adrift. Yet oddly they had the opposite effect. Rather, they distracted us from the reality of the situation. Each day and every day, he instigated and incised these sounds into his singing and they carried us away on a wave of euphoria since they fell so harmoniously on the ear. Anyway, need I add to the fact we failed him miserably by not noticing at the time his declining physical condition?

Since then, often we have asked ourselves whether it had been intentional on Mark's side or otherwise. Had it been so, of course, we would have every reason to believe Mark has within him a certain evasive self-destructive element even though we can't prove it, nor give reasons why. So it remains guesswork. Needless to add, we are much more aware of him since that terrible dysfunction occurred. But at the time, it had nearly been too late when the realisation dawned upon us. Tilly immediately headed for a breakdown. As for myself, I could scarcely keep my wits about me. And Mark; they rushed him away in an ambulance to the Coast Isolation Hospital where the worst, often untreatable, sickest children, many fatally ill, are admitted, confined and segregated into isolation wards. Over that period, we were only allowed visits from behind a thick wall of glass. Tilly became so disturbed at the prospects she could not forgive herself, blamed herself unreasonably. At the Coast Hospital, doctors resorted to guessing games. Simply were unable to diagnose accurately Mark's condition. Parrott's disease, anorexia, all included in the suppositions. Nothing helped. What made matters worse, he could not sing a note. Just managed a few crackily words in an unrecognisable enfeebled voice."

"Heartbreaking, Charles," Madame O ventured.

"A foreign doctor swore he recognised Mark speaking a few words in Aramaic or some such language. What else? We asked in desperation. Now his mind is going. That year in a hospital ward launched Mark on a journey into another unrecognisable world from which we believed at the time there would be no return. Towards the end of the year, one day we noticed Mark had rallied a little. His eyes glittered and scrutinised us. Shortly after, at our next visit, the doctors informed us they believed he had begun to fight his way to get better. Mind you, the extreme effort left him deplorably weak but, little by little, he gradually improved and finally the hospital agreed it in his best interests' to return home. We were told no more could be done for his condition. Nevertheless, we were warned the situation had been touch and go."

Charles Gorrick gulped, cleared his throat and looked out through the French windows for a few moments.

"Anyway, the positive outcome of such a horror story is that we set ourselves goals to achieve, in the full realisation that we must never let such a thing happen under our very eyes again. I took to staying at home for greater lengths of time to be near Mark, and that's when I got the idea to teach myself philosophy and it brought with it some home truths. For one thing it taught me just how little I knew, to use my powers of thought, especially when I studied some writings of Martin Buber for the first time – given to me by our neighbour, Nona – and I benefited greatly. It put me more at my ease knowing the boy's ways, his continued muteness – I mean silence – might be brought about by some self-induced state of torpor due to physical shock to help him recover. Imagine, not a sound forthcoming. We were frightened. His light remained left on throughout the night. His door usually locked. Whatever was going on in his room we were not permitted to know. We thought this 'self reprisal' or 'recovery system' or whatever you care to name it would not cease. So you can imagine the immense relief when, one day, we were awoken at dawn to hear the strains of Lucia's first aria. The one we, the family, all like so much. 'Regnava nel silenzio – In silence all lay slumbering'. The relief! It came as a breath of fresh air – a bonus.

Madame O sat totally entranced at Charles Gorrick's vivid description and gulped a quick intake of breath.

"I remember d saying how appropriate that melody had been coming as it did in a time of extreme doubt and worry. Toward the end of the aria though, Mark stopped, and the next thing we knew he had stolen into our room and sat at the foot of the bed. A touch shaky and worse for wear and registering a little surprise at his own superhuman effort. His cheeks flushed. His eyes glassy, near enough recognisable as the boy we thought we were about to lose. That dawn marked a breakthrough in all our lives. Mark had returned from the abyss. Tilly remarked he'd grown up mentally overnight, whereas I felt physically he had aged. Yet he still managed to bring into the room with him a timeless, magical glow. I remember how we watched, waited on tenterhooks, held our breath, not wanting to intrude upon his very personal reverie. Who knows, looking back, for a while we may even have imagined ourselves in the presence of a sleep walker!" Gorrick chuckled, "a phantom from the past. This unpredictable episode in our lives certainly set store to a slightly different way of looking at things. With more awareness that is. Anyhow, we knew our luck to have changed before our very eyes and that we at last were being rewarded after a terrible time of almost unendurable stress. At our bedside Mark sidled a little closer like a faithful puppy. You'd have sworn he had a tail and was wagging it and as he came over to us, he bent forward and looked closely into our eyes reassuringly with unfamiliar, age old concern. Compassion is the word I am looking for. The glazed expression on his face is difficult to describe even today, except to say it maintains a haunting aspect, which can actually sadden us if we dwell upon it, as if he is growing up too soon or knows too much for his years. Tilly and I were carried away with the combination of consuming sadness and joy. Mark smiled towards us but not with us, if you can understand my meaning. Not a word passed his lips, nor between us either." For a moment, Gorrick's eyes followed Madame O's as she gazed out through the French windows.

"From the brief time you've known him, Madame, you may well have noticed Mark rarely smiles? Well I can tell you this much, when he does finally smile, you know you are faced with the utmost truth because he reserves that smile for the most rarefied moments. Those moments when he knows and feels himself to be the only one answerable to his own uncompromising set of emotions."

"He doesn't smile for the sake of it is what you mean, Charles?"

"Exactly. One could say his smile is in effect symbolic of everything he holds to be sacred," Gorrick answered.

"But, a boy of that age affected by his emotions in such a deeply thought out manner!"

"Yes, it's true, Madame. He is forever taking himself to task," Gorrick replied without hesitation. "To put it another way, even his smile is an all embracing serious statement! That same smile speaks volumes more than words can tell. It is wholly encompassing. In my own eyes, it conjures up an almost mystical event."

As Madame O listened, mesmerised by the man's narration, she thought 'here is a person, in all seriousness, spelling out the meaning, of the virtues that lay behind a smile!' She observed the man's lean features, his finely shaped generous mouth, and then she believed herself no longer hearing the words, instead imagined herself plunged into a vacuum of thought, able to lip read. All is silent. The boy's soul having been spelt out in silence, Madame O had no need to speak, just watch and follow the 'movements' in order to understand everything the man had said; needed not to say.

Suddenly, Charles Gorrick broke off from what he had been saying and changed the subject. "Recently I read of some unfortunate persons whose aims worked against themselves. The left side of the mind, fighting the right, or vice versa. I've no idea what this illness is called but it struck me not unlike Mark on his bad days fighting with himself. At such times, I keep well away to escape his malice. He fights with himself, mentally that is, one side of his mind in combat with the other," Gorrick remarked with an air of finality, and stopped as if there were no point in continuing.

"Oh, what's the use of trying to explain this boy of ours. It will take a lifetime anyhow to iron him out". A slightly embarrassed expression reached across his face. "I'm sorry, I've overdone the 'doting father' bit, Madame, forgive me. You must be very bored, if not, you certainly have the right to be. I am sorry to have taken up so much of your time," he paused," but I suppose I felt, with, you I could let go of the reins. I've never actually spoken to anyone the way I've spoken to you today, and on second thoughts I shouldn't have embroiled you in a subject of such a highly personal nature for which only the boy's immediate family ought to be bridled with. However, it's too late now to change horses midstream," he sighed, a whimsical half smile playing across his features.

Madame O leaned forward. "May I say something, Charles?"

"Please do, Madame."

"It's this. If you can accept it. I believe you and I are kindred spirits and I, like you, have your son's voice and well being at heart and I should like to be of help as much as I can."

"But initially, at the Conservatorium Madame, we only came for a judgment on his voice and I've overstepped the mark. I guess it's because the boy is such a handful." Gorrick looked as though he were about to give up. His nerves more pronounced than any time that afternoon.

"Please let me help if I can, Charles. For myself I couldn't think of anything more rewarding, although naturally I realise the decision is yours."

"But, circumstances permitting, Madame. The Conservatorium? I would gladly accept your offer with open arms but unfortunately we are a little in financial straits at the moment."

"But, Charles, I and anyone else should be the ones to pay you a million pounds, and more for the privilege, every time Mark sings a note! What I meant is I would see him privately at my house free of charge."

"Your problem is that you are much too good, Madame."

In a gesture of mutual understanding, Gorrick took her hands in his. Madame O could no longer comment. "I'm at a loss for words, Madame." He looked down towards the garden and remarked distractedly to himself, "At such times something dies a little in him. You might liken the condition to someone's brain cells that are abused by alcohol or drugs and over time become a little more deteriorated. That same slow waning and lapping away process gnawing at his innards."

"Some are born to suffer, perhaps that is the obverse penalty for being endowed with any God given gift?" Madame consoled. "For the course of a noble life must suffer pain (Aeselylus – the children of Heracles). How ought I to put it to you Charles? A child while it lives it grows, absorbs and learns. There is so much substance to fill the empty vessel finally, sometimes to bursting point. Consider the premature death of many great composers. Schubert – dead at 31, Mozart at 35, Pergolesi at 26, Bellini at 34. Yet they managed to fill the flask to over-brimming, left eternal legacies, but paid the price with a short life crammed to overflowing. I'm certain as with Van Gogh their enthusiasm or 'madness' as the Dutch painter writes in a letter of himself, made them suffer, admittedly, 'divinely' – In other words, a 'divine' suffering. I believe at present, your son's vast weighty talent is more than his lightweight child's body weight can ably deal with. Hence, his fighting with the unknown quantity. In himself, he knows something extraordinary is happening but cannot quite conceive of it in everyday terms. It is also not only his voice that is already fully-fledged and existing. It is the unknown stealth, which accompanies that talent in which he now finds himself enveloped and which demands he singularly deal with. And he chooses to do so – solo, bravely without the advantage of a catalyst to set the tone of the music." Madame O continued, "I would surmise to be born with so abundant a gift is an immense onus, leading its possessor to be ultimately bedazzled by their very own existence."

"I'd already rather imagined such a thing," Gorrick answered, and added shamefacedly regarding the exquisitely arranged table.

"With all my talking your beautiful afternoon tea will be ruined Madame."

"On the contrary Charles, think nothing of it."

"I think we should leave Madam."

"Oh, but you will stay?"

"Shouldn't I just fetch him and leave by that side entrance, to save us further all round embarrassment."

"Not for my sake unless you feel it best. For myself, I am still hoping against hope. I think you know what for?" Madame O paused.

"All right, Madame," Gorrick managed a smile, "If you don't mind marking time a little longer?"

"Very well, whatever you suggest. I am used to treading water with my students!" Madame O responded. "Tell me, Charles, the name Gorrick. Is it French?"

"I like to think so, Madame. I so admire this most artistic nation on earth. No, I rather think the name is a touch common, a no man's land soubriquet. I can't imagine anyone special being called Gorrick. Sounds more like a gravedigger."

Madame O smiled away her thoughts. "I shouldn't bank on that," she remarked, her eyes twinkling.

"Could you just rekindle in my mind Madame what you said before about the fragile vessel becoming jammed full to near breaking point before its time?"

"Of course Charles, during this process the owner of that fragile vessel does not become deterred. He does not reject. The human receptacle goes on receiving and accepting, expands beyond limitation. Genius has no choice, it runs the full gamut of emotions and in so doing runs the risk of becoming 'waterlogged'. At this point it can easily snap, erupt and explode finally resulting in that same Van Goghian 'madness frenzy'.

Charles Gorrick whistled under his breath. "So you say, Madame, Mark cannot contain the flood once the sluice gates are opened?"

"Few could, let alone a mere child." She replied.

A cool breeze settled through the leaves and out onto the window panes in the garden. The leaves of the mimosas rustled casting a flickering glow that filtered through the pines and filled the room settling upon Madame O's finely wrought features.

"I have painted a dark picture, Madame, so I should add there also exists a sunnier side to his nature."

Madame O took account of the man's strong chiselled but gentle intelligent features and varied expressions. Gorrick read Madame O's wishes when he remarked, "He always returns, eventually. Revives, regains his equilibrium – self resuscitates. He will sing today, God willing, I can assure you. I think the 24-hour revolution is coming to an end. The crisis will soon be over. Are you alright Madame?"

"Yes, Charles, it just occurred to me that nothing short of wonderful ever came easily."

"He will sing today..." As the words escaped Gorrick, and as if he had heard, the boy at the fountain shuffled and frisked himself. Stood upright. Head bowed, slowly retraced his steps towards the house, bleary-eyed, entered through the French windows. Madame O grasped the arms of her chair, not daring to speak or acknowledge the boy for fear of making a wrong move. No word passed between the three whilst with lowered eyes, the boy seated himself down again at the table and

Madame O simultaneously experienced the inexplicable sensation of being in the presence of some rarefied, unidentifiable human object that had incontrovertibly strayed from its path. The boy's eyes gradually drifted upwards and across over the table, then travelled directly in a straight line ahead without once veering to left or right. For a second, Madame O followed his gaze, scarcely daring to breathe nor cast a further sideways glance at him, but when she could resist no longer she saw an enigmatic, half smile creep unexpectedly over the boy's face that had the power to supersede her worst forebodings and fill her with a warmth and hope that had lain lost and buried these past years. No mention is made of what occurred earlier on. Instead, the boy's virtual transformation is met with more than one sigh of relief. Everyone could now more or less be themselves again, even though the tension of such an unsettling event involving the risks of making a wrong move in the boy's presence had caught Madame O unawares and left her with a vague sense of apprehension and wondering what next to expect. For the following twenty minutes, Madame O presided over the tea without a hitch albeit with a minimum of conversation and, when they had finished, she tactfully suggested they might wish to adjourn to the music room leading off the conservatory.

There, father and son's attention had been immediately drawn to one corner near a window where stood an extraordinary life-like statue of a very tall, rather awkward man attired in sumptuous 17th century costume. As his father would say, 'Mark photographed every detail in his mind', whilst Madame O gave a running commentary on the statue's origins.

"Word has it that the impressive gentleman standing before you was, still is, considered the greatest singer of all time. Italian by birth, his name: Farinelli (1705-1782), born Carlo Broschi, Farinello being a pseudonym applied to the Broschi family who, it has been suggested, were slightly disreputable and whose origins with the passing of time we can't be certain of. In Italian 'Farinello' means rascal or rogue! You may wonder how the statue came to be here, again a family heirloom," Madame O explained. "He had to be smuggled out from Germany where he had stood for decades in our house. From all accounts by some who heard him, in those far-off times, the mystique and wonderment surrounding the singer has till now been enough to make him my own personal singing model par excellence. Written reports from the time have come down to us that he could do things vocally that have since never been equalled. That is..." Madame O did not finish the sentence unable to disguise her rapture. As Mark listened to her commentary, he continued to avidly scrutinize every detail from head to toe of the towering polychrome figure. Simultaneously the boy's hand unintentionally drifted over his own throat caressingly as he stretched his neck so that it elongated oddly. Madame O interpreted this unconscious gesture as a reassurance on the boy's part of what hidden riches he knew to be lying beneath the exterior. Or could it be he was tempting some hitherto hidden element out into the open once and for all before the opportunity no longer availed itself, or perhaps he was simply dreamily comparing himself to the statue – in other words fantasizing as children are apt to do in unselfconscious moments? Several times, as Madame O in the course of her commentary pronounced over again the name Farinelli, the boy silently shaped the name on his lips and as he did so swayed a little as if to some lilting tune, all the while digesting every vestige of information Madame O furnished about this strange gangling figure of a man who had taken the public by storm from his debut in 1720 to his retirement in 1737. "From all accounts, and we have no reason to disbelieve, Carlo Farinelli could sing whatsoever he wished. No constraints existed in that amazing vocal mechanism. His most celebrated feat being an aria di bravura 'Qual guerriero in campo armato which in those days came to be known as the 'Concerto for Larynx, a piece especially written by his brother Ricardo to accommodate Carlos's voice.

Charles Gorrick smiled inwardly, "Did anyone else attempt to sing the Larynx Concerto, Madame?"

"Interesting question, Charles. I'd not given that much thought. As far as I know there is no reference to another singer attempting this remarkable showpiece. In any case, I doubt very much if Farinelli's vocal gifts could have been emulated."

"I see," Gorrick replied stroking his chin thoughtfully whilst observing the intensity of expression on his son's face as Mark digested each word of the conversation, that faint lingering smile returning to inform his still unformed features, as he became only too aware that here he stood, in a rarefied musical atmosphere, within touching distance of a statue of the man said to be the greatest singer the world had ever heard.

Madame O, her suspicions now allayed, remembered Charles Gorrick's promise that the boy would 'return' and on that assumption alone she decided to throw caution to the wind and as a result recovered her lost equilibrium, self esteem and authority. She decided to rejoin Mark on an equal footing and became immensely relieved to note the earlier threatening stance he had adopted, thankfully no longer evident.

Now that the tension had died down, Madame O felt it opportune to mention her desire to record Mark's voice for the purpose, as she put it, of 'post vocal analysis'. "I usually ask my students if they mind me turning my recording machine on sometimes. After they have left it helps to better understand or discover certain facets of their voices I may have overlooked during the lesson. It's quite an advanced machine, created by a scientific engineer, Alfred Hertz. She uncovered the sleek, silver object for father and son to see, both of whom gazed on it with particular interest; becoming imbued with the idea. Although Mark may have appeared a little diffident at the prospect, his father was all for it. "That indeed would be a very interesting exercise to see how Mark's voice records, and you would like that wouldn't you, Sonny?"

The boy nodded affirmatively, the slightest semblance of a smile still lingering on his countenance.

"Good. Agreed. Shall we make a start?" Madame O said not bothering nor needing anymore to disguise her enthusiasm. Without adding anything further, confidently she went straight over to the piano and set to work. "So Mark. Can we make a short test. First I shall play some scales, and you sing anything you feel like."

Mark nodded his agreement. At last, he was on home territory. At her side, Madame O quickly regarded the recording spool. "What a golden opportunity we have here. Just imagine, the mechanics of this machine work on wire. Ah, by the way Mark, when I suggested you sing 'anything' I actually meant ornaments, embellishments and that type of thing," Madame O proceeded to give a demonstration of examples with her noticeably diminished vocal prowess.

Mark listened patiently and did not raise an eyebrow at the few short-lived badly misjudged notes upon which, Madame O realising her ineptitude, abruptly stopped and excused herself. "Of course, at my age, one's voice no longer comes up to expectation. Simply won't obey what is demanded of it."

A timely silence ensued after which Mark readied himself for the assault course ahead. Madame O loaded the recording spool and switched the machine on and then commenced to play a scale. Mark opened his mouth and whispered out the first note that could scarcely be heard. A natural method he usually deployed whenever he started to sing so as not to strain unduly. Madame O laboured to hear but Gorrick, who was familiar with this approach, attuned his ears and heard clearly, for he knew exactly what to listen for and expect, knowing only too well how that fragile first note is all part of a carefully planned 'swelling on the note' exercise whereby the boy's voice would increase in volume, firstly on that same note so that the whole room would inevitably resound with its power, after which Mark would take the note back to nothing. All of this undertaken on the same one long sustained breath, apparently without any undue effort on his behalf! Afterwards, Mark no longer waited, he simply continued in the same vein all the while ascending the scale and, as his voice arose, likewise so too did he increase vocally in volume. Never before had Madame O heard such an example of swelling on the note. She asked, "Mark, how do you hold the breath for so long and continue to increase in volume?" The boy's expression changed to one of bewilderment. He made no reply half smiling, just shook his head from side to side mutely.

Gorrick answered for him, "Mark has immense reserves of breath. He goes swimming and likes nothing better than swimming underwater for minutes at a time, but that's not exactly how he first learned to hold his breath, Madame."

He winked at her. Now it became Madame O's turn to look bewildered. She couldn't imagine telling her students to swim underwater to gain in breath control before she realised the actuality Gorrick alluded to. Hypoventilation. Next, Mark took the initiative and swiftly broke out into another powerful lung display singing with added vigour and unprecedented agility a series of astonishingly swift and impossibly difficult divisions and octave leaps that seemed beyond human endeavour, the exercise being brought to its conclusion on a beautifully poised and sustained high note. Madame O appeared unable to comment. She stole a glance at her watch and looked into the recording machine to ascertain the remarkable feat had been captured. By this time any comment seemed superfluous, nevertheless she felt obliged to say something to the boy, but when she looked up at him, she knew the greatest compliment was to let him continue without interruption now that he had found his voice. However, she could not resist telling both father and son, "In my day, that last top E Flat alone, not to mention what came before, would have won a singer an annuity accolade for life from any leading opera house."

As the afternoon wore on, Mark continued to reveal more hidden facets in his vocal emporium. Madame O remained tirelessly at the keyboard stunned by the onslaught. The afternoon had proved a revelation. As for the boy, his vocal prowess did not show the slightest sign of waning, convincing Madame O he was evidently endowed with endless reserves of strength and inspiration, using his voice like a well trained athlete. She replaced yet another blank spool of recording wire on the hi-tech recorder and then, feeling light-headed from the affects of the boy's singing, left the room telling father and son, more refreshments would be forthcoming. In the kitchen, she mopped her forehead in relief, and leaning against the back of the door drew a deep breath to regain her equilibrium and asked herself, 'What is happening? Am I honestly to believe my ears or am I in the midst of some waking dream? If I'm not mistaken, the boy has no idea of the affect he is creating with that stupendous vocal mechanism of his. One thing is certain, I can't teach the wonder anything. At best I can only listen.' Madame O delayed going back in for several minutes, remaining leaning her full weight against the back of the door before deciding to return. In the course of presiding over a second tea, she asked if Mark practised often with a piano.

"Yes, Madame, but it doesn't seem to be a leading factor, not a bother to him. As you've heard, he has a very finely attuned ear. It is virtually impossible for him to sing out of tune," Gorrick replied.

"Oh yes, I noticed that straight away."

"We have a funny old upright at home. All the tuning in the world doesn't help the decrepit old thing on its last legs, so Mark often as not makes do with his own reliable inner self tuning device. Mind you, it's not that we can't afford a new piano," Gorrick added unconvincingly, "it's just that we haven't got round to it, have we Mark?"

Madame O stole a tactful glance at Gorrick's frayed cuffs and dare not peer at his incongruously worn spats covering his well-worn shoes for fear of laughing, and declared to herself she liked the proud Charles Gorrick more and more.

Before Mark and his father left that afternoon it had been mutually agreed they would come to Madame O every other day from then on. What followed, usually entailed one session lasting four hours or more, so carried away everyone had become in the process. Over the next weeks, Mark's natural musical intelligence proved a complete revelation to Madame O and she gained fresh insights into his complex nature and soon detected his indwelling apprehension that his present voice was of an all too transient nature. With this fact borne in mind, Madame O found herself drawn closer to him and he to her. A liaison was created but nothing of the oncoming problem about the voice breaking was ever discussed openly. Instead everything between the two was understood inwardly. This suited and benefited the boy's natural reserve, extreme sensitivity and increasing vulnerability. Soon he started to lean towards Madame O and became only too glad to comply with her every request as a patient might seek his doctor's help and advice except in this instance not a single drop of medicine need be wasted. Throughout Mark thrived on new repertoire, which manifoldly increased. Madame O, baffled at this prodigious progress, sorted through her old record collection and let Mark choose and take whatever he wished, after which he would return with new pieces having extracted the best part of a particular singer's version, married with musical ideas of his own so that everything he incised into a specific piece improved it. Today he chose a record of Mozart's 'Laudate Dominum' sung by Ursula van Dieman. Tomorrow it will be a carbon copy of the same singer but with a surfeit of the boy's magic touches unintentionally added, to making the piece more memorable. Madame O now regarded him as a 'perfecting device'. Everything he sang being free of mannerism and cliché. Nothing contrived. He sang as nature intended yet with a voice that came from another unknown source altogether. Over the next week, Mark gave of his voice unstintingly as if it were his dearest wish to saturate Madame O's ears for all time with the flute like sounds at his command, causing her to forget every other voice she had previously heard.

"So, Mark, is it to be Chopin's favourite Bellini aria today? 'Ah non credea Mirarti' from 'Sonnambula'?"

"No, miss," he replied deferentially. "Could I first sing 'Laudate Dominum'?"

"Oh, I should love to hear that." Madame O looked towards the cameo of Mozart near the piano and commenced to play the introductory accompaniment from memory, as is often her practise. Mark's voice entered gently, similar to the way he prepared a scale. At that moment he may even have been imitating Madame O's playing as her fingers caressed the keyboard and made the notes literally float across the room. Throughout the short piece, Mark never allowed his voice to rise above 'mezza voce' obliging Madame O to listen carefully to each magical sound. This way the sweeping melody lingered and remained embedded in the senses of the listener, creating an intimate dialogue between singer and accompanist. If only she could hear him sing this piece with orchestra. Madame O promised herself one day she would. That same afternoon, Madam O made tape after tape, with Charles Gorrick keeping an eye on the machine. Each took turns to suggest an aria or song for Mark to sing. To Madame O, his knowledge of the 'Bel Canto' operas seemed inexhaustible. His musicality unquestionable. His sense of ornament and embellishment something she wished her other pupils possessed. Everything he sang, he invested with his own particular stamp of distinction and originality and, what is more, undertook everything he sang with utmost modesty 'without showing off either his virtuosity or his lack of exhibitionism. The rarest achievements of an artist'. (Hans Keller).

The day before Mark's 13th birthday, on their return home Mark and his father were met at the front door by an excited Tilly Gorrick. "Come quickly," she beckoned and led them into the sitting room. There in the middle of the room stood a small concert grand piano, as shiny as black ice, its gold letters spelling out 'Grotian Steinweg. Berlin'. His parents, stunned, looked on as Mark, speechless, walked over to the instrument as if drawn to a magnet, his eyes gliding over every surface of the bodywork. Noiselessly, he lifted the lid over the keyboard and skimmed his fingers across the keys and coaxed from the piano the first few bars of Mendelssohn's 'On Wings of Song' in a near perfect imitation of Madame O's playing. Tilly had been the first to speak. In her hand she held a large envelope, "Here, the delivery men brought this. It's addressed to Mark." Mark slowly pulled the score of Bach's 'St John Passion' out of the envelope, opened the front page and read the inscription. 'To my dear pupil, Rosealma - Your teacher Lilli Lehmann - 1902.' Underneath had been added in another hand, 'and to my dear pupil Mark who needs no teacher as such but who is in dire need of a piano to add lustre to its tone with his voice – a happy 13th birthday – Rosealma Oppenheimer – 1942.'

Mark refused to go to bed. Instead he stayed in the living room and spent the night on the sofa, his eyes cast on the piano, studying the ebony woodwork as it shone in the moonlight entering through the open window. Resting on the piano; the score of the 'St John Passion'.

At break of dawn, after a short sleep, he awoke, foraged over the keys whilst he softly hummed. By breakfast time he had become adept enough to sing and accompany himself, near enough note perfect. Such remarkable musical feats affected his parents whilst affording them an endless source of surprise never knowing what next to expect from his astonishing talent. At the next lesson with Madame O what could they say. On Mark's 13th birthday, the Gorricks and son couldn't wait to see Madame O. The piano and the rare autographed manuscript had been the most perfect gift. Words could not express their appreciation. Madame O appeared as thrilled as they both were but did not elaborate too much and tried to make as little of the gift as possible, curtailing the conversation finally by simply adding jokingly, "What could I possibly do with so many pianos? Anyway, none are more deserving than you three."

Gorrick looked slightly at odds with himself, and asked uncomfortably: "But we should dearly like to offer you something, Madame O".

Madame O feigned ignorance, then added in a serious tone of voice, "You've both offered more than I could ever imagine one person deserving in a whole lifetime."

Gorrick fumbled for the appropriate words. His voice choked. "Actually, by way of gratitude, Mark has prepared something for you, Madame." As he spoke he fetched the score of the 'St John Passion' Madame O had given Mark for his birthday, and opened it at item 58 and placed it upright above the keyboard. The contralto air 'All is fulfilled'. Madame O stalled. "I know of no more beautiful piece of music than 'Die grosse Johann's' work she declared. Then she looked closer and asked herself why, for reasons she could not give, this same air had haunted and played through her mind these last weeks. When such things happened the reason usually came later. Happily, Mark had gone straight to the aria without any true idea of what the piece meant to Madame O.

Gorrick spoke, "Mark tells me overnight he's read through the text but always irresistibly returned to this particular section."

Madame O shook her head. "I can scarcely wait to hear it," she said. As she searched the boy's face, she realised this sacred air meant a total turn around for his voice, "The long lines and phrases will pose no difficulties but I shall need to transpose up into a suitable soprano key to accommodate Mark's voice."

"I don't think that will be necessary," Gorrick offered, "Mark will simply lower his voice accordingly."

"Are you happy with that, Mark?" Madame O asked surprised. "After all it is written in the contralto key. The lowest range." The boy nodded back to her reassuringly and stole a glance of confirmation over to his father at the same time. Now he stood in readiness. Statue like, arms characteristically slack, hanging at his sides.

Not a sign of a breath.

His eyes glazed.

"Do you wish to follow the text with me, Mark?" Madame O asked as she motioned to him to stand closer. Gorrick knew Mark would pretend from innate modesty to agree, but the truth was the boy had already learnt the simple repetitive text and each and every note had been perfectly placed and formulated faultlessly in that astonishing catchment area of his child/adult's mind so that, if needs be, he could be relied on to sing note perfect the lengthy excerpt with his eyes closed.

As Madame O turned to peruse the score, Mark took the desired few steps forward and stood by her side at the piano. Madame O set about re-familiarising herself with the work and became lost in the exalted world of the 'Master of Eisenach'. Before starting, she deliberated at length on the aria. To Mark and his father describing thus… "The first part of this three tiered excerpt is written for continuo, organ and viola de gamba, an instrument which is smaller than a cello. The music begins 'molto adagio' and already, at the first entry, we are experiencing the dying phrases of Christ on the cross. 'All is fulfilled'. Ideally those last prophetic words should echo over the ages, timeless in their emotive power. There then follows a fast section (alla breve) with some coloratura deployed on the word prevailed – 'The Lion of Judah fought the fight and hath prevailed'. After which all the strings join in. The music returns to adagio upon which the voice returns with the solemn recapitulation and utters twice over the last words, 'It is finished'." Madame O's voice faded to a reverential whisper as she intoned a second time that last dying phrase, 'It is finished'.

As she prepared to let the piano take over the opening section for organ, viola de gamba and continuo Mark's voice, in a mood of deepest grief, materialised effortlessly, hovering and gliding in and over the haunting melody as he sang the words 'Hope to fainting souls extended… this mournful night shows me thy day of labour ended' allowing his voice in the last section to die away on a plaintive note of subdued finality with the twice repeated phrase 'It is finished'. Throughout, Mark's voice had sounded entirely transported. Solitary and remote, deep and clear, yet supplanted high above the world, engendered by a mysterious hidden force far removed from earthly involvement. Untouchable and distant. Ethereal and disembodied. For a time, after the last notes had diminished, no one present need comment. One word, any word, would have been painfully misjudged. In her mind Madame O likened the boy's spirituality in another way to the young Felix Mendelssohn who at 16 had composed his celebrated octet.

It is said the greatest tribute an artist can meet with is not with immediate applause but with sustained silence from an awestruck audience. Later when father and son had left, Madame O mulled over the way the boy had sung and again concluded as Hans Keller had said of the great Romanian pianist Clara Haskil when writing of her performance in a public concert, that the rarest achievement in an artist is to present himself without showing off his virtuosity or his lack of exhibitionism.

At the end of the next lesson, Charles Gorrick took Madame O aside whilst the boy walked on ahead. He mentioned the family intended taking the old restored Vauxhall with the dicky seat on a trial run to the Charontoll Lakes where they would stop off and spend a few days holiday. Gorrick explained that his wife needed a break to ease her migraine headaches, which had begun to reoccur. As for Mark, "he doesn't want to go yet. In the past he's talked of nothing else and now in the last few days what with the arrival of the new piano, he's completely changed his mind! Not only that, he's become so gloomy at the mere mention of Charontoll I wish I could leave him behind but Tilly won't hear of it. She's determined he needs the fresh air. As you may have noticed, he has lost his tan and is as pale as snow. Knowing Mark, he'll do everything in his power to sabotage the idea. Nothing short of deflating the tyres.

The news jolted Madame O and sent her into a state of anguish. As far as she were concerned, a few days away at this crucial stage in Mark's life spelt an eternity.

Madame O at length dwelt on De Vries's doom laden prophecy. 'Any day now the boy's voice can break'. Shatter into a million pieces like a priceless chandelier falling from a great height onto a stone floor below. It's true. By the time the family return, perish the thought, perhaps the voice will be no more.

"Should Tilly change her mind, Charles, in your absence I will gladly put Mark up in the spare room," Madame O offered.

"That's more than kind of you, Madame. I shall speak to Tilly but I doubt if she will give way. In that respect Mark takes after her. Stubborn to the core. For myself, I'm already tempted to postpone our planned trip or at least return earlier. Anyhow, come what may, you shall be the first person in our thoughts when we leave and when we return. So, if we do not meet again before we leave…"

"Just a moment, Charles, before you go then." Madame O went into the house. Gorrick waited on the veranda. Mark stood at the gate, his back to the house. Madame O returned with a book. "Perhaps you might like to take this with you?" she suggested. "Who knows, you may have some time on your hands. The reproductions will certainly appeal to Mark." Gorrick started to open the book but Madame O stopped him, placing her hand over his.

"Later, Charles, don't bother to look at it now." She appeared to want to leave suddenly. Gorrick glanced at the title, 'Colcancas – Coloraturas, Cantors and Castrati by Rosa Alma Oppenheimer'.

"You've written this book? What can I say, Madame? I shall treasure it, read each page twice," he promised as he thanked her several times over.

"Thank you, Charles, and I shall endeavour to play each tape of Mark's voice a million times each," she declared forcing a strained smile behind held back tears.

As Madame O accompanied Charles Gorrick the last few steps of the way, in jocular fashion, he remarked, "It's not everyday one is entrusted with a learned treatise from the authoress herself. It must have entailed immense knowledge and research."

For a moment, Madame O appeared not to digest his words. She stopped a moment. "I must say what a privilege these last weeks and months have been; to have been chosen to hear Mark sing is something I shall never forget," she said. She diversified back to the book, "It was written in response to a certain demand by colleagues, students and professional singers. As a result it also deals at length with the recorded legacy of great voices from 1900 onwards and before which will interest Mark, I'm certain."

"And me too I can assure you, Madame."

"However," she reflected, "As things stand at the present, I think I shall have to rethink my views."

"Why is that so, Madame?"

"Oh, I think you can guess, Charles. You see, taking into consideration the dearth of singers I have personally encountered and been acquainted with, and quite a glittering array they were, none so far have lived up to Mark's voice nor his perfect style of vocalising."

Gorrick looked down at the ground silently before replying, "What a wonderful thought to take on holiday, Madame. I'm overwhelmed."

By the time they rejoined Mark who had begun to walk on ahead, Gorrick said to the boy, "Well, Markomino of the cords, I bet your ears are burning after what Madame has just told me!"

Mark looked askance and fumbled awkwardly in his pockets, shuffling from one foot to the other. His cheeks flushed, a sheepish expression on his face, but not a vestige or sign of satisfaction, nor a smile revealed in response to his father's remark. Intent on watching the boy's reaction, Gorrick impulsively felt the inescapable need to laugh when, for no reason, he suddenly remembered a daft film in which a comedian, either Joan Davis or Judy Canova, played a dizzy cowgirl dressed in gingham with pigtails that stood out at quarter-to-four horizontally from her face. Approached by an equally comical cowhand admirer, the cowgirl reacted demurely, coyly lowering her eyes and dug her overlarge feet into the dust and, in a soft-shoe shuffle, coquettishly exclaimed 'Oh, shucks' with a grin a mile wide. Presently, in what should have been a solemn moment of introspection, Gorrick could smile outwardly at that recollection which at least signalled a happy, short lived response from Madame O and Mark instead of what could have been a sad, parting gesture.

"About six days we shall be away. Not long. Truth is, can't wait to get back," still grinning, Gorrick told Madame O.

"Well, I suppose we'd best be on our way, Madame."

For a second in time, instinctively Madame O took Mark's hand in hers and felt it slip lifelessly away as he addressed her with the longest sentence he had yet attempted, "I'm sorry I have to go, Miss," and left it at that, peering earnestly into her eyes. Before she had time to reply, he quickly turned away and walked on ahead again, but this time he did not look back. Only Charles Gorrick turned and waved and father and son soon disappeared from sight down the laneway. Madame O made her way back up the pathway, remained standing motionless at the same gate where similarly she had caught that last fleeting glimpse of Florrie Murgatroyd, bringing back even further memories of Theodor, her father, futilely grasping her hand before being forcibly thrown into a truck by the SS. Her mother, Aloysia, desperately tugging at her husband's arm with one last tenuous thread of hope before she herself being manhandled into another truck and all three separated. How Madame O finally escaped only weeks later – remained a miracle of conjecture that had left her scathed and guilt ridden these last years and rarely able to get a normal night's rest. Since that time, Madame O had nursed a distinct horror of saying goodbye. Not farewell, but fare thee well she would say in an attempt to soften the blow of parting. To say goodbye is to die a little, her mother impressed upon her daughter whenever she left home. As she looked into the distance, Madame O's mind pre-emptied, blurred into momentary oblivion, trying her best to eradicate the memory of that time when the Nazis invaded the cultural bastilles of that once magical musical world she had been born into. And still this infamy carries on whilst every endeavour to track down her parents ends in a blank of nothingness.

Europe is engulfed in a war that seeks to separate and drain every worthwhile human resource, aspiration and inspiration from the human psyche. Where and when shall it all end, she asks, still leaning forward on the front gate. It is her father's voice that rings out. A cantor from Murnau am Stafelsee, Germany, who had studied with Emerich in Prague and given his daughter her first taste of soaring coloratura singing in the grand manner. How ancient and guileless, Madame O remembered him. A wise counsellor who steeped the girl in history and song. A resilient man, pious and vulnerable. His last words, "I'm sorry Rosealma for the world."

Chapter Five

Return of the Prodigal

Over the next day or two, Madame O experienced an oppressive emptiness but nevertheless saw to it her time be fully taken up in teaching as much as possible, extending the duration of her lessons and exhausting herself in the process. Despite putting little heart into her work, it helped take her mind off matters. Meanwhile, each evening, without fail, she hastened home to listen to the recorded excerpts of Mark's singing; diligently spent long hours in making extra copies with the second machine as an extra precaution in case of loss or damage, and placed the finished results for safety in a securely locked steel trunk labelled 'Property of the Conservatorium of Music Archive'. With each passing day, she resolutely ticked off the date on her wall calendar. Presently it would only be a matter of 48 hours before the 'prodigal's' return. She prayed the boy's voice had remained unscathed and intact. Back at the Conservatorium in Madame O's music room, the matriarchal German prima donna assoluta and scholar, Frau Prof Lilli Lehmann, imperiously glared down from her frame on the wall, its brass plaque inscribed with her dates '1848-1929'.

"If only you knew, Frau Prof Lehmann, what your pupil and admirer has gained and heard these last weeks, you would be filled with envy and perhaps new-found humility," Madame O opined mischievously.

That same night, Madame O experienced violent stabbing pains in her head. Something she had never previously suffered. It felt as though an iron band were digging into her skull and temples. The strain of the last weeks is taking its toll. It frightened her to imagine she could pass away in the night with not a soul to come to her aid. Nevertheless, she sat quietly, meditated for a few minutes, thought of the priceless tapes amassed there in the trunk. In that moment, she decided to try and put aside her worst forebodings and instead select the 'St. John Passion' air, the last piece Mark had recorded, and carefully placed the spool on the turntable. Whilst allowing her eyes to rove over the astonishing recorded legacy of arias and songs he had sung over these last months in her presence: carefully catalogued in date order.

The ingenious hi-tech recording machines, decades ahead of their time, engineered by Alfred Hertz, indeed did justice to Mark's voice capturing every nuance of sound in its pristine vocal glory. She need only close her eyes to be transported and imagine the boy's presence there beside her at the piano, doing everything within his power not to fail her. Notwithstanding, the machine had also captured their conversations, intermittent laughter and silences. In fact, the total ambience of their meetings from first to last. Madame O vowed both father and son must hear these miraculous flights of the human singing voice on their return. Up until now they had not heard the recordings, simply because there had never been enough time for a replay. The lessons, time-wise, out of all proportion, lasting sometimes a minimum of four hours, a maximum of seven hours. Later that night, Madame O forgot what a headache could be, but by the next day it had returned full force with a vengeance. Once more she alleviated the problem by convincing herself into believing the merest sound of Mark's voice would do the trick and assuage the pain and work as a palliative so that eventually she found solace when she played Mark's version of Mendelssohn's 'On Wings of Song'. The singer and the song lulled her mind. She got to thinking that compared with her colleague the legendary soprano Irene Abendroth's rendition, Mark's approach seemed even more finely honed and distilled in its essential essence.

At last, the great day approached. Agog for Mark's return, Madame O did her utmost to remain level headed before phoning the Gorricks. The very idea she was about to again hear Mark's voice in person filled her to the point of exaltation. She had become addicted to the idea that all he need do was to open his mouth for an effulgence of luminous scales and notes to pour forth at the Conservatorium this afternoon. Madame O would be in no mood to concentrate on Mahler's 'Kindertotenlieder' at this afternoon's lesson. It would prove virtually unbearable to deal with Miss Cagliostro struggling with the difficult tessitura demanded of her inadequate contralto voice for the second song 'Oft denk....' Enough! Basta! I must telephone! No reply. Too early. Too enthusiastic. 'I must take a hold of my senses'.

Madame O set off for the Conservatorium where she decided to wait until the lunch break before making a second telephone call. Again no reply. They must be returning in the evening she consoled herself in German, near enough quoting the Mahler 'Kindertotenlieder' - 'They've gone on a journey'. Yesterday painfully she had listened to Miss Cagliostro struggle her way blindly through Mahler's 2nd Rückert song which now became totally bereft of its true meaning, partly due perhaps to the girl's lack of knowledge that Mahler had lost his daughter prematurely aged four.

By evening, the Gorricks phone still remained unanswered. The family had not returned and 'must have decided to extend their stay overnight. Well, I shan't telephone again tonight. It's nearly midnight.' Finally at 1:00 a.m., a worried Madame O took herself off to bed. Throughout the rest of the night, she tossed and turned in her sleep, dreamt she was standing in her studio at the Conservatorium. Upon the wall above the piano, next to the cameos of Bellini and Donizetti, she had just finished nailing a framed photograph of Mark to join the illustrious assemblage of artists from the Golden Age of singing when it fell and the glass shattered and showered into a myriad pieces over the highly polished surface of the piano, simultaneously smashing the vase holding the freshly picked zinnias that father and son had brought on the Sunday when they'd come for tea. Whilst Madame O attempted to clear up the damage, the broken shards of glass scratched across the piano's surface into the form of a swastika, glass became imbedded in her hands and, as she continued to clear the pieces, blood spurted in all directions from her palms. Furthermore, when she searched for the boy's photo, it had disappeared from its frame. No matter how and wherever she searched, it remained nowhere to be found and, in her panic, she banged sideways into the music stand knocking down all the music scores from the shelf into the open fire grate where the pages began to burn. Madame O looked on helplessly as Mendelssohn's score of 'Elijah' went up in flames, each page turning, aided by crude rough hidden hands. Horrified, she watched as the decipherable pages of the contralto air 'Woe unto them' went up in smoke and quickly burned to ashes. Untouched by the fire, a calendar remained propped up on a desk where she had pencilled in a red circle around the date '9 November 1938' and written underneath 'Die Reichskristall Nach' - 'The Night of Burning Books'. All that remained of the wall in her music room – an empty space, where her treasured music scores had once been housed, now a black empty void. A deathly silence reigned. Can she ever erase from her memory the anti-semitic Nazi slogans appearing all over Germany? "Wenns Judenblut vom Messer spritzt" (When Jewish blood spurts from the knife). (Death to the Jews!) "Jude verrecke!" not to mention the scurrilous, "Die Juden sind unser Ungluck!" (The Jews are our misfortune!) With these words Madame O recalls sadly how Germany robbed itself of an irreplaceable wealth of Jewish culture in art, writing and music, science, medicine and technology.

In the distance her father's voice intoning the Kaddish for the dead, whilst further away she hears in the background Mozart 'Laudate Dominum' sung in an unfamiliar half toned crackle of a voice, more as an eerie accompanying lament rather than the familiar resplendent piece Mozart composed for solo voice.

Next day, as usual, Madame O awoke at dawn, her head resting on a drenched pillow and her clothes soaked and clinging to her slight frame. It had been as much as she could do to raise herself. Eventually she took herself into the breakfast room. The nightmare having created an altogether unsettling change over her, listlessly she seated herself at the breakfast table and, for a time, mindlessly regarded last year's autumn leaves piling up in the back garden and building up on the outside windowsill; half wondered half dreamed of what had so stealthily occurred in her midst. Hair dishevelled, dark circles under her eyes, her face an indeterminate blur reflected in the half-light on the mirrored clock face opposite. As she remained at the table, hands held to her face with only her eyes bared, she dared peer out through the window at the fountain where lately the boy had passed a full solemn hour in silent isolation. Already, the hands of the clock pointed to well past the time of her first lesson, yet still she sat, not desiring to make a move. This loss of all sense of time had never happened before to the punctilious little professor.

Now the memory of Mark's voice haunted her to distraction, even to the point where she actually started to dislike her other pupils. As the weeks turned to months it seemed inconceivable that the boy and his father, 'these people she had helped', failed to contact her. Maybe they'd gone back to the country to live? No matter, whatever she suggested to herself, truth is they had gone, hook, line and sinker, without paying her a thought. Consequently, Madame O must get on with her life and compromise. It wouldn't be easy. She could of course take early retirement and settle down to writing her memoirs of pre-war Europe but this would have meant living in the shadow of that 'twelve-year-old overnight vocal wonder'. Now the truth dawned on her. By this time, wherever he was, the voice had broken! How she had looked forward to the return, she cried. Thank goodness however, she had the recorded testament at her disposal. Madame O's eyes kept clouding over with frustration and bitterness. Even the recorded legacy was not enough without the boy's presence. This shall not be the first time she has had to come to terms with harsh reality. She convinced herself she must put all else aside and make a start with numerous emendations to her book with a whole chapter devoted to Marcus Aurelius Gorrick. No one, of course, would believe her on hearsay alone, but she had the advantage with the recordings in her possession to verify the boy's voice, and of course the testimony of Anton de Vries. She must keep guard over the tapes 24 hours a day. For the purpose she expects 'Windermere Cottage' will become a bastille, a fortress, a preservation area for one voice. The Voice. She set store on the fact that shutters and locks must be reinforced. Unless of course, Mark made an impromptu return, his voice still intact. Each day, Madame O pleaded that this voice, above all others, will in time become the reality of her dreams, the acme of all her desires. Better still, she begins to believe and convince herself anew that nothing untoward has happened. If she tries hard enough, she pretends she cannot recall even what the boy looked like! Or his father. Anything to blur painful memories. Why though, she kept speculating, had they not dropped her a line? No! The sad truth remained. They were still there embedded in her thoughts. She could not brush the family aside just like that. Vividly she remembers every physical detail. Now she started searching for reasons. The Book – that was it. My book. Maybe they took offence at the chapter on the Castrati and imagined I was hinting and wanting to give them ideas.

Without Mark, Madame O intended giving notice to the directors of the Conservatorium of her desire to terminate her teaching post. She would give no reasons. In three months she decided to leave the place forever. Following her decision, she changed her whole attitude towards her students and to music generally. This showed itself in a form of illogical tyranny that few of her pupils and colleagues could satisfactorily deal with, nor wished to for that matter. At the Conservatorium, she vehemently set about expounding her views in an arrogant and wholly unacceptable manner on the one and only correct way to sing, addressing in particular the Greek contralto who in the past she had always handled with kid gloves. "To start with, you must have a voice!" she sternly reproached. Surprisingly, Miss Cagliostro turned on her teacher furiously, "So why have you bothered to teach me all these years if you don't think I have a voice?" Madame O turned on her serpent-like and retorted spitefully, her eyes narrowing into slits, "Because I enjoy it! That's why!" Cagliostro left, threatening never to return. With the Greek girl out of the way, Madame O now set about relieving herself of other 'unwanteds" for her clearing out process in view of her proposed resignation. This ought not to be a difficult matter should her own insulting behaviour been anything to go by. Within the next week Miss Berthron walked out in a huff, followed by yet another singer. In a peculiar way this permitted Madame O the desired allotted time she needed to re-think the recent 'disaster which had befallen her. The 'loss of her'star pupil. She did not hesitate to blame herself, but she did not know precisely for what. As if she were a detective, she started to go over in her mind from that very first day of Mark's appearance to the last, but it proved almost too painful and her mind afforded her no rest. Incessantly, she pictured father and son on that day making their way tentatively up the gravel driveway of the grounds of the Conservatorium and remembered dolefully how she had been in no particular frame of mind nor mood to hear a boy sing, added to which she had been irate at their lack of punctuality. Previously the father had set store upon his son by way of an absurd letter raving on about the amazing virtues of his 12 year old son's astonishing voice. Madame O sighed. 'Just goes to show', she reflected regretfully. She now cursed herself for that 'idiotic' indifference and ignorance and premature lack of initiative. However in retrospect she excuses herself, when later on she more than made up for that apathetic attitude and gave the boy her unmitigated attention. Never again would she take anything for granted. She rocked to and fro cradling her arms in front of her, humming indistinctly. She believed everything began to go wrong from the moment she failed to properly notice the peculiarly magical setting exuding in the grounds of the conservatorium on that propitious occasion denoting something altogether special about to happen. Presently she can vividly recall how the driveway in midsummer had been carpeted in a mystical glow of the last year's autumn leaves. Why is it that only now she should attach so much importance to the Autumn leaves? The reason is she had honestly come to the conclusion that on that day she had altogether missed the rarefied significance of father and son. Madame O kept blindly searching in the back of her mind for answers. How did it all go wrong? She repeatedly asked. How could I have been so blind? She questioned in desperation, her head spinning. No answers are forthcoming. If only it were possible to turn back the clock. Foremost playing through her mind she now began to invest magical connotation in the unearthly glow that played over the oak's shedded leaves. Yet as she dwells upon the still, unearthly light filtering through the branches in the afterglow of her convoluted thoughts, she is offered a further fading glimmer of hope. Today from her window the leaves remained strewn over the grounds. "That indeed tells me nothing has changed except myself, but is that of any consequence? She asks obliquely. Her mind is made up. There remains but one choice, to wait, endlessly wait. All day long, Madame O found herself returning to Mahler's haunting song. The one that Cagliostro could not, for the life of her, grasp and sing correctly, 'Nun seh ich wohl warum so dunkle flammen, but then how would the girl know the real life tragedy that lay behind this work, when the young woman had only been obsessed with her own foolish problems.

Madame O took out her diary and with an unemotional, meaningless smile written across her features began to haphazardly inscribe across the top of the page:

'The winter of my discontent. The Misses Cagliostro, Caliopsis, Berthron and Kapinsky are gone. At last giving more time to myself to think and prepare the day ahead. Common place lack lustre voices all!... Good riddance, I say - my worst fears - they will return to the fold-but I won't be there.'

Until recently, Madame O had prided herself, like De Vries, on upholding a distinct mission in life – to gauge and turf out all those undesirable modern day vocal habits and defects, distortions and mannerisms accruing with the passing of time so bountiful in each new generation. Is that not the reason she is there? Voices are her life-blood. Nowadays, however, she is about to find herself indifferently going along, rather than against, the misleading and damaging current tide of thought. It seemed by the wayside she herself were being robbed of that admirable tenacity and verve which spelt out the essential underpinnings and requirements that make a great teacher such a necessary, exacting and respected influence in the musical community. And so it shall be for the first time that 'en passant' Madame will fail to notice all those abject major and minor flaws and ailments that today plague the vocal cords of singers, and which in previous times she would never have permitted to go undetected. But now, singer and teacher will no longer be in rapport with each other. Among her colleagues word will soon circulate that Madame's standards are rapidly on the decline and that she has toppled from her hitherto unassailable pinnacle, where once she held sway like no other teacher of the human voice. Where once she demanded nothing less than perfection, now she no longer shows she remotely cares. Besides which, she has begun to carry on a vague insensate dialogue with herself, mostly in German, that no one understands. "Ich Kann es nich glauben, dars ich dich verboren hab"; vague incantations that cause concern and disruption amongst the other professors most of whom, wholeheartedly agree she is in dire need of a holiday, a long break away from the stresses of work. Now in her 62nd year, also they agree that in her present state she has made the correct decision by handing in her resignation, premature though it may be for one who until only recently still appears more agile and alive than her years. However, it has been stipulated Madame O leaves with the goodwill and the proviso, that should she see fit, she can return to her post at short notice, because there simply is no one to take her place. But Madame O is exhausted. Her once vast reserves of strength abysmally depleted. Her infallible ear unreliable. Her pitch, once perfect, wavers, so that she is no longer capable of warning off imminent vocal danger and defects in her pupils. This latter hearing condition is probably necessitated by days spent resolutely trying to correct at too close quarters to those of her pupils whose voices refuse to be tethered as they latch onto endemic and relentless overtones of ever louder and more clamorous histrionic vocalisations, especially those extrovert type singers she so deplores, who endlessly compete against one another in preparation for a shouting match on the operatic stage. In the past, Madame O rarely tired of advising them not to strain, and always cautioned them to aim for beauty of tone first and foremost, but bad habits die hard and she admitted defeat on her behalf in order to convince some of them. Over the next weeks, though these self same singers enjoyed a field day and could be heard in her studio masterclasses held every so often, blaring at the top of their lungs without interruption, regardless of their already sorely depleted vocal resources. In amongst them sat Madame O, blandly oblivious to their squawks. Where once she'd taken a dim view of such antics, now she doesn't as much as raise a dissenting eyebrow indifferently, adding the occasional remark, "Fine, fine! Carry on. Yes, very good."

De Vries quickly detected the, gradual overall change and decline in her teaching when she no longer sought his advice and, as far as the boy had been concerned, had perversely refused point blank to even mention his name or acknowledge anything about him. In the past both she and De Vries compared notes and together reached valuable teaching conclusions and exchanged ideas. Each always welcoming the other's advice and expertise. After all, Madame O had never been in the habit of blindly accepting just any old voice. Rather, she enjoyed specialising in taking on 'potential' voices sorely in need of 're-structuring' which, in her own spectacular way, she set about to work wonders. That individual deployment had been her great forte, the legendary 'Oppenheimer overall re-structuring Vocal Technique'. Moreover, another much respected book of hers had been published under that title which dealt at length, and in detail with this much needed process so that, due to her immense and exceptional knowledge, countless voice teachers and students alike (far and wide) stood to immeasurably gain in vocal instruction, improve upon, or regain lost voices by instilling the Oppenheimer method into their studying and, as a result, bring forth their pupils utmost potential. Experts and critics alike were not sparing in their praise of Frau Prof Rosa Oppenheimer, nor skimping in their use of the word 'genius' when referring to and acknowledging the woman's unique talent and contribution in her chosen field –

Chapter Six

Farinelli's Nightingle

One morning, exactly at 9:00, Madame O arrived at the Conservatorium and rushed into De Vries's studio, hugged him boisterously and in no uncertain terms announced,

"Anton, you are now looking at the happiest person around here. Would you believe it? Do you remember our long lost prodigal? Well, I have good news to report. He has returned and not only that, but with his voice intact!"

Anton de Vries's face lit up. "Mon dieu! Then let me be the first to congratulate you my dear dear friend. This is the best news, but may I ask is his voice truly still intact?"

"Yes, indeed Anton".

"Unbelivable! Marvellous, but tell me Rosa, when did this all happen?"

"At midnight-last night. I'd left the door unlocked and the family let themselves in on the stroke of twelve," she answered breathlessly, near unable to contain her joy.

"Well, I can see how happy you are. You're positively beaming."

"I know, Anton. I feel a different person. Mr Gorrick kept his word, when he promised I would be the first person they would see on their return. He called up to me from the bottom of the stairs at Windermere."

"But why so long, Rosealma?"

"Oh, I didn't bother to ask. I was so thrilled to see them all back in one piece. Mind you, seeing Mark standing so still there before me in the music room in front of the Farinelli statue – it was as if he were imitating the statue, and the moment I entered the room he wore that slow captivating smile of his which, as Mr Gorrick so succinctly put it, 'has to be earned'."

"Rosealma, if anyone deserved such a reward, it's you. You've been so patient these last months and it's been a long wait and we've all been worried about you."

Madame O ignored this last remark. "Anton, I still haven't got over the surprise. And hear you this, what do you think that dear boy prepared for me?"

De Vries shook his head, at midnight "I simply can't imagine, Rosealma. Something wonderful by the look on your face."

"Indeed - more than wonderful. Unaccompanied and in perfect Italian, he sang Farinelli's celebrated 'Nightingale Song'. You know the elaboration of the aria 'Quel usignola' from Giacomelli's opera 'Merope'. If you recall, Anton, it is one of the four songs Farinelli is said to have sung for King Philip of Spain every night for 10 years from midnight until 5 in the morning."

De Vries shook his head in disbelief. "But how did they know about it?"

"That's precisely what I dared ask myself, until I remembered the original manuscript kept at the Biblioteque National in Paris is reproduced in my book in the chapter on Castrati which I gave Charles Gorrick the day he left."

"But tell me, Rosa, how did he sing it?"

"Dare you ask? Well, I was and still am so carried away, dazed beyond belief, and shall I tell you why? Because he performed the piece in a way that contradicts all human vocal possibility. When he finished the piece in the original key, he started all over again and he re-sang it an octave higher turning the work into an awe-inspiring vocalization without words. Each note and phrase holding forth a new coloratura feat of ingenuity. By the time I'd got to bed I promise you, Anton, I slept undisturbed for the rest of the night, for the first time in two months at least."

"Had it been me it would have been the other way round. A sleepless night.

"The question remains on my lips, Rosa, when am I to receive the privilege of hearing him again for myself?"

"Ah, leave that to me, Anton. I can tell you this much though. It will not be at the Conservatorium ever again! That would only create havoc with all and sundry. From now on, he will always come to Windermere for private lessons. In any case, by then I shall have handed in my notice."

"Oh! and the voice? You say it remains the same?"

"Precisely – better in fact. But what is even stranger is his actual speaking voice is deeper."

"So what about the prime issue we previously discussed?"

"Do you mean the break in the voice? Well, I've just hinted haven't I? His speaking voice is only slightly deeper."

"I've just about heard of everything now, Rosealma, but this is something I would never have dreamt of and would not believe had you not told me. A voice, somehow breaking in half. It's uncanny."

"Yes, his father told me, that when he was on holiday at Charontoll the boy woke one morning and felt a strange sensation in his throat and, when he spoke at breakfast, the family were horrified to find his speaking voice temporarily down here somewhere." Madame O pointed to the ground at her feet.

"Awful!" De Vries nodded quietly.

"Yet when Mark 'felt' for his singing voice which he'd imagined by then no longer existed, it had become clearer, higher and more effortless than ever! And that you have my word for, Anton."

So in fact his voice never actually broke in the full sense?

Is that what you are expounding?

'The passaggio' - no break, or change in register?

'Exactly De Vries!'

Uncanny! So as I am to believe the voice did not truly alter?

How stupendous! - This indeed fells me with joy and surprise.

De Vries had never been so quite affected by the news of the outcome of a voice of which he had heard just the once.

Over the next weeks, each time De Vries asked when he would next hear the boy, Madame O promised, but somehow being so carried away and involved, she never actually got round to arranging a meeting. Instead, each time she met De Vries, she seemed bent on describing at great length how Mark's voice kept gaining in stature – daily as she put it - in one way or another. De Vries became endlessly frustrated yet increasingly intrigued as she avoided the issue.

"Soon, it may be too late," he tried to convince Madame O. "You can never be sure of a voice. Any day the death knell for Mark's voice could ring."

Madame O registered horror at this last remark. "Please, Anton, if you don't mind refraining from such vicious remarks. I've already told you it's broken successfully. Or should I say it did not break, there was no register change! There now, does that satisfy you?"

Shaking his head, De Vries knew when he had overstepped the mark. The mere mention of such a thing! He offered no reply but as he made to leave the room, he told her, "Then, if you must keep the boy's voice all to yourself, well and good, Rosa, but I do think you have a debt to society to let people hear young Mark." De Vries then excused himself and left to go downstairs, feeling somewhat mean spirited at his previous tactless show of candour, but more than that, he felt himself more frustrated than ever now that the boy was there to be heard but his whereabouts kept a secret.

As the weeks passed, de Vries saw less and less of his colleague. Furthermore, each time on the rare occasion they ran into each other, Madame O scurried off scarcely stopping for breath. Sometimes she didn't turn up at the conservatorium but then it didn't matter since she had no pupils to speak of and the apparent weight loss she sustained became another source of worry to the staff. Moreover, when the offer of food came, Madame O retaliated vehemently "Look here, if I want to eat I shall. Nobody tells me what to eat. I've better things to do. I don't like food, especially since all one sees these days are people munching like cows on a cud. Stuffing their faces with horrible concoctions when they should be feeding their minds instead. It seems to me no one can take a step without holding a bottle of something or other up to their lips. Think about it. Downright infantile I call it. Adults are still suckling. The very thought turns my stomach. Makes me heave."

Absent-mindedness also became a point of issue for Madame O. She left things everywhere. As to the few hours she spent at the Conservatorium, she determined to reach home that much earlier so news of her premature proposed retirement came somewhat as a welcome note to the directors, but it would also pose problems. A new regime would need to be engendered whereby students could be shuffled around to find different teachers. It soon became clear to de Vries that Mark is the cause of Madame O's behaviour. Even so, it pleased him to know there were still odd times when she reverted to form and returned to normality; became her approachable self again. Alas, these were short-lived moments.

How entirely changed Madame O had become from the woman who had adhered to the dictum that one must aim to sew the seeds of greatness wherever ordinariness and mediocrity have taken a hold, so that the student can at least experience some form of greatness, no matter how fleeting, and cling to the memory of a 'magic moment', Madame O had somewhat ambiguously written in her book, 'It is the teacher's foremost duty to mould the singer from within by means of an almost mystical application. Without this means the teacher and singer are at a loss and cannot take advantage of that enigmatic 'ether' that needs to be randomly snatched from around and within the pupils 'aureole' the discovery and outcome of which provides the possibility of reworking forth and replenishing, if needs be, the young person's individual soul. In effect, transforming the spirit into a second more vivid interior mould, so that ultimately the singer in question is rewarded beyond the confines of their self imposed, shackled ordinariness and hopefully ultimately lifted to the heights, depending upon the success of this all important teacher-student alliance.'

Madame O likened this 'metaphysical' act to 'artistic transcendentalism' which she goes on to describe in her book; "as a means of fortifying and revitalising that potential which lies dormant within the individual psyche. Expressed differently, gaining access to what already exists no matter how trivial or inaccessible, and finally bringing to light that which had previously remained hidden."

However, there are a number of factors to Madame O's teaching methods which until recently she had seen no reason to change, but now she is about to rethink and alter fast held concepts based on the discovery of the 'prime example's' marvellous natural way of singing. In the past she could not supply a living example in the flesh but could only provide a composite ideal in writing in her book, but all that had changed with Mark's emergence onto the scene. Soon she expected some of her carefully thought out teaching theories should best be put to one side. Indeed, at present she seemed less able to accept them since that overwhelming voice had arrived to exert such a profound influence over her. Throughout each of their meetings, Madame O opined she learnt more from the boy than she could ever teach him, so that in his absence she could not resist the temptation to frequently refer to him, regardless of inciting envy, frustration and jealousy amongst her two remaining pupils, Lorna Budge – and Joseph Rosenblatt the tenor. She was even prompted to go so far as to sometimes ridicule their efforts. Needless to add, nowadays they were led to suspect Madame O's hypo - vivid imagination to be at work, and ideally they too would like to hear the mystery singer in person. However, Madame O fended them off, indulgently, playing games, fully aware that had she so desired she could produce the 'genuine article' had it not been that, ironically, she did not want to share the 'anonymous voice' with another soul.

Madame O had indeed become chronically possessive of what she now saw to be her own new found 'prophetic skills'. In other words 'inventing' a vocal paragon before its actual inception. Since it is true, throughout her life she had vaguely dreamt of a 'certain type ideal voice' and accordingly lately had alluded to such in her book. If she were honest with herself she had always believed such a voice could only remain a daydream; one teacher's composite example of all the finest inherent vocal qualities.

In reality, a vocal impossibility not only due to such a voice's wide vocal range incorporating the lowest and highest notes, but also owing to its all round lack of defect, to which Madame O added great emphasis on musicianship and maturity. No! She admitted this particular boy's vocal supremacy would once have been well beyond her own powers of perception. Meanwhile, fully aware of the prevailing rumours, Madame O continued to enjoy the intrigue. Let them believe amongst themselves that Professor Oppenheimer had conveniently created a 'straw man' to enhance her own teaching! 'Why not? What do I care?' She even resented having let Anton de Vries share in the magical discovery and, with this attitude taking an ever firmer hold upon her, she launched out upon a process of systematically isolating herself and withdrawing altogether from her colleagues. Sooner or later she may even entertain delusions of being solely responsible for creating the vocal phenomenon herself! These days, before her oncoming self-imposed retirement, she is prone to continuously take her two surviving students to task, over their slightest shortcomings and confined herself to tactless and negative remarks such as 'My 'star singer' would never subscribe to such cheap effects' or 'I wish my 'star singer' were here to demonstrate the correct approach'. In effect, abiding by this inharmonious stance, Madame O set about contradicting her own teaching. After all, she had worked with these two students harmoniously over the years with never a harsh exchange of words between the three of them, but nowadays she entertained no qualms about interrupting them either in the middle of a piece to make yet another disturbing and superfluous comment, perhaps ludicrously upon their appearance. Furthermore, with each passing day, she grew progressively restless, more impatient and blatant in her assessments and attitudes, no longer indifferent, as of a few months previously, purposely setting out harsh objections to provoke her pupil's enmity. With her once beneficial sensitivity and tact at such a low ebb and an unfamiliar bitterness in the other's presence gaining an overall grip on her, not to mention the unacceptable incessant allusions to her 'star singer', it came as no surprise that Lorna Budge and Joseph Rosenblatt felt let down and were inclined to forego their lessons rather than encounter her head-on insults.

Compared with the same woman who, throughout the recent past, exemplified the moderate perfect teacher, now, because of Madame O's drastically changed outlook and ways, everything she expressed sounded alien, especially in the way she conducted her fast waning fortnightly master classes, where she resorted to unreasonably singling out some unsuspecting student to publicly take to task.

Chapter Seven

Lorna Budge

Lorna Budge must surely have been the professor's least talented yet most vulnerable student, owing to her innate inability to learn new repertoire, nowadays an item, that Madame tactlessly disregarded yet made show of, to perversely humiliate the girl. How different from their first encounter when Madame O and Lorna had formed a close bond owing to the fact that Madame O swiftly learnt much of Lorna's problem existed due to the shock at the premature loss of the girl's family. After all, no one qualified better than Madame O to help sort out a student's personal problems, whilst never once neglecting to bring out their hitherto undiscovered prime underlying musician's qualities. And thus, in certain knowing professional circles, it had become an easy guessing game as to who were the Oppenheimer trained singers. Needless to add, it is a clear advantage for the student to have Madame's name mentioned on their curriculum since, under her expert and sensitive guidance, it is well known the woman possessed the teaching talent to turn purely nondescript types into quite impressive personalities. How the professor so ably dealt with a students' hidden talents possessed of its very nature a certain air of mystery much envied in the musical profession. Nevertheless, Madame O had not been without one or two 'lame ducks', almost beyond even her help, to contend with, yet she was known to take a benevolent attitude towards them in the knowledge that there is little else she could do to correct their chances of improvement. In regards to Lorna Budge, Madame O had been reconciled to the fact that over the last five years the girl had repeatedly sung the same tired set pieces, which had presently dwindled to precisely four items! Even so, under the circumstances, Madame O had patiently abided by her own rule of not asking questions of such a pupil but rather to have answers ready. Using this approach, she saw to it that a nervous student is not put on the spot but led instead down successive avenues from which to seek and gain new horizons and vistas; so different is Madame O's perverse attitude today, when from the past so rightly she had overlooked Lorna's lack of voice and concentrated on the girl's innate depth of emotion; an inherent gift, that served to exert immense strain on her vulnerable young nature. Even so nowadays, Madame O is intent upon ignoring everything she had previously nurtured so carefully to bring out the best in this least talented and most vulnerable young woman.

Throughout one particularly disastrous lesson, Lorna Budge's throat completely clammed up and, for several frantic moments, she became incapable of swallowing. Madame O however appeared not to heed the warning signs and carried on regardless, with the outcome that Lorna started to dry retch. Still oblivious, Madame O took no notice, much to the girl's chagrin, except to dryly say, "Why do you cough so? You can't come to a lesson with a cold. You'll infect Rosenblatt". However, in the days to come, Lorna Budge's increasingly frustrated curiosity soon got the better of the girl and with some regained confidence Lorna decided outright to throw caution to the wind and ask if she might hear the 'star singer' so often illustriously referred to in Madame's lessons. Madame O's lips remained fiercely sealed and to Lorna's amazement her teacher terminated the lesson there and then half way through, leaving the girl traumatised and humiliated, but not before she had again taken up the attack alluding to Lorna no doubt, when she flagrantly decried - "those dreary neither-nor voices". Those impossible to place voices known in the profession as 'Bitzers', 'dogged voices', 'two or three indeterminable voices pitifully contained within the same depleted vessel', 'vocal patchworks', so that Lorna had been under no illusion as to whom Madame O referred. But that day Madame O had not finished with her diatribe as she bluntly asked "Do you know what a mongrel voice is Lorna? It's one with an incurable break in the middle, top and lower registers. The opposite to legato. Don't waste my time now but think about it when you leave here today," she added with downright malice.

How entirely different to the time Lorna first came to Madame O when it had been the girl's greatest desire to possess a coloratura voice, simply because a 'quack' teacher had dishonestly misinformed her that "with the correct study any voice can be totally altered beyond its former self. Tailor made in fact. Bespoke, if you like!" In her simple way, Lorna had believed in this nonsense. One day she hoped her wish would be granted and she would sing like the old French song 'Comme un Oiseau' – 'sing like a bird'. Unfortunately, with her limited vocal resources, that of course did not pose the slightest possibility. However, at the time of her first audition with the Frau Professor, naturally enough Madame O had not been impressed with the girl's limited voice, but noted positively something else which she referred to at the time in her personal notes as that 'ineffable element', that quality which the singer either has or has not - the means to move the listener far beyond the inadequacies of such vocal limitations. This happened to be the sole reason Madame O took Lorna on as her student.

For a woman of Madame O's profound sensitivities, she always lived in the hope of what she described as "discovering underlying virtues in the common place; rarified moments that have no rhyme or reason to be where they are. After all", she opined, "when all is said and done, what is a beautiful voice without the means of conveying depth? It is not enough. To be complete, a voice ought also to play upon the heart strings". And Madame O concluded that Lorna's lacklustre, unbeautiful voice did exactly that; peculiarly convey depth. So from their first encounter Madame O saw fit to forgive the girl for all her many vocal defects and shortcomings so that Lorna, over a period of time, soon lost some of her many inhibitions and usually sang at her best for Madame O, and once when Madame O, with her consummate skills of understanding the individual's needs, took Lorna aside, and in the process subtly alluded to certain 'nondescript voices nevertheless empowered with the divine, carrying their listeners to the heights," Lorna felt comforted and requited so that progress of a kind had been assured under Madame O's watchful and superior musical eye. Enough that is, to build up the girl's hopes and painlessly steer her clear of the futile desire 'to sing like a bird' and, from the beginning and throughout those following five years, Madame O frequently made a point of hinting without making too much of a show of it, at Lorna's rare ability to 'look inwardly and beyond' and, under that type of personal supervision, the girl became aware enough of her own "hidden depths" which ultimately served to substitute for her vocal deficiencies.

Madame O, with her intensive character searching, soon learned that Lorna from childhood nursed a tendency to believe in the unbelievable and, as such, had been given to seeing 'visions' and, well past childhood, indefatigably had put her faith in fairy tales. As she grew older Lorna attached increasing importance to coincidence and fate and, up until his death, enjoyed nothing better than to be taken aside by her father and be told extraordinary tales, products of his own vivid imagination, that stretched his and his daughters fantasy to the limits. At such times, Lorna became a little possessed and so it happened that throughout her childhood and onwards, Irene & Reginald Budge saw no harm in positively encouraging their daughter in her quiet pursuit of the 'unworldly'. Consequently, left to her own resources and locked into the occasional fantasy, Lorna became a model child. However had that enchanted world been forcibly wrested from her, who could tell what problems would have arisen? As to the 'visions', by the time Lorna reached her teens and read intensively, she responded passionately to a book by Franz Werfel about Bernadette Souberius, the girl who purported to see the 'Immaculate Conception' in a grotto. As a result, Lorna asked her parents if she could change her name to Bernadette. They suggested she wait a year or two, "You have so many wonderful visions of your own," they told the suggestible child, "without having to change your name." And so Lorna carried on in the same vein seeking out the things that affected and moved her most. By dint of this she came to opera and each time her parents took her to hear 'Madama Butterfly', 'Boheme and 'Traviata, she broke down near inconsolably and thus was paved the way for a departure into the world of the 'tragic muse'. And Lorna went on to create her own wholly believable, ever more inescapable private world – albeit a tragic one in which love, art and music featured prominently; a secret place where she saw herself vividly playing the heroine. The next step in 'her assumption', as she described in her diary, and with the advent into her life of Elizabeth Barrett Browning, Jane Austen and the Bronte sisters, Charlotte, Emily and Anne, Lorna managed to create her own 'Nirvana'. All this, with music nonetheless at the forefront of her dreams. Yet no matter how determined her efforts, operatic arias eluded her sparse little voice. A very few simple songs and some excerpts from oratorio suited her better and proved less problematical, especially those pieces that did not place too great a burden on her chronically limited vocal range. Into these carefully chosen pieces, she diligently ploughed all her energies and inspiration. The only element letting her down being her meagre voice. Nevertheless, on certain inspired occasions, she could make up for the vocal deficiency with will power alone, affecting some who heard her by the special depth with which she unwittingly imbued the music.

Lorna Budge's transition into 'adulthood' had not evolved without its fair share of difficulties not least because, since losing her family, she had desperately clung even more tenaciously to childhood in order to recapture and grasp a hold onto a happy past, even to the point of resorting to playing out childhood games. She could imagine in the silence of her surroundings her brother by her side. Gabriel in his spare time, created model planes out of Balsa wood or steeped himself in reading adventure stories including every volume of 'Biggles'. Today, Lorna's bedroom still retained all the features of that blissful past. The room remains a retreat away from oppressive learning problems brought on by her dyslexia, added to which she had 'caught a stammer' as she preferred to put it, a carry-over again, as fate would have it, from being parted with such dramatic finality from the members of her family. On her parents death she had been provided with enough means to support herself and carry on living in the modest family house, Ariel Court from where she rarely ventured forth, save on the day of her 'lifesaving' weekly lesson with Madame O.

In her house she saw that everything remained neat and tidy, just as her parents had left it on that last fateful day. Such is the solitary life imposed on the girl who, each day downstairs confined herself to practising her singing and piano playing on the baby grand piano in the music room. A room with its soft furnishings and mellow northern light shining through the large picture window. On the wall of the music room hung a reproduction of one of the few known portraits of Henry Purcell, its brass inscription denoting his dates (1659-1695). To Lorna, this greatest of all English composers who was by far and above her favourite. The simplicity of his melodies spoke to her directly and of all his 250 songs and works, one particular air moved her more than any other – Dido's Lament from his opera 'Dido and Aeneas'.

Lorna had claimed this for her own when as a chorister at a young ladies boarding school she took part in a performance of the work. These days Lorna liked to think Purcell's haunting song of farewell filled a vacant gap in her existence and even went as far as to believe that in another life the piece had been especially written with her in mind. In the lonely niche destiny had carved for her at home, she discovered she could permit her mind to fantasize at will and turn on and off from the world that had prematurely dealt her such a cruel blow. As a result, sometimes she could talk herself into believing her family had returned and were safely ensconced back at the house, even to the point of hearing their voices and laughter resounding throughout the now vacant rooms.

As Lorna's memory journeyed back over the last five years, she affectionately remembered in detail her first encounter with the spry little German professor, and how warmly she had been received as if she were an honoured guest. For her part, Madame Oppenheimer had been immediately struck by the 20 year old's unassuming manner. For that first audition Lorna had painstakingly prepared two extremely difficult Schubert songs learning the German text phonetically. The first song with its long phrases, 'Du bist die ruh', 'You are rest', had particular significance for Madam O Lorna learned later. And when Lorna came to sing the second verse and her breath control momentarily faltered on the worlds 'Ich weihe dir', 'I dedicate to you', 'voll lust und Schmetz, 'in joy and pain', Madame O had suddenly found herself deeply moved as if this particular girl's vocal shortcomings actually added to the depth of feeling underlying the song.

Subsequently, Madame O had been swift to recognise the inherent problems in such a vulnerable young person and, whilst keeping her own emotions in check, feigned not to notice the girl's wavering in the presence of such a difficult song. At the time Madame O didn't stop;- continued accompanying on the piano leaving Lorna to come to grips with the remainder of the work, succeeding to complete the song without further mishap. Afterwards Lorna believed her chances of being accepted for the professor's singing course, to be nil and shot Madame O an embarrassed glance and readied herself to leave. She was more than surprised to be met with a disarmingly frank smile. Madame O stood at the window and motioned to Lorna to come over to her side, "Take a little break, dear," the professor insisted. "Pause for some deep breathing," she suggested, adding, "You sang that song with all the depth of feeling it demands. Now, when you are ready, just give me a sign and we shall journey into your second choice, the world of 'Night and Dreams'". Lorna nodded blissfully and when the time came she began to vocalise less tentatively, but again characteristically floundered on the second verse. Once more, Madame O acted in a nonplussed fashion, which gave Lorna added incentive to continue singing on in reasonably good German –

'Nacht und Traume'

Die belauschen sie mit Lust

    They listen to them with joy

Rufen wenn der tag erwacht

    Cry when day awakes

Kehre wider heil'ge Nacht

Return Holy Night

Holde Traume Kehret wieder

Return sweet dreams.

This time, at the end of this second song, there followed a slightly edgy silence. Lorna dared not look at the professor. Meanwhile, in the girl's best interests Madame O tactfully decided to reserve judgement on Lorna's interpretative powers rather than comment on her wispy, thin little voice which, for all that, had still strangely moved Madame O. Thus without a further moment's hesitation Professor Oppenheimer conceded in a suitably professional tone of voice, appropriate to her authoritative position as former pupil of the imperious and illustrious German soprano, Lilli Lehman: "I suppose you would like to know where you stand, Miss Budge?" Lorna did not answer. Madame O continued, "Well let me say this, I should be most honoured to take you as my pupil." 'Honoured'? Lorna, who until then held no hope in her mind of gaining admission to a Conservatorium, could not believe her ears and found it difficult to restrain herself from embracing the woman. That day, she walked out from the Conservatorium into the broad daylight a changed person, more grown up, her peace of mind regained. As a direct consequence, with the passing of time, she became more or less dependent on Madame O who, in a matter of minutes, had accepted her and in so doing rescued the girl from a state of self-induced need that would eventually change her entire future outlook. Over the succeeding five years, Lorna and the professor increasingly confided in each other and during that same period Lorna gradually became familiar with Madame O's family background and its all too tragic ramifications. Likewise, Madame O slowly delved into the circumstances of Lorna"s childhood. Thus the two became kindred spirits, both women sharing the great loss of their respective families; Madame O almost becoming an idol for Lorna, and in the girls eyes secretly taking the place of her family, and as their relationship progressed, at certain lessons, Madame O might see fit to discuss Lorna's problems rather than undertake to hear the girl sing a single note. In Lorna's mind her teacher became 'Mado, no longer Madame O, or Prof. Oppenheimer.

However, today Lorna could only experience abject concern at the dramatic overall transformation in her mentor. Lately each proceeding lesson had of its nature become a trial of errors besetting Lorna's fraught nerves. The vital spark the two had shared systematically extinguished, and the once compatible relationship now in sharp decline. Indeed, as far as Lorna could envisage, spoilt beyond repair. How Madame O had become this alien presence that picked fault with every note is beyond Lorna's simple powers of comprehension though, ironically enough, under the strain of this abuse Lorna's singing grew more intense and heartfelt, but Madame O paid no heed.

Whether as an escape route, or as a last resort, Lorna decided to drastically impress Madame O with a new piece, that lay far beyond the girls' scope, namely Donna Anna's aria from Mozart's "Don Giovanni" – 'Non mir dir' - with its overtones of regret and despair. 'My grief will soon destroy me, one day maybe Heaven will hear me. Hear my prayer and pity me: 'Crudele, Non mi dir bel idol mio': 'Ich grausau? Sag mir nich O Heiligellichbter'. However from the outset Madame O had no intention of letting Lorna sing the aria. At the mere mention of it she had immediately scoffed at the idea.

"How absurd!" Madame O exclaimed. "Why, I doubt if you could even wade through the first few bars," and promptly, with little or no voice of her own, recklessly plunged into the piece herself, stopping abruptly after no more than half a minute to announce, "You couldn"t possibly attempt it. You're no Lilli Lehmann!" Lorna replied 'I don't want to be". Madame O cried out: "Now it appears we have delusions of grandeur to contend with as well. No! Enough is enough! Enough of Donna Anna!" Madame O added caustically.

Totally out of character, she seated herself impatiently at the piano and in an oddly alien and unfriendly tone demanded "Well, are you ready, Miss Budge, or would you prefer me to decide for you as usual? Come to that," Madame O dryly announced, "Would I be correct in presuming you wish to play the ever forsaken Dido, Queen of Carthage again? How very original. But why, why? I truly can't imagine." Stifling a mock yawn she continued, "Or is it to be our 'Blessed Virgin's Expostulation' for the umpteenth time?" Under this barrage of insults, Lorna Budge completely forgot about the music and remained awkwardly standing in the same place not able to move nor knowing where to look through her welling tears. "Do you know, Miss Budge, I'm about to tell you something that's been playing on my mind for an exhaustive amount of time. It is this. I've always felt that Purcell work far above and beyond you. So why do you still struggle with it? There! I've said it." Madame O had a glint in her eye and a self-congratulatory cruel smile on her bird like features. "Now should my 'star' pupil take a hold of such a work, that would result in something memorable indeed!"

That day, the teacher and pupil breakdown reached its nadir when Madame O took Lorna aside and thrust the score of Bellini's 'Norma' in the girl's face, then jerkily placed it on the piano rest and started playing unrhythmically. "Now, do as I tell you. Forget Mozart and Purcell. I want you to follow me. I am determined you should learn new pieces but the ones I choose!" Madame O commanded. "Do you hear me girl?" Madame O spoke in a menacing high-pitched voice that sent waves of panic through Lorna. "Today, you and I are going to sing the duet for Norma and Adalgisa. Here, look over my shoulder and follow." Madame O started:

Tell me, tell me,

Thou hast vanquished.

Once more I find a Friend.

Yes until the last hours

I shall be thy companion:

To shelter us together

The earth is wide enough;

With thee, against my fate,

I will firmly hold my head

Until I feel my heart

Vibrate upon thy own.

Lorna a poor sight-reader at the best of times, at Madame O's scolding insistence began shakily and, after just a few phrases broke down, her voice deserting her entirely. "No, please Madame, I can't," she pleaded, "My voice won't let me. I can't sing Bellini, never could."

Madame O's eyes narrowed angrily. "That's of no concern to me because I know you can't. And there are any number of things you can't sing!" she snapped and for a while she sang the beautiful melody in her broken instrument of a voice. Then she turned around to Lorna defiantly and declared spitefully, "I'm afraid, as a last resolve, Miss Budge, your limitations have reached a stalemate and I don't see any future at all for you!" She grimaced unkindly and continued, "There, I'm glad I came out with it! Am I getting across to you? I certainly hope so. No! As usual your powers of concentration are on holiday!"

Lorna, shocked and pained, made no reply. 'So this is how the end comes,' she told herself silently.

"Don't you have a tongue in your head? Can't you stand up for yourself? Heaven forbid have you also lost your speaking voice, Miss Budge?" Madame O didn't bother to wait for Lorna's reply to her questions. "Nothing to lose in that direction I expect," she added shrewishly. The sound of Madame's voice droning on relentlessly assaulted Lorna's senses in a way that left her quite dumbstruck, vague and irresolute, totally at odds with herself and unable to offer a word in her own defence.

"Perhaps you'd prefer that I answer for you in a more easily understood way, Miss Budge?" and without further warning Madame O started accompanying herself at the piano and began to sing 'When I have sung my songs I'll sing no more...' twice over, her aged sad woefully skimpy voice attempted the refrain but each time the voice strained and tumbled over itself in a horribly bitter-sweet but wholly ineffectual manner, suffocating in upon itself. Finally it dwindled off into a subdued crackle, until, with tears welling in her eyes, Madame O stopped altogether. Had Lorna not been so moved, she would have been desperately hurt. Instead she felt even more deeply for the woman whose personal tragedy remains reflected throughout the tired, old song. However, Madame O had not finished. Again she turned to address Lorna directly, in full operatic fashion, piling on the insults,

"Swans sing before they die. T'would be a good thing t'were some died before they sang," she declared irritably, then with utmost finality,

"Basta! Lesson over!" She stood up stiffly to attempt, near -unsuccessfully, to reach a height of 5 feet over the keyboard, her stance resembling a grim automata figure as she shut down the piano lid with an alien harshness hitherto unknown to Lorna.

What Lorna believed she had been witnessing these last minutes could not be her teacher but a pitiful tragedy queen re-enacting her own destiny in which everything worthwhile had changed for the worse. Still Madame O had not quite finished pouring scorn on troubled waters.

"I hope at least you have learned something today, Miss Budge, because I can assure you I certainly have not!"

With that last caustic remark, Madame O disappeared behind the curtain of the adjoining kitchenette and started to furiously clatter around in the background without reappearing. Lorna, embarrassed and deluded, waited indecisively for some sign, wondering whether to remain or let herself out. After ten minutes she chose to silently leave and, in that moment, experienced little or no desire to return anymore, except at the back of her mind curiously it occurred to her that what her teacher had said had not been directly addressed to her. Strangely enough, to Lorna's way of thinking, it seemed as though throughout that highly unpleasant meeting, the woman had almost been addressing herself, and had taken leave of her senses to destroy something deep down within, that personally meant so much to her own existence, whilst indirectly taking out her frustration on her hapless pupil. In fact, a punishing form of mental self flagellation she deployed to hurt herself. Later Lorna recalled the distraught expression in Madame O's eyes, and on second thoughts, decided her teacher's erratic behaviour is more likely due to the woman's declining health, eroding away at her sanity. Lorna felt herself plunged into a hopeless situation and convinced herself that Madame O's mean spirited attitude had been little more than a 'guise' that had nothing to do with the true Madame O who Lorna knew so well.

So much for the disastrous lesson Lorna had waited all week long for, albeit in vain and, as she sauntered down the driveway, it was difficult not to feel her body and mind battered into abject submission by Madame O's malicious verbal onslaught. Lorna asked why it had taken all of five years for her so-called 'best friend' to come out today with the painful truth regarding her pupil's sadly lacking singing abilities? In that surfeit of hurtful admonitions, Madame O had more or less conferred the death knell on her 'most vulnerable pupil'. Lorna wondered what the future would garner. Until the present she had sought refuge in her long serving fantasies, but that essential turn on valve that till now could be relied on to cover pent up emotions and gives her Dutch courage, presently seemed non-existent. A thing of the past. there and then, Lorna may gladly have relinquished her studies. However, in positive mode she demanded, if she were to 'survive', she must ward off 'stunned reality' as had always been her habit in times of adversity. Act the 'memories game' where she invoked her lost family to play a key role. 'What then am I to do?' she asked herself. But all she could hear as the gravel crunched underfoot was not Irene Budge's welcome reply; only Madame O's grotesque singing parody still brashly ringing out from over the piano. 'When I have sung my songs, I'll sing no more.' Despite the woman's obvious personal allusion to the girl, Lorna resolved she herself is not yet entirely ready to take to heart a 'sick woman's' advice. She kept telling herself that perhaps after all Madame O had not altogether meant what she'd told Lorna. Still, the urge to sing and summon forth from within her own nondescript little voice remained too great a compulsion and desire for Lorna. But now her mother's question to her father rose over the girl's thoughts, "Who will look after Lorna should anything happen to us? She will be utterly helpless!" Throughout the years, Irene Budge had repeatedly advised her daughter "Whatever befalls you in this life, Lorna, promise your father and I to fight on no matter how difficult the situation." Lorna recalls: "These words had stayed indelibly etched in the memory, not dissimilar to the words of a song, 'What 'ere befalls... Love will find a way."

"No – Yes!" Lorna vowed imagining her mother standing there beside her. She must faithfully carry out her parent's prophetic wishes to the best of her ability. Besides, had she not increasingly dedicated her singing to those two and, were she able to hallow their memory, had she not but one choice - to keep up with her singing? Her resolute mind continues to constantly demand she return to 'Dido's Lament', that one timeless melody above all others that meant so much to her. Impulsively she came to grips with herself and demanded why 'that other singer' Madame O permanently raved on about should be given precedence to ruin everything she, Lorna, had worked so resolutely to achieve? "No!" she persuaded herself aloud, remaining convinced that no matter how wonderful or unique the 'star' may be, Madame O still had no right to only consider herself and threaten Lorna by taking over her life. Lorna scolded tersely as she began to despise the anonymous singer. By the time she arrived home, she had succeeded more positively to adjust her mental state and better plot out her future since on the journey back, for the first time, she found within herself a hitherto undetected indwelling strength. After all, she urged, there is only one choice left she self-taunted theatrically. Fight on or perish. At the gate to Ariel Court she stopped to wonder from where she'd borrowed that phrase. Probably from the movies a whimsical half smile of irony played across her soft pale features, as she approached the front door accompanied at last, by a vague sense of relief.

Constantly her thoughts returned back to her teacher, her one time 'best friend' whose mind Lorna now remained convinced had been taken over by demons. How to go about rescuing this woman to whom she owed so much, who had always helped her in times of personal need. Maybe Lorna should first make it a duty to enquire into the existence of the 'infallible, self possessed, 'star' singer" to whom Madame O swore such blind allegiance. Hear in the flesh, this 'unimaginable voice', that had so clearly affected and changed beyond recognition Madame O's total character, had in fact turned a once solicitous, balanced woman into a tyrant now near enough bereft of the everyday human feelings. Only then, Lorna assumed her own mind would be put at rest, in the knowledge that her personal decision to continue singing would be the correct choice, failing which, she may decide at twenty five years old to escape and to discontinue singing altogether. Retire inwardly to her ideal fantasy retreat far from the outside world wherein she determined nothing, and no one could succeed to hurt or wound her ever again. Whilst her eyes scanned the interior of her bedroom, Lorna contented herself that not a single soul knew better than she to what lengths one can go as a means of deploying fantasy through self deception in order daily to pacify and protect a disturbed state of mind. For the present she foresaw every strategically placed object in her room answered to some pressing incumbent foreboding assailing her thoughts in respect that is, to past, present and future doubts and events.

Chapter Eight

Nightmare

Repeatedly Lorna's mind returned to reconsider her teacher whom she now genuinely believes has lost touch with reality, no longer recognises the difference between kindness and cruelty. Speculation and supposition absorbed the girl's mind to overflowing. Abruptly she maintained that Madame O in her present unstable state has purposely created a non-existent 'straw man'. A product of the imagination continuously entrenched in the woman's fantasy who conveniently acts as a supreme vocal model of excellence, a magical type emblem who possibly stood to prompt and inspire Madame's students onto higher levels of aspiration! By dusk that day Lorna had decided on a definite course of action.

Down the tree-lined laneway Lorna made her way towards 'Windermere' Cottage. When she reached the house, not a sign of life stirred. She carried on walking straight ahead. At the last moment, despondently changed her mind and resolved to return home. In such moments how she longed for her parents and her brother Gabriel. Had they never left she believed none of this would be happening to her today.

Throughout the next day, Lorna scarcely bothered to eat a morsel. Rather she fed upon a sense of starved anticipation and that afternoon decided upon a second visit to 'Windermere' purely on the off-chance of at least catching a glimpse of Madame O's fabled 'wonder singer', should, that is, 'she' exist at all. This time when Lorna arrived at the cottage she did not hesitate to carry out her plan. Stealthily she made her way up behind some shrubs and cautiously took up a position inside the derelict summer house, crouching down in wait so as not to be detected amongst the tall grass and weeds that reached up and spread around and over the verandas and through into the creaking, rotting wooden floorboards. From here she strained to listen; hung onto the merest sound in the hope of hearing the much-extolled 'star' and, as she did so, she romanticised nervously on what she might expect if anything at all. She recalled Madame O's oft repeated thrilling account of the silvery voiced Australian soprano Nellie Melba being discovered in Paris by the most acclaimed singing teacher of the time, Mathilde Marchesi (1821-1913) a singer who, in her prime, had been a mezzo soprano of some renown. The story went that Nellie arrived in London on 1 May 1886 and shortly after, bearing a letter of introduction to Madame Marchesi, left for Paris. In the Marchesi household on the Rue Jouffroy, the then Nellie Armstrong was shown into a room for her audition and ordered to stand on a tiny platform. Asked what she wished to sing, Nellie replied "Violetta's aria from 'La Traviata', 'Ah! Fors e Lui, 'Ah! Was it he'", but before she had finished singing the aria, Madame Marchesi, a small grey haired woman dressed in black stopped, turned and asked the unknown singer. "Why do you screech your top notes? Can't you sing them piano?" the girl responded and sang as softly as she could the top B. "Higher!" Madame demanded from the piano striking the C, and then onto the E Flat pianissimo, upon which Marchesi rushed from the room leaving Nellie still trembling on the platform. Later on, as the newly named Madame Melba, Nellie learned Madame Marchesi at the time of their first encounter had scrambled up the stairs to excitedly tell her husband, "Salvatore, j'ai enfin une etoile!". "Salvatore, at last I have found a star!" Thus a legend was born.

For some little time Lorna relished the tale whilst noting the front window of 'Windermere' cottage remained unlit in the fading half-light of dusk. As darkness approached and the air became quite brisk for midsummer, she took from a flask a few nips of brandy to provide the necessary courage and warmth needed for her lone, clandestine vigil. When the moon rose, Lorna raised herself and took a few steps up onto the platformed weatherboard veranda making certain not to attract attention. There she secluded herself behind a climbing Wisteria and breathed in the heavy perfume. The combination of wisteria and brandy subsequently promoting a sense of welcome euphoria as she peered into the room beyond. It took a minute or so to accustom her eyes to the gloomy interior. What appeared next nearly sent her toppling backwards, but she managed to catch a hold of the Wisteria vine and steady herself in the shadows. Suddenly from behind the window materialised an immensely tall, sinister figure of a man. She felt his penetrating eyes riveting and leering through an eerie smile directly towards her. In abject horror, Lorna's heart skipped a beat as she automatically crouched down further away from his gaze at eye level with the sill. The moonlight shone through a side window behind the man and streamed down over one side of his face and oddly elongated figure. The veil curtain semi-draping and gently billowing to stroke his countenance, simultaneously enswathing and caressing his peculiar old-fashioned apparel. Lorna felt exposed. Her entire body being seized up in a paroxysm of fear, nevertheless, she seemed unable to resist a last, tentative parting glance at the figure, before attempting a hasty retreat back down into the garden. Too late. One of his arms appeared to rise from the darkness and reach out, a massive open palm thrusting towards her. With each passing second, the figure looming larger and increasingly menacing in Lorna's eyes. At any moment his clenching fist would crash its way through the half opened glass pane and smack directly into her face answering to the girl's worst fears; an encounter with a real life stone man. Her imagination running rampant, she envisages the Commendatore from 'Don Giovanni' now assailing her very lifeblood! She stifled a scream and ducked to avoid the hand she asserts is reaching out to seize her, lift her into the air, and pull her back into the house through the jagged glass, severing her jugular vein. Automatically she held her hand up to her neck. In her panic, the man's face suggested to her something that had terrified her since childhood – the hideous Goya painting of the giant about to devour the naked form of one of his own children. Lorna's mind wrestled at the sight of the colour of the man's skin which with each added movement changed from a sickening enamel greenish hue to a crude Goyescarish crimson. Momentarily, a dark cloud covered the moon. The veil curtains billowing forth in shadow and moonlight returned to envelope the figure in a shroud like effect, but he made no effort to draw them aside. Instead, he remained leering at her, his eyes two black hollows capturing her in their hypnotic gaze, affording her but one option, to hold her breath in alarm and dread. Fleetingly, she shielded her eyes to stifle out the image. As the moon grew brighter, the man's expression changed. The purple gaping mouth enlarged by the shadows, exhibited a ghostly grimace tethered across his features. Now he beckoned to her. For a split second Lorna regarded the period attire before rapidly stepping backwards away from his clutches.

What followed next sent her reeling over the corner of the veranda onto the wet overgrown tangle of grass and knee-high weeds and nettles. A scream echoed overhead and resounded on all sides as the wind increased and several slates from the roof smashed down onto the wooden verandah resembling the clanking of stone footsteps in her pursuit. 'Che inferno che terror – ah!' The breathing grew stronger, pounding filled her chest, and Lorna helplessly lifted one leaden foot before the other. A wild flurry of wings brushed her cheeks, furiously beat over the top of her head as she dodged down. Next she pushed herself up from the sodden grass, felt the blood rush through her veins. Once back on her feet again, she stumbled, tripped and fell headlong into some brambles scratching and cutting her shins, cheeks and the palms of her hands. Regaining her balance, she tripped again and dislodged a shoe, which flew out into the darkness, as she stumbled down through the overgrowth into a giant cobweb. Screech owls and Nightjars had taken up rival positions in an overhanging birch tree, their screams and taunts following her from above. To add to the ordeal, a nightmare cacophony of cats joined in the screeching session, resulting in an unholy din. Lorna began running for all she was worth.

With one good shoe clasped to her chest, she sprinted off until, heaving for breath, she halted in her tracks. She was ridding her face of cobwebs when a portly policeman with a handlebar moustache appeared under the lamplight and, reaching out a beefy hand, laid it on her shoulder. Lorna yelled so loudly he snatched it back as though he'd touched hot coals, nearly lost his balance, and swayed backwards supported by his truncheon, simultaneously straightening his helmet lurching over one eye, as he sat on the ground, holding onto Lorna for extra support.

"Hello, what have we here? What the Dickens is this one up to?" he cried. Lorna shocked, jerked away from him and with what little breath she'd regained, yelled "There's something wrong down at Jamberoo Lane, - Windermere Cottage". The policeman repeated after her, "Jamberoo Lane? Windermere Cottage?" Lorna only wanted to get away and managed to splurt out at the baffled constable as she tugged away, "A man! A murderer! A burglar!" she shouted. "He's there now. An intruder!" The words stammering forth the first things that came to her mind. In a final outburst she warned "Hurry! Or it will be too late!" She kept a safe distance from the constable giving him a wide berth. Had he not been so heavy he may have grabbed her again but instead he stopped to wipe the sweat from his face, "One too many, eh, and only a young'un at that. Start early these days," he exclaimed looking in Lorna's direction as he sniffed the air and smelt a waft of brandy enter his nostrils. "Hang on, Ronald," he said to himself, "A murder? An intruder? 'Windermere Cottage? That"s our lady Professor"s old ruin of a place with all them wild trees and weeds and shrubs growing everywheres." Lorna took a few swift and furtive steps backwards. "Yes, yes!" she moaned in frustration. "Did I hear rightly? A murder. A burglary?" But Lorna had scampered off into the darkness. "Here, come back!" Constable Ronald Lascelles called after her, "Just a minute, Miss!" but Lorna had already disappeared, the sound of heavy plodding footsteps dying off behind her leaving the constable to make a mental note of what she had told him.

At last, when she reached her front door, she could hear the whimpering of Bertie, the mongrel dog who had made himself at home the previous year. Sheepishly, still not quite confident of his position, he welcomed her as a guest might the host. Lorna slinked against the inner front door, and unthinkingly left it unlocked. Bertie waited looking at her inquiringly and diffidently followed behind as slowly she mounted the staircase leading to her bedroom where she divested her dishevelled clothing and gratefully climbed into bed. Bertie, at the foot of the bed, waited for her to put out the light and settle in for the rest of the night but the moment she dared shut her eyes, the ghastly vision of the man at 'Windermere' returned to terrorise and haunt Lorna, and subject her to her worst fears. "What will become of Madame O?" she whimpered under the bedclothes blaming herself for not staying on to help. The man's sinister waxen features remain vividly encapsulated in her mind, his head sporting a bizarre full length elaborate wig trailing down upon his shoulders, or at least that is what Lorna remembered. The weirdly elongated clumsy body glistening unnaturally in the eerie light of the moon, a blurred picture that emerged evoking a ghostly underwater cavern staying etched in her memory. She pulled the bedclothes up closer to her face and stared up at the ceiling. What if he had murdered her teacher? Lorna spluttered, and her body stiffened. Her mind raced off at a tangent. Tentatively she pulled the bed quilt up over her head. And what if she awoke during the night and found the monster towering over her? He could easily have followed her back here with his long legs, keeping to the shadows so as not to be seen, and finally discover her. Lorna, in her desperate efforts to get home quickly, had not once thought to look back. Now she suddenly remembered she had not secured the front door. By now though she was far too rigid with fear to move. Bertie would bark and warn her. Already the dog is dozing. Lorna imagined that green face pressed up against her own and, as a last resolve, attempted to persuade herself that perhaps she had been mistaken. Mistaken about what? That the half man, half beast standing so threateningly at Madame O's cottage may not have wished her ill! Try though she may, she failed to satisfy herself and throughout the latter part of the night, her temples burning, two new images haunted and pounded at her senses, the one superimposed on the other. In her mind the man became a dark indistinct figure lurking in the adjoining alleyway to Jamberoo Lane and, having spied her, left at exactly the same moment as she had, running at a safe distance from her to follow her home. Next, again she envisaged the bloodied spectacle of Goya's mad child eating giant thrusting and devouring one of his own children into his gaping mouth, eyes wild, murderous, aglow.

Whilst these images of horror persisted, Lorna listened to the wind outside gathering momentum until sleep overtook her. Slowly, the door to her bedroom creaked open of its own accord. A tall figure entered the room soundlessly appearing from the shadows and clambered down over the bedclothes leaving a trail of blood on the snow-white quilt. No longer is Lorna dreaming! The figure proceeded to snort, and lick out lasciviously with its repulsive and salivating tongue that flopped out steamily as it caressed the flesh on her face and hands, covering her in a glutinous mess. Then, ever so slowly, the monster set to work to throttle her and finish her off. The mouth opened, underwater reptilian jaws retracting, revealing the huge crimson void of slimy membrane awaiting the girl's head to be roughly positioned into it. Wider and wider the mouth gaped until from the depths it produced a nauseous, pungent odour accompanied by an increasingly deafening hollow bellow. Lorna recognised the Bull Roarer, a musical instrument she'd heard played in 'corroborees' put on by the Aborigines, and knew at once her ears were about to be deafened for all time, never to hear another note of music. Her mind and body anaesthetised by acid fluid, the acrid odour of the monster's volcanic breath heaving forth in scalding bursts basting in turn every bodily surface and function, cooking her alive with his boiling breath in preparation before masticating her body between voracious glass sharp fangs. Lorna is bodily lifted upward by the scruff of the neck in readiness to be thrust headfirst into the immense steamy, jagged cauldron. Inside, on all sides her eyes settle on stalactites and stalagmites abounding in the crimson interior on and off turning to indigo and magenta, gore dripping as his hands press her further down into his throat, on her journey into the depths of the cavern. Digging into her skull the needle sharp embers bake her temples, crunching through her hair and scalp, followed by the immense strike of an outsized outstretched palm of the beast's hand on her backside. For a moment, she is airborne, after which she is gripped tightly by the waist to be smothered forthwith by his 'mouth of mouths' with its exquisitely swollen protruding lips. Thus she shall be consumed in that obscene whirlpool of frothy broth and saliva as the creeping flesh is systematically scorified from her flayed body; ultimately being divested of its existence in an endless series of agonising strips. Throughout, she will refuse to die despite being eaten alive, but fate decrees die she must under this horrific rampage, not noisily but in the last instance quickly, to quell, her hopeless screams. Only a few bones shall remain, a reminder that a human once dwelt in this place. Now her feet dangle uselessly above the ground and no matter how she screams, her wails will be deadened deep down within the predator's throat. His tongue will mop away at hers so that all her efforts to call out are rendered muffled and blurred, softened and saliva drowned, suppressed into a silent murky void, finally as the Colossus's tongue sets forth upon it penultimate handiwork, Lorna grows smaller, diminishes in body volume as the man increases in size, and before she is completely digested and swallowed, she is yet to experience within the last throes whereupon she will agonise in a crimson mess and purple sea of salty, bitter sludge that fills her nostrils to capacity and blinds her vision forever, whilst the last vestige of breath expires until she is no more.

In that endless night, Lorna's wetted hair became entangled in the blankets. A sheet secured tautly around her neck. She tugged with all her might to disengage herself as the sheet threatened to strangle and squeeze the last remnants of lifeblood from her. Bertie, one paw on her forehead, remained dutifully licking and nuzzling away at the beads of perspiration from his mistress's face, his eyes meeting Lorna's as hers opened in abject horror. From earliest dawn, Lorna sat bolt upright in bed shaking uncontrollably from her nocturnal ordeal, remains too terrified to get out of bed. Hours later, she struggled to phone the Conservatorium for news of Madame O, relieved at least to learn lessons were to be resumed as planned. She is assured by the superintendent at the Conservatorium, that Madame O's life has not been threatened nor, for that matter, had been in any danger whatsoever. For the rest of the morning, unable to make a move, Lorna remained in her bed pondering listlessly upon the horrific events of the previous evening at 'Windermere' cottage and throughout the rest of the early hours at Ariel Court till the dawn. By late afternoon, when finally she arose and looked at herself in the badly deteriorating antique mirror, she could well imagine peering into a frayed, life-size photo of a much older woman, the wearer of whose jaded expression peered back at her through dimmed eyes, a shadow of her former self. Her mind wandered back to 'Windermere' where the night before no sound had ushered from within the portals, not even from the 'green man' who had horribly materialised before her, Phantom-like, to endlessly haunt her, but what in effect disturbed her even more, being the fact that presently she found the terror of seeing him again, momentarily irresistible, as if drawn to her own demise. Several days were to pass before she dared return to the cottage.

When her next lesson took place, Madame O, in a blind rage, met Lorna and wildly confronted the girl with any number of accusations. "Do you not realise that I know what you've been up to? Don't think for one moment I am not aware of you victimising me in the safety of my own home without imagining for one minute that Constable Lascelles doesn't keep me abreast of such matters? Oh yes, the local constabulary informed me that a girl, drunk and in a sorry state, answering precisely to your description, down to an account of the clothes you wore, not only screamed abuse at Constable Lascelles, but let it be known that I had murdered someone! At my own house! Preposterous! Not only that, mention was made of an interloper, a murderous looking man and a burglar to boot! As if I mix with criminals! It's an outrage. I know better than anyone that not a soul entered my house nor do I have a lodger, nor a guest, nor is anything missing! Now what have you to say for yourself? I warn you I will not tolerate such behaviour from a student, nor anyone else for that matter." From a drawer, she produced Lorna's missing shoe. "There is the evidence.

Own up to it. It is yours, isn't it? I found it in the garden. There's no mistaking red tartan leather patent. Haven't you caused enough trouble? Letting 'them' go off like that." Whoever Madame O saw fit to refer to as 'them' Lorna felt too ill and shocked to guess or give the matter a second thought. Nor did she dare to offer the truth of what occurred that night. Rather, she remained tongue-tied, not wishing to divulge her whereabouts on the evening spent at 'Windermere', even under pressure. In future, when going to the cottage, she would wear Gabriel's clothes and dress up her skimpy figure like a boy until she had satisfied herself exactly what was going on. Monster or no monster, she must catch a glimpse of him again to assure herself she had not hallucinated. How she considered, without implicating herself, is she to tell her teacher there had been a genuine prowler lurking in the woman's music room? She simply could not for fear of retribution. Curiously enough, Madame O seemed satisfied, without resort to explanation and unpredictably almost meekly told Lorna to leave, warning her to be doubly punctual for the next lesson. Her teacher's behaviour confirmed to Lorna that Madame O had become completely illogical and altogether erratic.

Chapter Nine

The Ecstasy in the Garden

Days later come the next lesson, her head swimming, by telephone Lorna proposed not attending, but Madame O would hear none of it, insisting adamantly that it was imperative that under no circumstances Lorna should miss a lesson! Lorna yielded to Madame O's demand and nervously appeared punctually and eventually regretted every minute of the lesson, which once more prematurely and unexpectedly Madame O terminated. Meanwhile, when the woman again accused Lorna of misconduct in some form or another, surprisingly she made no mention of the previous week. It must be true Madame O had succumbed to some indeterminate form of gross mental upset. During the lunch hour, Lorna agreed with her friend Joseph Rosenblatt who is of the same opinion. Others at the 'Con' agreed Joseph informed Lorna. Lorna did not care to divulge anything of her visit to 'Windermere' but both she and Joseph set out on a plan of sorts hopefully in order to help improve Madame O's disturbing condition, despite the fact neither knew exactly the best way to go about dealing with someone so irrational and manic; nice one minute, nasty the next. Throughout the last two lessons, Lorna hardly got the chance to sing a note, yet each time Madame O stringently insisted the girl arrive punctually, only to erratically announce halfway through the lesson.

"I must rush off home. My star pupil is due to arrive within the hour and Charles Gorrick wishes to discuss with me pressing questions of utmost importance. Apart from which, my 'coloratura' has consented to give me a private performance of the celebrated Aria di Bravura, that until now, only Farinelli could sing – some 200 years ago. It promises to be a vocal display of fireworks, the like of which has never been heard in our time."

Lorna plucked up courage enough to comment, "But how do you know if you've never heard the aria before?"

"And who, miss, has the audacity to suggest I haven't heard the aria before? For goodness sake, don't say such foolish things," Madame O impatiently retorted, "I've already experienced a similar vocal display and I know what I am to expect! This performance is more or less a repeat performance. Now be off."

With that, Madame O ushered Lorna from the studio as one would an uninvited guest, impetuously and irritably.

At the mere mention of the name Charles Gorrick! Lorna's mind recoiled immediately to the sighting of the 'apparition', or whatever it had been, on her second visit to 'Windermere Cottage'. Today she remained baffled but nevertheless began to predict this same man may even play a key role in relation to the singer. No, that's not possible! She quickly put the idea out of her head. The terrifying spectre couldn't be Charles Gorrick. As for Joseph Rosenblatt, she would continue to conceal her plans from him for the time being and carry on with her own private detective work. For her intended third visit to the cottage, she would be disguised as a boy in Gabriel Budge's overalls. Should the sinister man make a return appearance and threaten her, above all she must endeavour to get matters in perspective since her prime concern is for Madame O's well-being, and secondly to confirm her own personal suspicions that Madame O's singing 'wonder' is a product of pure fiction and even worse, that Madame O in her present state may be honestly unaware of a monster prowling around the cottage. For the third time in a fortnight, her new identity intact, Lorna bravely trekked back to Jamberoo Lane, but this time she placed a pot of pepper in one of the deep pockets of Gabriel's overalls to throw into the face of the 'Goya' monster should he appear again to try and take her by force.

On the way she deduced, not for a moment did she expect to succeed in hearing the 'imagined' spectacular 'star' singer. Yet while the slightest possibility prevailed, that beyond the walls of a dilapidated old cottage there existed a vocal mystery of such mammoth import, and who could actually sing the legendary Farinelli 'Aria di Bravura' an aria that lay beyond the possibilities of every living singer, then Lorna could not resist going to any lengths to be present, such is the overwhelming sense of expectation she is experiencing. At the end of the laneway, surprisingly Lorna noted the windows of the cottage ablaze with light and estimated this evening it would be more difficult to hide. Next as if from loudspeakers over the garden Madame O's voice rang out in conversation with a man's speaking voice. Lorna shuddered and determined nervously this time not to venture further than the summer house where visibility, amongst the tall grass even in the bright light, amounted to almost nil but, more importantly, to where the sound carried satisfactorily.

Shortly after she heard Madame O mutter a few words in German followed by the piano imitating the harp in the opening introduction to Lucia's first aria, goose-pimples went down over Lorna's arms as she prepared herself hopefully for the soloist's entrance. But no voice appeared. Madame O stopped playing and uttered more indistinguishable words, again followed by the piano, her voice intermittently interrupting throughout. How strange! Thought Lorna. The clock had struck twelve, yet it's only six o'clock in the evening. Her teacher's clock is probably just as neglected as the house, Lorna thought, feeling slightly calmer. Then a few more notes on the piano interrupted by the most ungodly screech. Silence, then peels of laughter, a man's voice, a long pause, and another voice, bell like clear – that of a young girl? In the next moment there followed some barely audible soft notes ascending the scale. Lorna's verdict, the sounds made were unimpressive to say the least. Even dull! Colourless! Lorna admitted disappointment. Then the phone rang in the house and afterwards the man ventured forth with a few lean comments that Lorna could not decipher. Lorna concluded if that amounted to all she was going to hear then she need not stay. To her ears the so-called 'star voice' if that is what she'd supposedly heard had to be a very mediocre instrument indeed. Lorna thanked her lucky stars she had at least been spared the ordeal of again encountering the terrifying spectral figure from her last nerve-racking visit. Perversely, something deep down within Lorna's psyche prompted her to actually wish "the voice", in fact, was the odd product of her teacher's imagination. She guessed: at least it would put her mind at rest. For a singer, with Lorna's low self-esteem, due no doubt to her own inadequate voice, it is always hurtful to realise other talents exist of such unimaginable magnitude. Yet, Lorna thought, without all those magnificent recorded historical voices from 1900 onwards to listen to, the world, especially for singers, vocally would be a poorer and a far less exciting place. Seeing that her expectations had risen to a zenith, if she were honest with herself, Lorna still yearned against hope to experience the 'uncanny and the sublime' that Madame O promised, and should that only succeed to be a mere figment of Madame O's imagination, Lorna convinced herself, well and good, then there is nothing much left to look forward to. So be it!

Distracted from her rambling thoughts, Lorna had just noticed the intriguing phosphoric glow rising up from the earth and settling over decaying wood in this wilderness garden, giving the place an air of enchantment that fitted nicely to her own personal demands of fantasy and setting her mind off at the oft desired tangent. If these are the 'Fairy sparks' Madame O often mentioned, then Lorna at least knew them to exist after all, and Madame O is not altogether given over to total exaggeration. Now all that was missing is the presence of Madame O's elusive champion. At best so far, Madame O's star had only produced a unnerving screech and a few unwieldy colourless notes. But not to be thwarted Lorna conjured up her own magic. Let's see, she thought, how best to imagine a magical voice, a cross between all those great sopranos of the past, added to which that special, unfathomable something that knows no barriers. That latter description tallying with Madame O's own description of the ideal composite voice. After giving the matter some thought, Lorna concluded that whoever is about to sing, if at all, is in hesitant mood. Never mind, she would wait a while longer and then leave. After a lull, with no mention of the telephone call, Madame O briefly continued the conversation then struck a solitary note on the piano.

"Dear me, all right, if you wish. Another octave higher if you think that wise. Can be quite a strain, that top E Flat. Not an easy note to follow even at the best of times, and dangerous territory for the uninitiated, but nonetheless a most desirable note when successfully executed," she commented doubtfully. This time, without further ado, the singer immediately responded to Madame O's statement and gently, ever so gently, coaxed the voice to ascend the scale, peculiarly enough creating an inexplicable fluttering sensation in Lorna's ears which she likened to the soft fall of leaves rather than a climbing upwards sensation, an unusual effect she had not experienced before. Odd, she thought, how sounds can play such tricks on the senses. Especially out here in the open air.

"Well done!" Madame O's voice blurted through the window. "Yes, my dear, indeed that was the top E Flat you requested to sing, and might I add, reached so softly and effortlessly," the woman commented distractedly. Then as an afterthought, added "Very unusual. Indeed quite something by way of its execution!"

Outside in the chill air, Lorna agreed as she recalled the famous interlude between Madame Melba and Madame Marchesi, which Madame O, from time to time, enjoyed recounting at lessons. Growing increasingly interested, for the next five minutes Lorna failed to catch further details of the following snippets of conversations, which she assumed to be a discussion on the merits of the singer's aptitude in the higher voice regions. Already something inside stirred and propelled her thoughts in another alien direction, curiously detached thoughts not unlike that last perfectly conceived, velvety note the impact of which somehow she likened to a lithesome, streamlined cat stalking its prey through the dense undergrowth before silently pouncing and taking a hold of its victim unawares.

Lorna digressed at the type of singer she had just heard who possibly and unknowingly treats their voice as an entrapping machine and possessed within themselves the power to take the unwary listener by stealth so that no longer do a few spare random notes spell out the ordinary, or the meaningless, but instead invest an eight note scale plucked spontaneously from the blue to change and take an overall grip on the listener's senses, waylaying and manoeuvring the listeners' preconceived thoughts, be they wrong or right, into a peculiar admixture of one or more nameless new found indeterminate revelations due to which, Lorna now felt the flesh on her body slightly tingling; found herself seeped into the hitherto alien, oddly prolapsed state of floundering, not in water but in mid-air. She wished she had her diary with her, she would be able to accurately quote Madame O's words: by peeling away successive layers of inner emotions one rises to the original surface. The 'Pentimente'. In the brisk night air and the unearthly glow, Lorna felt herself being systematically drawn into an eerie physical state of suspension whereby the sounds of a voice ascending an eight note scale could successfully cast a mild spell over the body's surface supplanting it between two worlds. The known and the unknown. The known inhabiting the world of sounds, the unknown the world of fantasy and intermittent silence. If only she could go inside and join the trio of people, but she must bide her time, wait and hide until the moment is ripe.

Presently the piano is given over to the final section of Lucia's Fountain aria 'Quando rapita in estasi' which Madame O referred to as the 'ecstasy' aria. Next 'the voice' made its reappearance, ever modest but this time far from hesitant and on the word 'ecstasy' proceeded to gently trill or rather ripple, and there again on the word 'sorrow – 'ardone' practically sighed and supplied forth another exacting sublime moment in the form of a wholly unprepared trill, incorporating at its insistence a world of meaning, innervating Lorna's being, and as the aria progressed the voice effulgently, flowed forth confident and radiant. The previous mild shock waves it had instilled in Lorna's ears now turned more to alarm signals alerting the girl's primordial senses by way of a scintillating array of effortlessly improvised vocal embellishments prompting the girl's whole system into an enforced state of wonderment. She felt herself swaying as though gently rocking to and fro on a bark and, by the time the aria neared its conclusion with the words 'mayst thou never rue this day', Lorna felt her whole world turned around, perhaps transported even beyond recall. Instead of remaining stultified in a vacuum as she had hours before at home, these hitherto unknown clarion notes shimmering and ringing in her ears would change her whole outlook as she absorbed the last note that meant to bring the aria to its conclusion. Unexpectedly however, on the spur of the moment, 'the voice spontaneously decided to climb a full octave, further extending the E Flat in alt and sustaining it for a full twenty seconds! Madame O's superimposed cry of disbelief came as no surprise. The idea of such a rare vocal innovation set Lorna's mind alight with visions of all the aforesaid illustrious singers of the past (mentioned in Madame's 'Colcancas", the singer's creed) queuing to pay homage to this one magnificent 'Etoile. Evoking for Lorna a charming silhouette of a young girl, substituting for the one that hung in Madame O's studio of Franz Schubert; "the composer king of melody in heaven, being paid homage by a cavalcade of great composers." For some time, her ears reverberating, Lorna remained mute, not desiring to move. Had it been suggested she would in such a short space of time succumb to the mercy of a singer's voice, she would not have believed it, but here indeed she is actually being faced with the presence of this vocal 'wonder' and finds herself living out the full reality. From within the cottage, Madame O's speaking voice emerged resonant and clear, no longer resembling the tired, strained crackle of recent weeks, and that disturbingly rasping cough of hers that had caused so much concern at the Conservatorium now is non-existent! Happily, Lorna also noted how, once ensconced in her own surroundings, Madame O reverted to her former self with not the merest apparent sign of aggression anymore. For the time being it is all Lorna can do to return, with effort, to mundane reality and quantify her teacher's unfamiliar teaching method of putting this particular singer through the rigours of the most gruelling scales. After all it struck Lorna that it had never been Madame O's teaching procedure, nor her intention, to allow her other students to attempt such complex vocal extravaganzas, largely for fear of damaging the ultra sensitive vocal cords. Tonight though, Madame O entertained no such qualms about uncompromisingly steering her 'star singer' through an impossibly difficult obstacle course which apparently did not remotely affect the virtuoso voice, in fact strengthened it. And at last it occurred to Lorna exactly what her teacher had meant by 'star singer.

"Where do you suppose these baffling supernatural high notes come from, Charles?" she heard Madame O ask excitedly.

"You tell me, Madame, neither my wife nor I have a clue," the man responded.

So that's it. The silent singer is none other than the man"s wife, Lorna assumed as the tale began to vaguely unravel.

An uncompromising silence ensued.

"Oh please, don"t stop yet "La Marca", Lorna pleaded inwardly.

Just then she heard Madame O chip in, "If its not too much "Marca", (Madame O's chosen pronunciation for the singer's name), "May we have a repeat of that last cadenza in the Lucia aria again? Or something similar?"

The singer eagerly complied and the bell like, seemingly 'amplified' voice re-echoed and escaped to remarkable effect through the open window and over the garden, bewitching Lorna's ears and again enveloping her in its primal wake. Turning her legs to water and her knees to jelly, before that is Lorna could recuperate and before she could resist a peek into the room to glimpse the singer, Madame O was at the window, her hands resting on the sill. She peered out over the neglected garden, as if in answer to some distant call or object attracting her attention. Lorna, remaining unseen, managed just in time to step further sideways behind the Wisteria as her teacher's voice, again now suddenly tired and weary, barely trickled forth.

"Is anyone there? Have you returned?" the woman asked in a listless dull tone of voice. Lorna momentarily managed to make out an expression of exaltation on her teacher's trance-like face, as she noted also that Madame O's breathing came in short hoarse gasps. Despite the chill evening air, Lorna puzzled how unlike her teacher to leave a window wide open when so prone to overheated rooms. In fact, tonight Lorna became aware of a number of elements in Madame O's behaviour and reactions that did not tally, but soon she overlooked the observation telling herself any minute now she may well anticipate that 'voice of voices' would recommence its warbling where it had previously left off. She was not to be disappointed. The piano again signalled the 'unknown' singer's involvement, answered by a powerful surge of prolonged staccato notes from the voice resembling not so much a human voice as a musical instrument, swiftly pursued by a succession of seamless trumpeted scales, so impossibly difficult and improbable ushering forth as they did, if they did, from within a human throat, so that Lorna could only marvel at such a likelihood. Could this then explain the mysterious 'Concerto for Larynx' Madame O so frequently and ecstatically mentioned during the lessons of the last weeks?

Presently, Lorna heard her teacher's voice comment zealously, "Yes, now I mustn't forget to re-read that chapter I'd written in my book in which I referred to the Italian singer, Farinelli. You see if I'm not altogether mistaken, I could swear to it, those self same scales and cadenzas we heard just now are identical. In fact..." Madame O's voice tapered off indecisively as the man's voice asked, "Who? Who did you say Madame? Fara-Nelly?"

"Exactly, Charles. Farinelli, a celebrated singer in the early part of the 18th century who took the musical world by storm," Madame O hurriedly interjected, too aroused to stop from her playing as she further explained within the room certain points to the singer, who began creating ever more pronouncedly astounding feats. Lorna absorbed every perfectly focussed note until finally, after what must have been two hours duration, the lights were abruptly extinguished within the house. Lorna could not recall how long she remained there sitting outside in the semi-darkness waiting and watching the hypnotic phosphorescent glow arising on all sides, her ears tempered by the memory of the unassailable, the indescribable vocal mechanism, at best she futilely waited an endlessly long time for the singer's return as, one by one, the fairy lights diminished into total darkness and she had no further reason to prolong her stay. She had indeed experienced the uncanny and the sublime. 'The rest is silence' she told herself resolutely quoting Hamlet's parting words as in a daze she walked home.

Later that night at Ariel Court, Lorna settled into the comfort of her own bedroom, disrobed out of her brother's damp overalls, stoked the fire and thawed herself out in front of the grate. The 'voice of voices' still rang forth in her ears as she urgently leafed through the pages of her copy of Madame O's book until she found the chapter headed 'Celebrated Castrati' and discovered an extended section devoted to Farinelli relating how he had been born Carlo Broschi (1705-1782) in Andrea near Bari, Italy. How as a seven year old, his family had portentously decided on his future when they permitted the child to succumb to the castrator's knife. At the time, no one could have predicted the result of this decision. Later the boy became known simply as Farinelli, by far the most venerated and idolised singer of the period, and possibly of all time, his legendary status gained through vocal feats, which have never been equalled.

The year is 1942, two hundred and thirty seven years after Farinelli's birthdate and, as she reads on, Lorna is convinced the mantle of the illustrious Carlo has indeed fallen on another, a certain woman who for convenience's sake she names 'La Marca', who she and two others have heard first hand. Tonight, all Lorna can guess at this stage of her investigation is the singer's voice obviously belongs to a healthy young woman, who is probably married to a man named Gorrick (Charles). 'La Marca Gorrick" she repeats, or 'La Marca Gorricka', even better, a romantic title she has coined in her enthusiasm for the 'supreme coloratura of all time'. Lorna reads on and is surprised to learn that Farinelli's range only climbed to the E that, she knows full well, is well behind 'La Marca's' range but then that is only to be expected. A male singer, even a castrato, could never hope to challenge the range of a female coloratura soprano. Where Farinelli probably would have won on points was due to his endless breath control, utilised by the immense bellows like lungs of the male castrato, which no woman could hope to compete with. Whereas Lorna recalled the singer at 'Windermere Cottage' scarcely stopped at all for breath. As to the vast volume of sound that the voice produced, Lorna might be forgiven for thinking the singer had indeed been equipped with loudspeakers in her throat! Trumpets, sirens, clarions, those were the words that beseeched and inveigled Lorna's mind. By now, the girl insisted that this particular voice she had heard tonight ran the full gamut of everything technically and emotionally that answered to a singer's dream voice and yet again she calculated the voice to be young and fresh. A voice unlike any other known woman's voice or human voice for that matter she'd heard, or even heard mention of, if that is, Lorna's ears did not totally deceive her. Presently, she questioned, had Madame O singularly discovered this virtuoso; whose voice is, perhaps the result, or part product, of a special rarefied vocal technique that brings out the full scope of the singer's potential; since the remarkable low notes were equally as effortless as the top ones. In which category could such a voice possibly be placed? In no category! Just by itself on its own multi-faceted golden pinnacle far from the reaches and influence of men. That was it! That is exactly where such a supernatural voice belonged, Lorna convinced herself. Not of this world but high above it in the stratosphere where the air remains crystalline pure. Had Madame O been responsible for incorporating into that divine modern day instrument a long forgotten technique gained from the 18th century Golden Age and marvellously carried over into the 20th century? - emphasising the fact that the little German woman then owned to being the greatest teacher of singing ever in this world. Lorna's mind raced on ahead of itself, conjuring up and gathering en route any number of other wild speculations and suppositions. And why? Because Lorna needed readily available answers to her own vocal predicament involving her sorely depleted vocal resources, and she yearns to know first hand just how recently Madame O had made the singer's acquaintance. She thought back and remembered that only lately Madame O had made mention of her 'Etoile. However, Lorna supposed such a virtuoso vocal technique would take several years to accomplish and it could not be conjured up overnight out of thin air, as it sounded to her on first hearing this evening. Then again, since the voice is so young and fresh it may be that it is totally untrained? Possessing a purely natural facility. No! No! Lorna did not want that. She needed hope for herself. She wanted to believe Madame O, in her prolonged life long researches, had stumbled on a hitherto 'lost vocal technique, one which she might pass on to Lorna. Lorna''s eyes glittered with yearning and hope as she watched the embers dying in the grate. The mere thought that such a possibility existed whereby she might extend her own voice beyond its woeful limitations and likewise increase her lung capacity and gain extra breath control filled her with expectation. Permitted the opportunity she would work night and day to fulfil that dream and achieve those much desired ends, anything in order to attain that which until now did not bear thinking about, the hitherto unattainable, involving a journey into the 'nether' regions of the vocal goals where in the future the possibilities might prove endless. Enamoured with the idea that one day she might indeed 'sing like the birds' her voice powerful and clear reaching up to the tree tops no less with the greatest of ease, Lorna would tackle and conquer new repertoire. Intoxicated with these thoughts, whilst fed on the unknown singer's 'unearthly sounds", at last Lorna knew exactly how Madame O had felt exposed to the mercy of a sublime voice. The difference being in Lorna's situation the girl is compelled and driven by an otherwise unknown voice she has heard just the once, and which possesses the power to breathe instant new life into her. In a few days time, her next lesson is scheduled with Madame O and she is under no illusion that it could prove to be her last due to the extenuating circumstances. However, because of Madame O's present state, Lorna expected the worst. Nevertheless, at the forthcoming lesson she planned to drop a hint or two in regards Madame"s 'star" and hopefully effect an introduction. Nevertheless, she still puzzled over how uncharacteristic it has been of her teacher to act so suspiciously towards her these last days, when in the recent past the two had behaved openly to each other more in the capacity of mother and daughter.

Far into the night Lorna avidly read Madame O"s book. A specific section (The Singer's creed) vividly drew her attention and caught her imagination. It is the remarkable account as outlined by Madame O of a competition between Farinelli and a trumpet player wherein both musicians blessed with assorted degrees of virtuosity, competed before an audience, to outshine one another, swelling and shaking together in thirds for such an inordinate length of time that both musicians appeared worn out from their efforts. At one stage the trumpeter, believing Farinelli, like himself, to be exhausted, relaxed but the singer, with fresh strength in his voice started off again accomplishing ever more difficult divisions and vocal marvels, sustained trills, octave leaps, repeated notes and brilliant arpeggios, etc in a manner which usually lay far beyond the possibilities of the human voice and eventually left the trumpeter behind, finishing off on a high E. However Lorna deduced again that the unknown singer of today touched on any number of stratospheric notes. Was it a C sharp in alt in Lucia for instance? A whole octave higher than what was expected, and even at one stage amidst a series of roulades went as far as the highest note on the piano. Lorna could scarcely conceive what other wonders lay in store. In her diary she gave her own account, in a heading: "The miracle in the wilderness garden":

'Dear Diary. Little by little in the short time I listened, 'La Marca"'s" voice chameleon like, changed by leaps and bounds into another altogether unrecognisable voice. One with a brilliant diamond like thrust ringing through the silence, fluttering and falling upon the night air and my disbelieving ears to be met by that unearthly phosphoric glow surrounding me in the garden. The whole event not of this time. Had I been in the midst of experiencing an actual true life fairy tale? Or had I been journeying light years backwards in time? After this evening I doubt anything can surprise me anymore. My temples are still burning'.

Now addicted to the mystery voice that almost haunted her every move and pause, Lorna, in a not unpleasant prolapsed state, turned from her writing to re-read a description quoted in Madame O's book that tallied with her own experience. In effect Lorna might be reading her own thoughts. Paolo Antonio Rolli, an Italian student in London wrote: 'Until I heard Farinelli, I realised I had only heard a small part of what human singing can achieve, whereas now I conceive myself to have heard all there is to hear!' Lorna stopped abruptly, by this time barely able to hold the pen steadily, and added an afterthought footnote to her diary,

'In 1942 A.D, an extravagant vocal comet made its presence felt, not in the public arena nor in a great opera house, but through the open window of a rambling old cottage tucked away in the heart of nowhere, of all places adjoining a rifle range!'

Two days later, as dusk settled over the neglected overgrown grounds of 'Windermere", Lorna resumed her cramped vigil, wedged in between the walls of the dilapidated summerhouse, having previously resisted the temptation to eavesdrop in broad daylight.

As yet, not a sound had issued forth from within the confines of the cottage, leaving respite for Lorna to carry out what she always did best in an idle moment when left to her own resources, that being to give vent to her bountiful imagination and duly escape into her world of fantasy which in no time at all transported her back into another era, plunged her into the midst of the golden age of singing. The date is July 4th 1886. The event is 'La Traviata at the Royal Opera House, Covent Garden. The House is festooned with every conceivable type of sweet smelling flower; Narcissi and Lilac, etc. The bejewelled audience is agog for the arrival of the most celebrated prima donna of the day. Her name – Adelina Juana Maria Patti (b. 19 Feb 1843). As with this legend, Lorna too first found her own voice when just seven years old!

Lorna peruses the silk souvenir programme, which is identical to the one framed in Madame O's studio. Before the houselights dim, she has a brief moment to read the programme. The conductor is signor Costa. Soon all is seeped in darkness leaving the empty stage aglow. An immutable silence charges the house with immense tension and, inasmuch as Lorna finds a moment to reckon on what the prima donna will wear, nothing could have prepared her for the sudden, deafening roar of applause reaching and rumbling to the rafters, threatening to shake the fine building to its foundations. It is as if the audience is already aware of the presence of the star of the evening who is not yet visible in the wings. The inspired moment arrives. Onto the stage steps the silvery slight figure of a girl. No more than eighteen years old, and of remarkably graceful and confident bearing. She makes her way in exaggeratedly slow motion toward the footlights, clad in a diamond encrusted body cuirass. Her elaborate gown is a combination of billowing lilac taffeta and lace, and reveals voluminous skirts glittering with extra diamonds sewn onto every square inch. Firmly placed on her head is a tiara embedded with even more countless diamonds producing the effect of a totally unreal vision of light, 'Lumine de Lumiere'. Unbeknownst to the audience, in the wings are two bodyguards who have accompanied the singer to safeguard her jewels and who remain in constant attendance watching over her every move throughout the performance.

Meanwhile, each step she takes reveals dainty sparkling silver satin slippers and is accompanied by fresh waves of applause. The diminutive singer's progress is made all the more entrancing since she appears to glide rather than walk across to the footlights, till she comes to a standstill, waits and strikes a suitable pose that informs a totally overwhelmed audience they are welcome to admire the resplendent flickering array of breathtaking jewels bedecking her from head to foot, each jewel set on tiny invisible intricately crafted springs that move remotely to catch the light and twinkle over the footlights into the darkened auditorium. Soon the deafening roar, customary on such rare occasions, begins to subside and nearly settles, were it not for a lone maverick who yells at the top of his voice from the gods, "Brava, brava. La Prima donna del mondo!" awakening a fresh wave of fervent applause from the enthusiastic audience. The singer gracefully bows in acknowledgement so that her face remains temporarily hidden whilst only the top of her dazzling coronet of tiered jewels carefully secured upon her elaborately coiffured hairdo is visible. Presently, in charismatic fashion, she lifts into the air one bejewelled gauntleted arm, a gesture, which has the almost immediate effect of silencing the vast audience who are agog for her every signal in readiness for the performance to commence.

As this fleeting 'tableaux vivant from an age of past grandeur in the theatre vanished, it is replaced by Madame O's voice emerging from within the confines of the cottage walls bringing Lorna back to everyday reality. As one might expect of an expert voice teacher, Madame O's voice is clearly projected and delivered, again sounding to Lorna as if transmitted over loudspeakers. The woman enquired of her guests,

"I wonder if either of you have read the charming story of 'The Wizard of Oz? It made quite a stir in Vienna where at the time I had been studying Greek and Latin."

At this moment, Madame O may well have been addressing Lorna personally since at the girl's second lesson years back she had asked Lorna this identical question, and had gone on to present her with a copy of the book telling Lorna how touched she had been by Lorna's innate ability to bring out the underlying solemnity of those two Schubert songs the girl had prepared for her first audition on that auspicious occasion.

Madame O continued, "Well, had you read the book, Charles, you would recall the tragedy of the Tin Man who carried a can of oil with him to remedy the squeaks in his joints, but above all he craved a heart to enable him to cry and laugh at will."

"And did he succeed in finding this heart, Madame?" Charles Gorrick inquired dutifully.

"Yes, but it took some little time and certain dedication, - and decision I suppose," Madame O added. "Mind you, everyone who wishes enough for something and is willing to make the effort to search for it, usually succeeds. So there you have it, Charles! Although having said as much, there is also a twist along the line if one recalls what Schopenhauer said: 'A man can surely do what he wills to do, but he cannot determine what he wills.

Lorna listened intently and began to wonder if Madame O talked that way to all her students. At that moment, she no longer felt herself unique in Madame O's eyes. If that is, she had ever been.

Madame O continued, "To further the cause of the artist and art in all its many manifestations, that should be the goal. Take this particular piece of music resting on the piano stand. 'Dido's Lament. Now if any work required the most heartfelt approach, it is this and yet, once the singer wears her heart on her sleeve when singing it, she has as good as lost the true inherent factor underlying the work. Do you know the piece, Charles?"

"Can't say we do, Madame," the man replied matter-of-factly acting as spokesman for both himself and Mark who, as yet had not spoken. A Lament? Isn't that something sung at funerals?"

Madame O failed to reply, seemingly passing the question off as an irrelevance. Instead, she continued.

"Very few are able to do justice to such a solemn work with the necessary desired simplicity that is entailed, not to mention the much vaunted restraint befitting Dido's tragedy wherein immense constraints are demanded of the singer. Let's say drawing the singer between two poles for argument's sake. Restraint and effulgence – a difficult double proposition!" She paused.

"I'm afraid I'm diverting. Poor Charles! Forgive me. If anything, today in my dotage I guess I'm taking on the role of student. In such illustrious company I am probably trying to convince and impress upon myself my own worth, or lack of it. I don't know which anymore."

Another of those indeterminably long pauses followed without further comment. Lorna felt tears of frustration and anger welling up. Why, she asked, was her teacher recommending to another what she had been brought to believe solely belonged to her? In Lorna's eyes a pact had not only been broken but also she believed herself betrayed, especially when she heard Madame O remark,

"Charles, it would indeed be of utmost interest to hear such a generously endowed voice as Marc-a's deal with the work.

"You mean Marco?" the man interrupted and laughed.

"Of course, Marco", Madame O replied unthinkingly.

The truth was that Madame O paid scant attention to names. In fact, usually she quickly forgot them and needed reminding, unlike her specialty, the human voice, every detail of which, after hearing once she never forgot. Just a single note from a gramophone recording being enough for her to identify any singer.

Madame O continued, repeating herself, "Yes, Charles, it would indeed be fascinating to hear such a voice delving into hitherto unknown territory, so to speak."

But Charles Gorrick seemed intent on light-heartedly getting his son"s name in the correct focus, "Well, shall we meet halfway, Madame, and refer to 'our singer" here as Marco Mara – rr" rolling the r"s as he did so in his best imitation of Sir Harry Lauder's Scot's accent so that to Lorna's ears the name now sounded like MacNamara.

"Whew! What a tongue-twister, eh Marco? Excellent, sounds wonderful," the man skylarked facetiously as he now pronounced tongue-trippingly Marcomara – or is it Manamara. The tail end of the name, which Lorna still could not be certain of. At any rate, the most she could think of for the moment being the fact that Madame O wanted to entrust to the newly acquainted singer the special piece of music she, Lorna, had made her own. Momentarily, Lorna's sometime allegiance to the wonder voice began to fade, replaced by a surge of bitterness overtaking her. Meanwhile, Madame O, oblivious to Gorrick"s jest, continued on in the same vein.

"Marca would, I believe, sing the "Lament" with all the restrained emotion required," she declared. Branding Lorna's face with a hot iron could not have succeeded better. At this final remark Lorna could scarce contain her disapproval. "No!" she uttered aloud, simultaneously placing her hands over her mouth to stem the impulsive cry drawing Madame O's attention to the open window. Hidden from view, Lorna watched as Madame O peered out into the darkness.

"Nightjars, I expect," she remarked before returning to her guests. Inside Madame O explained how Purcell's opera 'Dido & Aeneas' had come to be composed.

"Will she never stop?" Lorna objected.

"First privately performed in 1689 composed for the pupils of a young ladies' school. Today the work is regarded as the first English opera". At this stage Lorna left, not wishing to stay another minute. No longer did the most noble outcry in the history of English music interest her, having been dispossessed of that one precious element she had been encouraged to nurture over these last years. Never again did she wish to sing the "Lament". Lorna took herself off at breakneck speed. Sudden blustery gusts of wind blowing her hair into her eyes. As she ran, she clasped both hands to her ears as if to rid herself of the conversation that had just transpired at 'Windermere' between her teacher, the singer and her 'husband'. However, had she stayed on she would have been witness to a number of revelations concerning herself, addressed as they were to Madame O's formidable guests. Swiftly Lorna made her way down the narrow laneway in the siding next to the cottage, and with a determined effort escaped into the nearby parkland where she found a bench to sit on and attempt to regain her lost equilibrium. As if these last days had not proven enough to deal with her mentor's vicious tirades and onslaughts, now Lorna even questioned her teacher's integrity; especially since the woman had confided to Lorna that if she had her own way no one else except Lorna would be permitted to sing 'Dido''s Lament". In the past, the wonderful compliment had done more to bolster the girl's confidence than any previous remark about her voice that had been addressed to her. Indeed, in a small way, had even helped reconcile her to the daunting loss of her family. However, in one swift fateful jerk now everything she'd esteemed paled, into insignificance; her already fragile world toppled, pulled asunder due to the events of the evening. A sense of delayed emptiness gnawed at her as she fulminated at length on presently what she deemed to have been her own wholly uneventful past, fed upon false notions about her own worth. As such, Lorna felt a vague compulsion to rid herself of all further close proximity to her teacher – even to music! And whilst plunged into this negative state of mind, perversely allowed, in fact desired, the increasingly chill night air to seep through her damp clothing and settle upon her flesh like the early frost laying on the ground at her feet. The wind continued to enshroud and freeze her bare arms and ankles, penetrate through the open sandals onto her feet and toes. How long she remained thus she had no idea. Her mind bountifully entrapped in misgiving, repeatedly compounding and confounding her thoughts, drawn between herself, a teacher and an unknown singer, the latter of whom continued to play havoc with Lorna"s senses. Thus, filled with contrition, she visualised herself doing penitence alone for some nagging unknown wrong. An ancient/young mariner all alone, alone on a wide sea.

To think these last five years at the Conservatorium had served in many respects to conquer her grief, and now Lorna honestly believed and blamed herself for being an impostor who permitted herself to be carried away for all the wrong reasons – emotional rather than artistic. Again Lorna's misgivings repeatedly essayed Madame O's malicious remarks. The woman's 'falsehoods' that continued to consume Lorna with ever more doubt and bitter resentment. Now she took a wilful pleasure in the dried, icy autumn leaves crackling and swirling around her open sandals. Then, just as suddenly as it had started, the wind ceased to blow. The moon and stars were clearly visible in the bitingly cold clear skies. Lorna arose, took her leave of the place and made her way homewards.

Chapter Ten

Delirium

At the conservatorium today, Madame O is as "mad as a hatter". The room is sweltering. The professor no longer responsible for her actions and Lorna is at the centre of her ire. Lorna must leave if she is not to be sick. She gasps for air but the windows are tightly shut. For one unpleasant moment she envisaged the ghoulish man at Windermere superimposed over Madame O's features. His dilated eyes fiercely glinting at Lorna.

When Lorna came to, she lay full length on the carpet, her head resting on a cushion, Madame O bending over her. A cool hand resting on the girl's forehead. "Ah ma mensch!" she sighed. "My poor Ophelia, where have you been? I looked around and there you were. Here, where you'd fallen. Whatever came over you, dear?" Now Madame O placed a cool tissue soaked in cologne on the girl's forehead and proffered water to her lips. "Dear girl, you had me so worried." Lorna struggled up onto one elbow but could find no words to reply. "Here, let me help you to the settee. You're still dazed." For sometime, Lorna lay on the settee absorbing Madame O's words of assurance and wondering all the while what had overtaken her in Madame O's presence. Thankfully, probably from shock, her teacher had been transformed back into the familiar Mado she knew and liked best.

"I've opened the window, Lorna dear. I'm afraid I must be more careful in future. You were gasping for breath and before I could utter a word you lay here on the ground," she repeated nervously. "Fortunately, you landed on the heap of clothing I left on the floor so that cushioned your fall. Do you feel better? Shall I pay for a taxi to take you home?"

"No, please, Madame!" Lorna sipped some more water scarcely managing to mouth the words. "I shall be all right, I'm sure." She hesitated. "May I stay for my lesson?" A note of false confidence overtaking her at the sight of Madame O's accelerated transformation back into her old familiar self.

"Of course you may, Lorna that is if you truly feel up to it!"

Lorna nodded her approval, confident in the knowledge that to stay on meant she also stood to resolve certain other pressing matters. She drank the remains of the water. "There, I've left the door ajar, Lorna, so that the through-draught keeps you cool."

At so swift a change in her teacher, Lorna might be forgiven for thinking her own vivid imagination to be at fault, had run amok, until Madame O again seated herself at the piano and all problems passed into music with its assuaging powers of healing. Over the playing Madame O carried on in a soft-grained voice so that Lorna felt pleasantly reassured, not dissimilar to the way she imagined one being put under hypnosis. As in a dream, she allowed herself to settle back on the settee, watching through half closed eyes. The diminutive figure of her teacher bowed over the keyboard oblivious to everything around her as she concentrated all her energies into the music, her face deathly pale, her voice filled with exaltation.

"Here is Lucia's Delirium," she cried. Lorna cringed. Her heart sank.

"Come, let me hear you, dear. Allow your voice to ring forth in the grand tradition that you are so familiar with," and Madame O began to reiterate firstly the Italian text to her own accompaniment, then the English

'Spargi damaro pianto il mio

Terrestre veto mentre lassui

'Cast on my grave a flower but let

there be no weeping.'

Madame O cupped one bony hand to her ear. "I can't hear you, my dear. As you know, I love soft singing but I'm afraid I can't hear you at all." She stopped and again went back to the beginning of the aria. "Ah, yes, that's better," she said. Lorna flinched at the sight of Madame O looking sideways, totally unaware of Lorna's presence. For a moment the woman laughed. "The way I see it, Donizetti and Mozart are composers in close configuration." Now a section of Mozart's Mass in C, the Laudate Dominum, issued forth. Madame O had fetched the score and laid it on the piano rest, then, impulsively took it over to show Lorna. "See here -! The same hymn" she exclaimed, "he was quite correct in estimating the similarities." She looked around, "Where's he gone now? The moment one averts one's gaze he disappears, the scamp." Lorna watched in growing dismay, she, the sole spectator to another's entombed inner world of conflict being re-enacted out aloud. Suddenly Madame O stopped, held out both her hands to the girl. "Tell me, pitying angel, what is the matter?"

Bewildered, Lorna faced her teacher. "Well, there is actually something Madame which I feel I ought not keep to myself any longer," but before Lorna had time to divulge a word, Madame O answered in a girlish confidential tone of voice, "Yes, I'm sure you have much to tell me, but first there's also a little matter I myself can't wait to tell you about. It won't take a second," she declared excitedly, leaving Lorna to nod her approval, knowing full well that when Madame O wished to intercede on the conversation, little choice remained but for the listener to comply.

"I am about to let you into a secret which you must promise not to divulge to anyone – my 'star singer' is a boy! Just imagine a mere stripling of a boy," Madame O continued breathlessly without a pause. "However, any time now his present-day voice will break and not a soul has any idea how it will sound."

Lorna gazed in disbelief at Madame O. A boy! Lorna hesitated and paused. "Who then," she unthinkingly asked, "is Macnamara, or Marcomara?"

"Who?" Madame asked, genuinely puzzled. "I'm afraid I don't follow you, Lorna."

Lorna softly repeated the name 'Mara'. At this stage she was not about to admit that from behind the summer house at 'Windermere' she had heard with her own ears Madame O address the singer as 'Mara'. In any case, no boy's voice as good as it might be, had or ever could sound remotely like the voice Lorna had heard. Meanwhile, Lorna decided to go along with Madame O and listen carefully to what else her teacher had to say. "Well what does any sane person do under such circumstances?"

Lorna shook her head. "I don't know Madame."

"Well, I shall tell you. If they have a vestige of commonsense they set about capturing the voice for posterity, and that is exactly what I have made provision for. The voice has been recorded in all its pristine state by me. Yes, I have seen to it and I thank my lucky stars Lorna that I had the forethought to do so. Each moment of every encounter has been captured without distortion on tape because the equipment I've used is, by modern day standards, the very finest. Now everyone will have the same opportunity to hear that voice. Some fifty hours at least all told!" A protracted silence ensued whilst Madame O went to the window giving Lorna time to digest the astonishing tale, which if true, meant nothing had been lost and Madame O has done the world of music an inestimable favour. Lorna experienced the same wave of excitement when irresistibly she reverted to that last memorable evening at Windermere Cottage. Perhaps, one day, that is, if Madame O is not altogether fancifully deluding herself she will play a recording for me of that same magical last concert. For Lorna it could not be soon enough. She had become addicted, nay overtaken by a 'voice' and somehow nothing else mattered, satisfying herself that her own 'fast fading lacklustre' instrument held little interest or value for herself anymore. Even more so since Madame O's brutal verbal attack earlier which she cannot forget. At least, Lorna determined she had completely accepted the truth about her own self-deception and can only stand to gain from this self-acceptance.

Madame O was still silently standing at the window leaning out over the sill. She pointed down onto the gravel driveway and cried, "It's them, Eccola! Horch!" She cupped one of her hands to her ears and beckoned Lorna over with the other hand. Lorna hesitated. "Too late, they've gone. Ah but that voice still cries out to me," said Madame O,

O giusto – so – cie – lo

O sight of sorrow

She kept weakly repeating, first in German "|Horch!" then in Italian, "Ec – co – la" then in English,"See she comes".

Lorna found herself dizzily joining the woman, both in mind and body even though she could not see what Madame O purportedly saw. In fact, just a chorus of leaves murmuring restlessly in the ancient oak. Moreover, it didn't matter anymore. Something magical is abroad – that Lorna could envisage even if she could not point a finger to it. Presently Madame O continued to recite in a peculiarly empowered dirge like voice, phonetically in Italian.

"Si si li – ra del ciel si si lira del ciel," then in English:

"Ah yes – sad was her fate".

Lorna automatically placed one protective hand softly on Madame O's bony shoulder to steady the woman from toppling as though the very framework of the professor's fragile body no longer is able to sustain the force of some invisible spectre tormenting her from beyond the grave. Regaining her equilibrium she leant on Lorna, an unexpected air of optimism written in her eyes.

"How fortunate, Lorna, that you and I could share this moment. I knew straight away by the look on your face that you heard it too. It's about time I should make us some tea? Oh, and that reminds me, I must remember to give you something." Her depleted energy regained, she nimbly darted off behind the curtains into the adjoining kitchenette returning with a tray, tea and a gift box.

"Go on, open it," Madame O said. Lorna undid the ribbon to reveal a tartan cashmere shawl, "All the way from Lammermoor Castle specially woven for you! I may add, dear, you'll need it on these cold nights."

"I'm not going to wait to put it on," Lorna answered as she draped herself in the folds. "It's absolute perfection, Madame. I don't know what to say!"

Madame O smiled benignly and changed the subject. "Do you know, Lorna, these last weeks have been very troublesome," she confided.

"Sometimes I've almost felt at the end of my tether and it's only now I feel able to share that awful dispossessing experience with anyone. As you will have gathered, it is all to do with the singer who in due course I must arrange to let you hear in person. That is, before it is too late. I can't say beyond what I have told you how everything fell in on top of me."

Lorna detected in Madame O"s words a lucidity that had not been there earlier today. She listened carefully.

"At night time, Lorna, I truly believed myself wandering and lost in amongst marshes and lakes. A place from which it became impossible to retrace my steps. For the present it is too painful to go into details. Suffice to say when I escaped from that horrible place I came away with an enduring sense of loss which, dare I say, has remained with me ever since."

Lorna did her utmost to understand by putting herself in Madame O's situation and in so doing instantly felt herself journeying on the outskirts of that dark world that did not seem unfamiliar. Madame O continued, "Over this period many awful ideas occurred to me. One concerned you Lorna. I firmly believed you wished to desert me. I was wrong, there you are, here, and you're not bearing any grievances. I mustn't forget. It's just struck me. You said earlier on you had something you wished to disclose to me?"

"Oh, it wasn't important," Lorna quietly responded, "In fact, it was so unimportant I can"t remember."

"Another time then, dear!" Madame O offered her hand to Lorna who became reassured as her teacher's weightless, childlike hand rested in hers, and she accepted the pain that Madame O told her she had gone through these last months. Neither spoke for some time until Madame O uttered in a perfectly sane matter of fact voice, "So now, may I suggest, we have Lucia"s aria in its entirety!"

Now, Lorna not knowing what to expect next, looked at Madame O disbelievingly and speculated helplessly. No one knows better than she my capabilities vocally, she thought, and yet here she is again torturing me! Madame O continued in a barely audible voice to hum the opening bars of the beginning of Lucia's aria to her own accompaniment intermittently abandoning herself to a declamation on the virtues of the music by paralleling the work with Mozart's 'Laudate Dominum'. "Yes, it is quite true what you said young man. Donizetti composed this aria in the form of a hymn. As the lyrics suggest". She intoned in a cracked faded voice:

"Ah l"inno suona di Nozze

Ah 'tis the hymn of our nuptial," immediately after, launching into the "Praise Ye"- Laudate Dominum from Mozart's Mass in C, as though both pieces were one and the same aria. Lorna, transfixed, listened to Madame O's macabre vocal potpourris, uncomfortably aware that again the woman now remained temporarily oblivious to Lorna's presence; aware only of an absent young 'man whom Madame O now engaged in imaginary conversation,

"Very well, my boy, shall we go onto the aria beginning with:

'Ardon glincensi

The incense rises.'

The burning tapers. "Ah yes, accompanying flutes. Hark! Where are the flutes? But please don't hesitate. No matter what, the singer must continue, always come in on cue. Never let down the audience. Remember memory lapses can always be covered up from the prompter's box," Madame O diverted, "However if the voice itself fails, well doubtless that can be a major problem." She smiled contentedly to herself.

Lorna shuddered when Madame O unexpectedly gesticulated in her direction for her to sing. In that same childish singsong banter, she suddenly addressed Lorna, quoting from the Blessed Virgins expostulation. "Tell me, tell me some pitying angel," increasingly embarrassing the girl and leading Lorna to speculate that Madame O acted as though she imagined herself to be 'Lucia di Lammermoor". Again Madame O diversified in a matter-of-fact tone of voice, "I"ve always nursed a deep regret that even in my prime I could not attempt Lucia di Lammermoor in the Opera House, nor anywhere else for that matter. Such is life!" she added longingly in a far off voice. Later on Madame O continued to abstractedly inter-splice English, Latin and Italian texts into a vocal melange of musical works finally reciting in its entirety, the Latin text of Gounod"s adaptation of Bach"s 1st Prelude, for Ave Maria.

Ave Maria, gratia plena,

Dominus tecum.

Benedictav tu in mulieribus

Et benedictus fructus ventris tui

Jesus, Sancta Maria

Mater Dei, ora pro nobis peccatoribus,

Nunc, et in hora mortis nostrae. Amen.

Chapter Eleven

Confession

Until she had returned to a more rational state Madame O began to carry on the same conversation with Lorna where they'd previously left off.

"You had something you wished to disclose to me?"

This time Lorna did not hesitate to make a stand and answered: "I've always wanted to know Madame, why you let me go on singing these last five years when evidently you had no faith in what I did?" At Lorna's question, for a moment, Madame O appeared genuinely baffled. Lorna blundered on, "By staying the distance, I've made a mess of the whole business because I've not been able to do justice even to those so called trifling pieces I chose to endlessly sing since I had no talent to do otherwise. Can you imagine, Madame, the awful reality of never living up to expectation? You yourself had a professional career, but I've never once appeared in public," Lorna added near tears,

"But my dear child…" Madame O interrupted.

"No, let me finish. Not living up to expectation," Lorna repeated, "for fear of disappointing my parents and – you. It would seem under the circumstances I've been at loggerheads ever since that audition with you five years ago"

"But Lorna, how mistaken you are! Can't you realise that until now, your whole life, every aspect of it, has been magically sublimated to that purpose. How you may well ask? I hear you think. Exactly! By the implementation of those four magical pieces into your life"s blood and existence. Trifling? Quaint? Do I hear you say miserable? Handel? Purcell? Thomas Moore? Hardly Lorna! How can I set about convincing you otherwise? Don't you see, Lorna, nothing has been wasted. Not for a moment and I for one won't hear of it! You are mistaken should you think a teacher does not observe such positive things? And also do you not think a teacher must also keep many things to themselves. Well they do until that is, as of now, the pupil demands an explanation and the teacher is obliged to put their cards on the table and confess."

Lorna listened intently.

"In doing so the teacher is constrained to lay bare her existing fast held inner feelings and beliefs." Madame O paused perusing the photos of a past golden age of singers hanging on the wall above the piano. "It is no easy matter. Then nor is this life of ours. And why should it be? It is inevitable at some time we are bound to suffer. As for you and myself, we have had our share of suffering, haven't we? Everything starts with our parents and for some, ends with their parents. However, we persevere on and survive as best we can. In fact, we have little option than to do otherwise. You, Lorna, since the loss of your family have chosen to become what you are, a solo act. Without any help over these last years to repeatedly sing, you have, I believe, unknowingly set up your own very personal assignation post taking the form of an innocent and veritable cri de coeur from the very depths of your being. And as to how you have achieved this – it has come about in the guise of various forms primarily by your choice of repertoire and a personal retrenchment – a looking backwards and forwards, an addressing yourself. A poetic self-observation of the finer values induced through your singing, taking your voice on repeated journeys of renewal through the same set pieces. No mean task may I assure you."

"But, Madame," Lorna interrupted, "This is exactly what you did not condone. You advised I learn new repertoire!"

Madame O appeared puzzled. "Let me continue, Lorna," she said hurriedly as if her time of lucid thought were at a premium and she must hasten to express herself before the clock struck the witching hour. Think of a work such as 'Dido"s Lament" filled with resignation and farewell, or the piety and innocence of "The blessed Virgins Expostulation." The longing and pain of things past expressed in the Thomas Moore song, and all incurred in Handel's. 'With plaintive note'. Does it not make sense what I say?"

Lorna responded with a diffusive nod. "No."

Madame O expounded. "Genius does not always have a ready recall or explanation."

"Genius?" Lorna failed to understand this last tenuous remark.

"Lorna, dear, it is not necessarily always the voice that makes the singer, but what lies behind the voice. Of course we should all wish for both, but the gods usually give to one to ironically take away from the other."

"But I'd always wanted to sing like the birds," Lorna piped up.

"But sometimes, Lorna, we must be content to just sing to them."

For the first time Lorna managed a vague, embarrassed yet near-enough satisfied smile.

"You know yourself, some things cannot be taught, Lorna. For instance, artistry is either there or is not there. In your disarmingly simple fashion you undoubtedly possess a rare gift – artlessness."

Lorna flinched. How can artlessness be a rare gift she thought to herself.

"That is a wholly natural resource," Madame O said, "the opposite to archness, that which is best described as a thoroughly contrived, unnatural element which I'm afraid many of the so-called great and famous – correction – infamous, carry around with them like a money-belt tied around their waist for fear of theft. If only they knew that a young girl can be equipped with that elusive quality whose existence they seem not to know of. Believe me, Lorna, look upon these qualities as your own rewarding personal assets! Now the question: Why did I take you on, at the outset of our relationship? Because, I foresaw in you those self same properties that cannot be taught. It stands to reason, I hasten to add, this paved the way of musical discovery. Often as not fate has called the tune, since you were gifted from the start in that particular exclusive region. Consider others less fortunate, Lorna, who must struggle to reach 'de profundis' whereas 'de profundis' reached out to you, unbeknownst to you, and those four pieces you chose all became inter-joined by what I like to estimate as 'a mystical thread forming a supernal pact, extracted from the same mould of your inner feelings. So you see, Lorna, although you are probably the last person to realise your 'meagre' repertoire, when put together, spells out 'Lorna's – artistic musical blueprint,'- in other words your very own sets of transcendental stepping-stones. Each of the four pieces unlimited in fact, running the gamut of human emotions. Why am I telling you all this, Lorna? Shall I tell you why? Firstly, because of your low self-esteem and secondly because of the misguided idea that you are inadequate."

Madame O continued to diversify, "Some may ask Lorna why you have chosen as your theme 'de Profundis'. It merely means, my dear Lorna, you have chosen to walk down a certain lonely path whereby you have positioned and directed your sorrow into a creative outlet that feeds the needs of the deeper emotions which in turn succeed in moving the people listening to you, such as myself and one or two others who chance to hear you sing. For example from most accounts, many around here probably acknowledge Miss Caliopsis as being physically attractive." Lorna winced, failing to see the beauty in such emptiness. Since meeting Madame O, Lorna had come to possess her own very predetermined views on whom or what she considered beautiful, although few would agree with her and, as she regarded Madame O, she saw in the woman a type of beauty that she placed far and above the so called near-perfect physical features of a Caliopsis despite Madame O's face far from answering by any means to the general precept of beauty. On the contrary, taken singularly Madame O's features were quite disproportionate but what mostly shone through is the glowing spiritual force compounded by an overall sadness allied to a wisdom of 2000 years that invests the woman's face with softness. Sometimes this rare admixture almost took Lorna's breath away. Bearing these thoughts in mind, Lorna began better to comprehend Madame O's views on what a beautiful voice, or possibly a more than merely beautiful voice might offer.

"Of course, Lorna, we venerate and love such exceptional voices, but there are still those amongst us who tend to cherish depth of feeling, in any form it takes, far and above the merely beautiful."

Listening thus to Madame O speak the truth, a surge of relief and confidence stole over Lorna.

Madame O diverted. "Anyhow, Lorna, if we need go further and laugh with happiness, if we wish to rejoice at being alive, what more could we ask for than a marvellous Strauss waltz?"

Exactly that type of comment is what made Madame O so approachable to Lorna. Madame O's world encompassed such a great deal, evoked so many different aspects and made Lorna remember her parents' two favourite composers, Johann Strauss and Tchaikovsky, and how most days Reginald and Irene danced and frolicked together to records of 'Swan Lake and 'The Sleeping Beauty" most days and in particular whenever celebrating a birthday or anniversary or Christmas at Ariel Court, then Reginald might call on Lorna to wind up the old vocalian gramophone and put a record of his favourite conductor Felix Weingartner on the turntable. Next moment 'Wine, Women & Song" or perhaps 'Voices of Spring" would thrill those present and fill the house to overflowing with exhilaration. In those days not a care in the world has been permitted in the family. At every opportunity, music simply took over, inspiring and affording everyone unalloyed pleasure, bringing out the best in them.

Suddenly Madame O's voice brought Lorna back into the present. "That's good, Lorna. That's the way I like to see you – with a smile playing across your face." She continued to reassure the girl at this time when she believed Lorna most in need of assurance.

"My father always reminded me, Madame, that Brahms copied in a guest book the beginning of the music to The Blue Danube".

'Unfortunately not written by me he wrote. "True Lorna, and one conceives every other great composer would have wished the same! To have composed such perfection." Madame O responded, "but returning to my chosen subject, Lorna, let me say this about you. I know I've harped on about the 'star singer' to the point of distraction, but don't be put off by that fact. Of course the prospects are exciting to someone like me, but so too is the idea for me in the piecing together of your quartet of chosen pieces of music. I look upon this process of yours as a gradual undertaking of artistic absorption and integrity. The slow distillation of the essential oil, or essence, similar to the way a great perfumer would envisage."

Lorna wondered why Madame O had today chosen to become so insistent in her views regarding her 'least talented' pupil, her most 'inadequate' pupil at that. As usual Madame O read Lorna's mind and continued with her pronouncements.

"Metaphorically speaking, little by little I see you have linked different phrases borrowed from 'the one work' to beneficially give to another. Over the years hopefully a meaningful sentence is spelt out, or better still perhaps a complete paragraph. It doesn't matter which, as long as one arrives at a meaningful distillation of ideas."

Lorna tried her best to understand what Madame O alluded to but finally desisted. Instead she allowed herself to be absorbed taken over by Madame O's insistent voice.

"As to inadequacy…!" Lorna"s ears pricked up at the mere mention of the word. "Look at it this way. How does one measure inadequacy? For example by the range of the voice, judged by the least number of notes in a limited voice, or by the most number of notes in an unlimited voice wrongly deployed? Both can be inadequate for any number of varying reasons, but not always for the most obvious ones. Let me give you an example, Lorna. Years ago, I received a letter requesting an appointment with me. Judging by her appearance, the girl who entered my studio might be from anywhere. When she drew that first breath to sing some may have thought the voice vastly inadequate. For me, that soft voice arose like a mist over the water. My heart stopped beating."

Madame O hesitated.

"Enough to say, I shall never forget the effect of that so called 'inadequate' little voice. There you have it in a nutshell. You see, often as not, greatness has no creditable measure. It either is or isn"t. By this I mean for example: it's not just the all over impact of a Schubert song or its words, but the hidden meaning lying dormant beneath the surface. The unassuming if you wish. No, Lorna, never imagine inadequacy is singularly measured in small numbers. Personally speaking, for myself, I am of the school, which prefers less well done, than more done wrongly. That is why I prefer a Japanese Haiku, or a short fairy tale to an epic, seemingly without end. My tiny oil painting of 'Stella Vespertina by Georges Rouault preferable to a monster Rubens. The difference being not that one is better - just different. One is more immediate and readily available, the other less so to the likes of myself. Having said that, who is to say which one took the longest to create the miniature or the mammoth? In these instances, time or size is by no means the criterion nor the prevaricator! Returning to your set medley of four pieces which you have chosen to sing, and unfortunately which you also choose to demean yourself by when referring to them as 'limited'. I like to think of them as four transcendental studies repeatedly nurturing your soul! Each an intrinsic part of the other moulded into an integral whole. One not to be separated from the other. How to put it succinctly? A whole life spelt out in a four-part symphony for voice. A veritable four-part Song of Destiny – a Schicksalslied. Quite an achievement which one might even parallel to the stages of man. Did you never think of your 'limited' repertoire in such terms. Of course not. Thankfully dear you were too busy acting upon your rare intuition! Take for instance "Oft in the stilly night". Do you know what I hear, Lorna, when I listen to that melody? The second movement of Mozart's adagio Kv491 C minor Piano Concerto, and who drew my attention to the fact? You of course, when you'd heard the Mozart work at the conservatorium." Madame O continued, "One wouldn't go too far astray to liken the recessional of Mozart's 'Laudate Dominum" to a section of 'Lucia". Working on such premises I believe most things as diverse as Chopin's F minor Piano Concerto or the chausson 'Poeme de L"amor" are often inextricably tied with the same knot. If only we could experience a recapitulation in life as in music. Journey far enough backwards in time to trace and recognise important elements or landmarks as they first appeared at source before being overtaken by development and inevitable change."

Madame O again paused to take mental stock before continuing with her monologue. "Forgive me for repeating myself, Lorna, but you do not measure restriction in quantity as you've led yourself to believe. By that I mean to say there is no reason to disbelieve for instance that your very few chosen pieces cannot spell out that most desirable and sublime and preordained timelessness that touches our souls. As I am convinced you have on occasion actually realised. Indeed I repeat by the choice of those four quintessential pieces you have succeeded to create of them a mystical tone poem or ode in answering to your own deeply felt inner needs."

Although the idea captivated Lorna, suddenly she became entrenched in the present when out of the blue she blurted accusingly, "But then why did you suggest someone else sing Dido"s Lament?"

"I did? Who?" Madame O replied with a helpless expression of surprise engrained on her face. A look, which may even have spelt out 'no longer am I responsible.' "Where did you get that idea from? How could you suggest such a thing, Lorna?"

Lorna is forced to admit to herself because she had overheard the conversation with the 'star' pupil at Windermere. Madame O insisted, "Had I wished someone else to sing 'your' Lament I would have, as I have already done, been immediately disposed to give you as a prime example of how it should be sung! How that is I truly believe Dido's solemn air comes closest to the composer's intentions." Lorna no longer knew what to believe. Here is Madame O near enough blatantly contradicting everything she had said earlier on. Normally Lorna should need have no reason to doubt Madame O"s integrity but now she supposed herself to be doing exactly that, and it pained her to dwell upon the fact; failed to find the words to reply to what she assumed had been meant as a laudatory compliment. Besides over these last days and weeks, Madame O had been responsible for uttering so many contradicting pronouncements that Lorna no longer exactly knew what Madame O actually meant and whether to believe her or not. "You know, Lorna, sometimes I feel like a motherless child who wishes to remain asleep in her dreams. 'Holde träume kernet wieder' symptomatic of Schubert's central character in 'Nacht und Traum".

Lorna needed to reconcile herself to the fact that these days Madame O could dramatically change from one moment to the next, and she attempted to understand what sparked the problem and how best to deal with it. At such times Lorna might at worst deviate between feeling incapable and unworthy or at best magically transported after a well-meaning word of praise coming from her teacher.

"Oh, don't think I didn't discover your worth in that first audition, Lorna, even before you'd sung a note," Madame O said.

Lorna felt her heart sink at this remark that made no mention of her singing voice. "I so admired the unassuming manner in which you conducted yourself," Madame O continued peering into the girl's face. She noted the disappointment in her eyes and with an air of finality, advised, "You must never lose heart, Lorna. Try to remember the good things and if you can ignore the negative side, you've won."

Now the words fell on Lorna's ears balm-like but soon affected her in another way as an indeterminate sadness overtook her, because she detected in Madame O's words everything there that needed to be said. Even so, Lorna is determined to still seek out answers. She listened to her own voice pipe up questioningly, "But five years, that's too long a time to put up with a talentless pupil!"

Madame O searched Lorna's face, "At twenty five years old you have no grounds for saying such things, Lorna, believe me. I've waited all my life."

Madame O pronounced these words with a surprising touch of optimism together with an expression of resigned fortitude wedded to a hint of whimsy before she turned around from Lorna to the piano, her hands weightlessly hovering over the keyboard and, without as much as a cursory preparatory movement, effortless coaxed a gentle bass note from deep down within the keys. Lorna had never heard playing quite so immediately disembodied, in that moment reality subsided and all but ceased to exist. But before Lorna had gained an opportunity to be further seduced and absorbed by the playing, Madame O wilfully stopped in her tracks as if what she had just been responsible for had been irrelevant.

"As you may have detected, in the past I have usually endeavoured to apply and lay down certain rules, one being not to wear one's heart on one's sleeve. The singer who controls her emotions, rather than be controlled by them, more times than not conveys to the listener the essential essence and soul of the music. As we like to say, 'Music first and foremost.' I mention this en passant by way of getting around to something that involves you personally. And this is, if ever you nursed misgivings about your own capacity to project the music, take it from your teacher, do not hold onto such doubts. And if you will forgive me, let me add that without the terrible tragedy that beset you I maintain you could not have succeeded to invest your singing with such depth, and maturity. One reason being, because you, of necessity through circumstance had to grow up quickly, despite the fact that you have remained, in another all important sense – a child. Now have I convinced once and for all my doubting Thomas-ina?"

Lorna nodded a little vacuously in semi-affirmation.

"Why have I waited so long to tell you, Lorna you may well ask? I suppose there is a time for everything but, for myself, at this very moment I believe it opportune to break the rules and wear my own heart on my sleeve. As you know, Lorna, I'm averse to the use of the word 'interpretation' especially in singing. Once accepted, this failing allows the wrong singers to take unfair advantage of both text and composer. Thus contrivance and archness creeps into the music so I prefer to keep to the word 'singing' and that is why your singing of Purcell's timeless ode has moved me deeply." Madame O's words hit Lorna in the pit of the diaphragm with a sense of revelation. It did not matter that they were addressed to Lorna or not. The fact of the matter is that Lorna need only guess in what context they were meant. Madame O is collectively addressing a whole congregation of singers past and present. A whole universe of music.

On such occasions, Lorna usually looked down at her feet, anywhere other than risk the penetrating gaze of Madame O's all seeing vision for fear of discovering something that she could not live up to, but such is the finality and inevitability echoing forth in Madame O's words that Lorna felt herself inwardly repeating her teacher's words. "Your singing of Purcell's timeless ode has moved me deeply – more than words can express!" If only her parents had lived to hear Madame O's opinion of their daughter. But what Madame O said next nearly overtook the girls emotions, in contradiction to what Madame O consistently advised; to control your emotions.

"Bear with me Lorna when I state that hearing you sing the Lament, reminds me of one's fragile mortality. It is as if I am witness to my own testament. A cynosure of all that has meant the most to me throughout my life of music and art."

Again there followed one of those long sustained pauses. A characteristic feature of the way in which Madame O expressed herself in conversation.

"There it is Lorna! I've managed to say to you, put into words, what has remained locked up inside me these last years."

Madame O remained facing the keyboard so that neither she nor Lorna could read each other's expressions, only thoughts. Next she lifted her hands as if in an act of supplication and proceeded to caress the keys ever more gently, again giving both life and flight to the ancient air to release it from its moorings and final deliverance.

At the section where Dido, the Queen of Carthage, enters to extol her sister Belinda to make ready the 'memento mori''opening section of the final big scene:

> Thy hand, Belinda, darkness shades me,
>
> On thy bosom let me rest,
>
> More I would, but Death invades me;
>
> Death is now a welcome guest.

Madame O momentarily stopped reached over and took Lorna's hand in her own before releasing it and continuing to play. Lorna stood to attention. "Do you hear it Belinda-Lorna?"

Lorna nodded and concentrated all her energies, listened inwardly to a disembodied far away voice accompanying the piano with each meaningful parting phrase. "Darkness shades me, on thy bosom let me rest," until the time arrived for the last note to transcend and deliver itself, and fade from the light.

"Remember me.

Remember me"

Madame O slowly and silently closed the piano lid and remained seated for what seemed an eternity as dusk approached and a dark pall enveloped the room.

Over the next few days that last meeting with Madame O rarely strayed from Lorna's mind, nor did that 'magisterial voice' that came from nowhere – within – without? No longer did she know.

Lorna noted in her diary the wonderful tartan Cashmere shawl Madame O had made a gift of to her, and her teacher's advice never to give up, no matter how difficult: 'Follow and nurture your heart, otherwise in its absence there can be no spiritual dialogue with the soul on earth.'

Chapter Twelve

Renewal

Just days before her next lesson fell due Lorna received a call from the Almoner at the Conservatorium stating that Professor Oppenheimer had unexpectedly taken ill. Nothing serious – just a slight indisposition the message advised and went on to add, all being well, the professor would most probably be absent for no longer than a week and any previous pre-arranged lessons would automatically be carried over to exactly the same time the following week when, it was to be hoped, Professor Oppenheimer would resume her normal teaching schedule. During the five-year span Lorna had studied under Madame O, she could not recall her teacher ever having experienced a day's illness so it had not been without a certain amount of surprise and trepidation that she received the announcement.

Midweek Lorna decided to bring Madame O some food and for the purpose, and despite having caught a slight chill herself, she did not hesitate to pay a visit to Windermere late one afternoon. As she made her way along the overgrown pathway, through the high pampas grass and climbed up onto the weatherboard porch of the house, she was taken by the unkempt profusion of lavender and sprays of purple heather that, for all she knew, may have showered down from the skies. For a moment she stood still to savour the pungent scent of the blue catmint known to drive cats into a state of torpor and rapture. But just as she were about to knock on the door, she stopped short when she heard coming from within the house that same familiar man's speaking voice joined in conversation with her teacher. Quietly, she withdrew to the side of the house, behind the wisteria where without being seen she managed to catch a snippet of sentences and heard the man exclaim, "Indeed, what a wonderful surprise, Madame."

Madame O, who sounded far from ill, in fact sounded positively glowing, as she rejoined, "Surprise, Charles? I can't imagine." Again the man's voice, "Just wonderful, wonderful!" followed by, "I'm so pleased, Charles," laughter played through the last remark, "And we also have a surprise in store, Madame!"

Madame O suddenly spoke in German "Eine überraschung für mich?" Then in English "A surprise for me?" The woman's voice wavered slightly whilst becoming less audible. Another minor silence prevailed. Lorna did not move, instead remained straining onto every word. Then Madame O's voice returned from somewhere further back in the house.

"If you bear with me a moment I shall need to transpose the music upwards to accommodate your voice."

"No," the man answered. "Marco doesn't wish to change the key."

"Oh?" Madame O questioned, "that rather surprises me, Charles, as the tessitura lies much too low for the soprano voice to even begin to cope. However if you wish, so be it." Another pause followed this last remark, and then Madame O continued, "If I recall correctly, Johann Sebastian wrote this solemn air with viola de gamba and continuo in mind. Having said as much as you suggest, shall we begin then in the original key?"

The first distinctive notes of the work flowed gently forth from the piano and immediately captured Lorna's imagination. Curiously enough in the past rarely had she paid scant attention to her teacher's piano playing even though Lorna took piano lessons as a second subject. To Lorna's way of thinking, the piano's prime appeal had simply been in its being there as a necessary accompaniment to her own voice. Furthermore, at the time she had been far too self-obsessed to notice anything that did not concern her other than her own singing; yet if she carefully thought back to an occasion some three years ago when she chanced to overhear through a half open door Madame O rehearsing on the day of the evening the professor had been due to play Beethoven's Piano Concerto No 4 at a student's concert in the recital hall, Lorna recalled how Madame O's playing of both soloist and orchestral sections incorporated the most subtle musical interplay imaginable.

Again today, Lorna found herself reliving a similar musical amalgamation. This time the same pianist and an unknown singer interacting with each other in total rapport. Lorna continued to give her undivided attention to the introductory piano sounds emanating from within the cottage, however after an unexpected pause in the playing, Madame O apologised a little shakily. "Forgive me, I quite forgot myself. You see for me such music comes closest to what we call in German, Ewigheit, and it always strikes me as a source of wonder that a mere mortal has been responsible for its composition. Here, with your consent, let me begin again," and Lorna found herself being rewarded a second time with an even more subtle repetition of the introduction entrusted into Madame O's hands.

Making doubly certain not to be discovered, Lorna huddled and pressed against the outer wall and allowed herself to be absorbed and carried away by the haunting strains of the piano, growing increasingly richer and more sonorous. Momentarily no longer aware of the true reason for her visit, Lorna allowed the piano to caress her ears as she came to thinking just how many chances she had missed over these last years by failing to notice such sublime playing. Madame O had always insisted, "the piano is a singing, rather than a percussive instrument", the latter "as many a misguided pianist is prone to make of it."

Now as dusk approached Lorna began to digest the full impact of her teacher's words, so much so that she became oblivious to the unusual chill in the midsummer air. The more Lorna dwelt upon the piano playing, the more she convinced herself how further mature and qualified as a musician she might be today, had she paid more attention to the instrument. Nonetheless, she consoled herself with the fact that possibly being too young at the time she had not been altogether ready to absorb the depth of feeling demanded by Madame O's advanced outlook on music. Yet now as the music unfolded and overtook her in its grip, Lorna found herself experiencing greater comprehension. Perhaps this fleeting magical piano encounter presaged a change in Lorna. In fact already might be responsible for sewing the first seeds of a healthy self-discontent and conversion. It may be just a matter of time before Lorna dispenses with singing and instead concentrates and devotes all her efforts into the piano as a first subject. Meanwhile, a contralto voice of unparalleled splendour, more unearthly than human, rang forth to effortlessly merge at one with the piano, enunciating with utmost clarity several times over the opening words of the solemn biblical text: "All is fulfilled".

Lorna, rapt as never before, marvelled anew as she let herself succumb to each faultlessly executed note and phrase falling upon the night air. A voice whose innate appeal to the spirit instantly addressed Lorna directly and carried her along on a transcendent beam of light, briefly reminding her of Mary Garden's reminiscence of Nellie Melba's unearthly voice echoing throughout the Royal Opera House, Covent Garden in a performance of 'La Boheme'. And now Lorna is experiencing first hand another type of musical transfiguration, involving an out of body experience few earthbound persons are rarely permitted to realise even once in a lifetime. Transported beyond the present, Lorna gained a far off vision of herself airborne, at once hovering and caught in ecstatic mid-flight, no longer weighted by any form of vicissitude to the ground beneath her. But before she could reckon further she not only glimpsed, but felt herself slowly floating back down upon that exact place she had ascended from. All the while the omniscient voice, beckoning and leading her onwards through and into an untrodden universe of soft, velvety shadow and raiment until she found herself back on the landing at the top of the stairs at Ariel Court, directly opposite the place where her mother's reinterpreted tapestry of the 'Issenheimer altar' hung. Lorna gazed at the heavily worked intricate fabric, her eyes coming to rest on the veiled swaying figure of the Magdalene who, with both hands raised in lamentation, faced the Cross. So realistic had her mother's portrayal become in Lorna's mind that she even believed herself to be hearing the soft rustling of the amply folded robes of 'the holy woman of Magdala', as Irene Budge referred to this figure, to whom she had bequeathed so much of her own personal artistry.

Meanwhile, throughout this confrontation, 'the voice', scarcely mortal in its inference and impact, rang out in Lorna's ears. It exercised an overall supernal spell to presently deliver a prophetic message of fulfilment so that one by one each meaningful word and music note sought to dispel Lorna's fast held personal fears gathered up over the years. Although launched into a state of exhilaration, by way of contrast Lorna is repeatedly urged into experiencing the deepest affirmation of longing and despair with which the mysterious contralto voice proceeded to invest the music, resulting for Lorna in a painful releasing of those underlying emotions of acute loneliness, loss and regret which due to time passing had taken a firm hold upon her. Nevertheless as she allowed her thoughts to be assuaged and her mind to be immersed and taken over by those indwelling yet ubiquitous sounds emanating forth.

She became convinced this voice succeeded like no other to encompass every possible profound emotion, and similar to herself, borrow from an inner source of light in order to ultimately rise above and be freed from disturbing thoughts of engulfing darkness. Whilst Lorna continued to listen, she found herself taking in and absorbing the inference of the simplified words rather than be able to memorise them, as otherwise she would ideally wish. Moreover she kept chanting to herself a certain meaningful phrase in the aria, the impact of which brought her back to that night five years ago that so dramatically altered her life. Etched potently in her memory, Lorna recalled the event when two police officers, one male, and the other female, arrived at the front door of Ariel Court. They excused themselves for arriving at midnight explaining that it had been imperative to get certain facts detailed as soon as possible. Lorna remembered the erring but sympathetic expressions on their faces, and when the male officer suggested Lorna might prefer to sit down, whilst his colleague found the kitchen in order to make the girl a cup of tea, Lorna complied and in that moment knew to expect the worst. Launched into a confused state she learned that the family car, with everyone inside, had careered down a slope and plunged headlong into a ravine dangerously swollen with floodwater. No one survived. If only fate had curtailed that last seriously flawed time Lorna endlessly lamented, she would have accompanied her parents and today she would be with them. However at the time she had been obliged to sit for exams. The tragedy left Lorna with deep depression. Each night ever since, dead on twelve o'clock, she promptly awoke unable to sleep further until the early hours when she might at last get some rest. However, as usual, Lorna sought respite in music. For the present allowed the rest of the words of the aria to temporarily cancel out the horror of past events.

"All is fulfilled and hope to fainting souls extended, this mournful night shows me thy day of labour," thus she hears the voice echoing the dying phrase of the Saviour, followed by the passionate middle section of the aria, taken as the music demands at a faster pace, "The Lion of Judah fought the fight and hath prevailed." Lastly, the third section involving a short recapitulation of the first section whereby the voice softly re-echoes mournfully, yet resplendently, twice over that last dying phrase, "It is finished," before fading into rapt silence.

That night at 'Windermere a stunned Lorna waited, agog for what further musical riches lay in store despite thinking everything had been said in the short space of time it took to start and finish Bach's magisterial aria; but no sound emanated from within the cottage. The lights appeared dimmed through the curtains. The room seemingly unoccupied with the window remaining open. Feeling herself an interloper and now ill at ease, Lorna decided to leave. From under the trees she strolled out into the light of the old fashioned gas lamps that had served the walk for nigh on a century, passed by the Rifle Range and turned down into Guilfoyle Avenue where one or two street lamps had petered out. Lorna braced herself against the jasmine filled noticeably less chilled air. Above, a crescent moon glowed. With her mind somewhere else and her body not unpleasantly tingling, and her head filled to overflowing by the never-to-be-forgotten thrill of those last irascible moments, Lorna made her way out through Jamberoo Lane, where under another ancient street lamp she consulted her watch but it had stopped, leaving her to guess the time of night.

On her return home, increasingly embroiled in that readily available escapist world of fantasy and the spirit, she had so eventfully self-created, Lorna set out in her diary to recapture every indelible fact and memory of the evening's proceedings.

Subsequently for the remainder of the night, with a dictionary at her side and dyslexia to harden her task, she laboured over the exact wording and spelling for the transcript. After all she conceived, what she wrote tonight would serve in the future as a definitive personal reminder of a unique 'double' revelation.

Her diary heading: "A Piano and a Voice:

My initial recollection of the evening had been those unique notes emanating forth from the keyboard. I distinctly recall questioning just how a piano could possibly be made to sound more like a cello or a harp. That evening, those silvery tones had done much to sew the first seeds of what would become an all encompassing mysterious event, encouraging me to concentrate and listen as never before. In effect, paving the way for the second revelation that transpired next when a wonderfully transparent voice, almost defying description, made its presence felt, and set about imitating those same instrumental piano sounds. Light-headed as I had become, I reacted as one enswathed in some magical robe whose properties immediately transformed me foremost into a more receptive and attuned person in my attitude to channelling musical sounds and resonances. In truth I believe from that moment onwards, for want of a better description, I saw myself 'enslaved' between two instruments – a piano and a voice – which, it seemed to me at the time once experienced, the listener could not easily return to reality. However after the initial shock waves subsided (only slightly) and I recovered my equilibrium, Madame O, just as she had done a few nights back, skimpily and unsuitably dressed for the cold, suddenly shocked me when she appeared at the window. For one awful moment I thought she'd caught sight of me. After all, we were only a few feet apart and I believed myself not entirely concealed behind the wisteria. I need not have worried, she didn't even look in my direction. In fact I gained the impression, as she stood there trancelike that even had she seen me she has been in no state of mind to register. Her thoughts were concentrated further a field, when she called over into the garden in an odd enfeebled unfamiliar voice: "Are you there, are you there? I do wish you would let me know!" Had she been calling to a cat or dog she owned? Who knows? All I can add is she sounded sad and distraught and in that instant I wanted to reach out to comfort her, but she'd darted away from the window back into the room and in the next minute or so I was confronted with what I conceded to be an altogether new version of Madame O's speaking voice, resembling that of a much younger woman.

"I know the heat affects Mara! (Mara?). Never mind – I have seen to it the window stays wide open to let the air come in and circulate!"

Only a moment ago Madame O's voice dejected and flat struck me as tired and alien as I would imagine a tired actor might speak, continuously familiarising himself with a new script. Now she is another woman. However I soon forgot these minor details so taken had I become with the magical musical alliance she and the singer had been mutually responsible for, not to mention myself being fortunate enough to experience the event. I could understand Madame O being carried away, or even more, obsessed with the possessor of two independently astonishing voices, a contralto no less attuned to a coloratura soprano running the gamut of the keyboard range! Who would not be? It is evident that Madame O whose obsession with this singer now, probably and rightfully so, had little or no time for anything else. For instance just days ago down in the canteen where once a week I meet him, Rosenblatt, expressed concern as to Madame O's sanity, which as from tonight thankfully I must add, is still fully intact. In the course of our conversation, he also went on to suggest that Madame O's 'star singer', she is in the habit of talking about at lessons, probably had been a fantasy by-product of her overwrought imagination that for some unknown reason had incontrovertibly gone 'haywire'. At the time I tended to vaguely agree with Joseph since recently we both compared having shared similarly odd unforeseen experiences at the hands of our teacher at each of our separate lessons. When for example on several different occasions she had turned the studio heating up so high that Joseph and I became completely stifled; our throats dried up so that neither of us could continue singing. Joseph informed me that halfway through one particular lesson he had no choice but to complain, whereupon Madame O impulsively opened the studio door and ill-temperedly advised him to leave at once and take a dip in the ocean to cool off!

Joseph and I both agreed this simply did not answer to our idea of the solicitous Madame O whom we both venerated. Rather it occurred to us she appeared as a person possessed, acting under some form of indeterminate personality change so that, over a short period of time each of us had grown more unsettled due to her odd behaviour. Nonetheless at this stage I dare not confide yet to Joseph that I had actually gone to 'Windermere' Cottage with the intention of taking her some food, nor for that matter that I had happened to eavesdrop and hear for myself the 'star' pupil of whom, I would have enjoyed telling Joseph about and who, Madame O had every good reason to rave over. For the time being I had decided to leave matters in abeyance and instead wait until the time is ripe before I reveal to Joseph what I already know, otherwise he might think I'm also hearing voices or witnessing visions, to both of which these days I've been secretly prone!

After tonight I've concluded Madame O's physical health has improved. In fact, happily I even nurse a hunch she used sickness as a pretext to give her undivided attention to what is the singer's name? Mara? Yes. Mara – Madame Mara?" As for the singer being a boy. Preposterous!

Exalted from the night before, next morning Lorna still wide awake felt a positive surge of renewal overtake her physically and mentally, releasing her from those past self-imposed fetters that had frequently taken their toll upon her. Now transported as a direct consequence of experiencing 'that voice' ringing throughout her whole being, Lorna is consciously attuned to the overall possibilities and inherent change involving a new musical vocation which she is decidedly in the process of seeking out for herself. She can scarcely contain her excitement at the prospect of singularly devoting herself to the art of piano playing, a venture whereby she secretly intends to emulate her teacher's playing, hopefully without yet letting Madame O realize. Lorna satisfies herself if she were not to sing like the incomparable contralto/coloratura, then there simply exists no better choice for her to make. After all, she surmised, she had lived a quarter of a century, most of which had been devoted to singing, and overnight here she is entertaining overall unnerving change. It is an odd feeling this mind propulsion that foretells Lorna Mary Budge, that by way of her own volition she is on the threshold of performing a 'terrifying" volte face mid-stream. Convinced, after making the vital turn around she will look back without regret on former days when she 'bore a cross' and uselessly laboured to achieve that which she had little or no chance of accomplishing. However, now she is doubly aware of the fact, since hearing the possessor of the unbelievable 'voice of voices'.

Elated at her new found decisiveness, Lorna anticipated Madame O's reaction at her forthcoming lesson and wondered whether her teacher would encourage or deter the change-over in her 'least accomplished' pupil, who even so, better than any of her other students, can "plumb the depths" regardless of her sorely limited voice, but who failed miserably when demands were made upon her to enlarge her woefully limited repertoire. Lorna resolved, Madame O with her sixth sense would probably guess immediately what lurked at the back of Lorna's mind, since nothing rarely escaped the woman's keenly observant eyes that retained the power to inwardly regard another with all the perception of a great painter making a portrait, an act of artistic creation Madame O once described to Lorna as "one man's foolproof understanding of another". In fact the same way, in which Madame O sought to unlock and liberate her pupil's minds.

Today Lorna's mind is compulsively adrift with certain misgivings should it eventuate Madame O not agree to the change. There is nothing much left to Lorna by way of choice, but worse, the idea that Madame O would fail to agree with Lorna might mean the bond between the two could be severed. Lorna realised she was walking a tightrope of her own making. However her confidence remained intact when she again permitted herself to inwardly ruminate upon Madame O, being a superior human being, and it is not without good reason that Lorna is continuously drawn to reflect on the woman's uncanny knack of solving whatever unanswered question arises. During the course of an encounter, Madame O's usually correct decisions were always based on one premise alone, the truth. This the woman referred to in musical matters, as the 'criterion mode' and on more numerous occasions than she cares to remember, Lorna recalls Madame O instilling into the girl's mind the dictum that truth is the spiritual force and foundation of all art. Indeed truth, Lorna submits is permanently at the forefront of Madame O's comprehension of everything. Without this strict moral code how else could she succeed to teach? Madame O would designate, that if anyone believed they knew better, then they should go their own way. The final result being they either came round to her uncompromising way of thinking in all matters musical and artistic, or were welcome to take their leave of her vast knowledge and experience, and go elsewhere and make their own stand whether it be wrong or right, or failing that take the least productive route and stop in their tracks altogether. The indomitable Madame O undeterred would continue with her practice of excavating the depth of her singer's psyche much in the way one might expect of an anthroposophist such as her one time colleague, Rudolf Steiner (1861-1925), also a former Theosophist, both sciences of which over an extended period of time Madame O had made of herself a knowledgeable adherent.

"Come, come, my dear!" Madame O coaxed, "Come out with it." She was apt to knowingly tease in her gentlest tone of voice, giving the students confidence. "What can be so terrible that you cannot confide your problems to an old woman like me? 'Eine alte dame' ."

The upshot of such an encounter perhaps might culminate in Madame O proclaiming to any fledgling wishing to change roles, "Very well then, you may depend on me to give you every assistance..." If only this could be so Lorna anguished to herself. Thus equipped with the required bountiful helpings of solicitude at the forefront of her dealings with her students, a hitherto locked door is invitingly opened wide enabling Madame O as she liked to state "to pave the way to sort and seek out the fons origo of the pupil's different problems". Consequently, as a direct result of this attitude, Madame O had on occasion been responsible for averting amongst other problems a suicide when the highly motivated and volatile Edita Caliopolis, due to a double crossing lover, had threatened to do away with herself had it not been that is, for Madame O's last minute intervention, telling the girl "No one is worth taking away the gift of a precious life."

Lorna is continuously drawn to recalling how Madame O dealt so understandingly in matters of the human condition, invariably succeeding to assuage a student's soul and inner spiritual force.

As the morning wore on Lorna seated herself before the triple mirrored dressing table and pleasurably noted the return of a long absent glimmer in her eyes and whilst proceeding to add the finishing touches to styling her hair, seemed bent on searching out another non-existent telltale grey hair. "No" she decided at age twenty five. "I've gained a reprieve for another day." Presently she stood up and walked over to the full-length mirror at the rear end of the bedroom. Imagined herself walking confidently into Madame O's studio, all past grievances settled and dispelled between the two. Madame O would greet her as though nothing had gone amiss, welcoming and lavishing praise on the girl's decision, "Admirable! Admirable!" she would repeat just as she had in the past so often remarked on Lorna's best singing days. And Lorna relishing Madame O's comments would not be further made to harbour self-regrets or feel inadequate anymore. Finally Madame O would accede to Lorna's enforced new artistic craving to become a pianist. Lorna saw herself, under Madame O's tutelage, attaining her new found ambition, shedding the relics of her old voice in exchange for learning a catalogue of new and exciting piano works if that is at all possible with her limited means of learning and remembering. "Never mind," she self-extolled optimistically, "Madame O will teach me to outstretch myself!" For a moment she hesitated before adding with forbearance, "I know she will."

And if Lorna is to succeed she needed to transact a hasty start since she would want to make up for years lost if she were to overcome her present limitation as a 'mere singer' of no particular worth, a singer 'non grata'.

Before the dressing table mirror, Lorna searched the reflected image questioning the dramatic overnight change of events. A ray of light strayed over one of the mirrors and beamed into her eyes and down over one side of her face so that she adjudged her profile in the adjoining mirror to be quite passable. Lorna rarely paid attention to her looks. This morning she seemed more aware, albeit in a detached way, of what the mirror told her. Now instead of neglecting her appearance she felt inclined to pay more attention to herself than she had tended to do in the past. When well groomed, even elegant, she would carry herself with a certain 'éclat" if the occasion demanded, yet her appearance so easily could deteriorate to dowdiness and untidiness especially when she became overly involved in singing. Fortunately though she did not set too much store about what others thought, since her major concern would always be music. Again today persistently she dwelt on the fact that her dire vocal limitations had been altogether responsible for her slow progress, stultifying and imprisoning her in an ever-widening sea of self-doubt. Lorna is now aware of this shortcoming, especially since Madame O already from the outset had subtly intimated, "Eventually you will find your own way. It's just a matter of time." However in those days Lorna had paid scant attention to the implications of Madame O's comments. Nevertheless the seeded notion remained dormant, tucked away in the farthest reaches of Lorna's mind ready to emerge from the chrysalis when most required.

In the meantime, Lorna must make ready for the intended all-important changeover. To think only days ago her foremost desire had still been to sing like the birds and now, above all else, instead she 'wished to play to them on the piano'. Again she resolved, if she could not hope to even remotely sing like the 'star' then she must at all costs try to emulate Madame O's playing.

In positive mood Lorna promised herself not to let the previous five years of study go unheeded or wasted. The indispensable musical training gained from Madame O had afforded the necessary groundwork and should be utilised to the full no matter what future difficulties are encountered. Thus with good fortune and fortitude on her side Lorna, hopefully shall make the necessary break from singer to pianist without too much agonising and be transformed into that rarest and desirous of musicians, the 'bel canto' pianist-accompanist! As such, enjoy a privileged and prestigious niche in the music world and on special occasions accompany the finest voices. Underlying this dream venture, the idea also, that one day, she might make the acquaintance of the remarkable 'star singer' to work with.

In the mirror Lorna noted that the play of light in her eyes made them appear glassy and unusually bright, more luminous and intense against the unnatural combination of pallor and glow in her cheeks and again she came to thinking that Madame O had been correct when she had stipulated "all in good time the fledgling shall desert the nest and find its own way", likewise Irene Budge's words when she quoted Omar and a different bird of flight, "The bird of time has but a short way to fly".

In her diary Lorna wrote in semi-poetic vein:

Hopefully the overall significant musical change from singer to pianist shall be undertaken without too great a drain on my limited musical resources and I shall be free to follow in my role model's sublime skills that turn the piano into a singing instrument, in other words an extension of the human voice, inextricably linked with the spirit of music.

When she finished, already Lorna somehow envisaged herself empowered with a little of the vastly appealing mystic sensitivity her teacher possessed, what in fact Lorna and others assumed to be, an abundant supply of 'divination'. The idea that there existed such a force and energy still motivated and spurred Lorna on to greater objectives. In her mind abstractedly she hummed a suddenly remembered Mozart aria from the 'Seraglio'. "I was heedless in my rapture" and a little later got to thinking about the prospects of a return visit to 'Windermere' but as much as she wished, she dare not venture there until after her next proposed lesson. Instead she decided she would bide her time and wait for word from Madame O who she guessed may now be aware Lorna had probably heard the 'star singer' since she would have found Lorna's food parcel left on the kitchen windowsill.

Lorna hummed to the words:

"Over my slumber your loving

watch keep – Rock me to

sleep mother; rock me to sleep."   [Elizabeth Akers Allen]

Soon she sang herself to sleep.

This morning, carried away with her future plans, Lorna had forgotten that throughout the night intermittently she had woken, coughing and spluttering. A dull pain racking her chest necessitating she heave up and down to catch her breath. She had all but neglected to take into account the creeping damp at 'Windermere' rising on all sides around her. When dressed in little more than a flimsy cardigan and dress to protect her from the elements, she had succumbed to a chill. At first a mere sniffle, but before long her forehead started to burn and her teeth chattered. Several times, this morning she attempted to clamber from her bed in a vain endeavour to make a hot drink, but each time she listlessly fell back upon the pillow. From one moment to the next, her head throbbing, she could swear her bedroom being in the process of changing colour before her eyes, firstly to a garish admixture of bright yellows and dirty orange fraught with lashings of crimson streaking across the normally white walls and dripping down onto the bedcovers reminding Lorna of an oozing open wound.

All day she lay in bed, feeling progressively worse, whilst another nightmare returned to reek vengeance, and overtake her. Gusts of wind blew through the open bedroom window. Lorna pulled the blankets high above her head, held her hands pressed firmly over her ears to suppress the noise of branches cracking. Her eyes shut tight, she lay deathly quiet in the darkness, in her thoughts felt her way blindly around, entrapped in a dark labyrinth. Before long, a crescent moon emerged. Slowly her eyes opened, only to be met with spectral curtains, which blew and billowed, swathed and intertwined around her slight frame. In desperation she cried out, "Gabriel! Gabriel!" but her mute throat remained unable to emit either sound or murmur. Soon the wind blew the bedclothes away from her altogether. In an instant before her she sees a vast deserted bleached-out peneplain, spreading as far as eye can see. The sound of water lapping against a distant shore. Lorna takes a few indeterminate awkward steps forward. Immediately swamp and marshland violently pull and engulf her ever downwards until she is totally submerged, then just as abruptly she is bodily thrust upwards. Sand, foam and leaves swirling about her bare feet, till unexpectedly she finds herself back indoors downstairs.

A loud rapping on the front door unsettles her. As she is about to turn the key in the lock, she gabbles hoarsely, "Who is there?" and waits to receive an answer.

A stony voice admonishes her – "I am afraid" - and before she dare open the door, she retreats instead and flees in the opposite direction and races towards the semi-lit landing at the top of the staircase. Lorna's attention is diverted when she notices how her mother's tapestry instead of catching the first light of dawn is bathed in sombre shadows. For a brief moment she regards the depicted figure of the expectant virgin whose temples are crowned with flames and who, surrounded by the light of her own halo, is waiting submissively for the appointed hour whilst two angels hover in the semi-darkness bearing the crown and sceptre of the 'Casta Diva' merging into the light. Lorna lurches away, convinced footsteps have followed her. She forces the bedroom door handle and scampers inside securely locking the door behind her before falling prostrate on the bed. As her head touches the pillow that same menacingly hoarse deep voice rises amplified above the gale, enters and lodges within her head refusing to depart. Soon those other all engulfing siren-like sounds coming from a different direction re-emerge increasingly growing in volume, taking on a sinister meaning and threatening to swamp and burst her eardrums, deafen her once and for all so that she shall never hear another note of music. Another nightmare ends.

It is the morning of her lesson, previously cancelled because of Madame O's indisposition. Lorna awoke bleary-eyed, her chest still heaving, scarcely aware of the previous night except that her ears still buzzed and hummed and her hands and feet are icy cold. In a daze she more or less simulated dressing and did not bother to take breakfast. The mere thought of food precipitated a feeling of biliousness. Even the slightest sip of tea would fail to agree with her present state, rather she dosed herself with aspirin in an attempt to ward off the debilitating emptiness arising and issuing deep from within, racking both brain and body in the process. With a taste of bile in her mouth, she might decide to forego the once eagerly awaited lesson at which she planned to announce her decision to renounce singing altogether. Today her voice is near enough non-existent, barely a crackle; her throat burning and parched. To sing a single note would pose both a veritable physical and psychological impossibility.

She crept back into bed.

Outside in the driveway the sound of a car engine, reminiscent of her parents' great majestic Humber. Lorna could have swooned at the idea of her parents and

Gabriel returning from an outing, to the point of actually overhearing a voice ask: "Anyone at home?" or at least she thought she heard an unfamiliar muffled voice call through the bellowing wind. She waited - mistaken? Rising from her bed and pulling aside the curtain, her first reaction had been to peer up at the overcast sky after which she spotted some distance away, as much as she could make out, half hidden in the bushes by the short driveway, a black hearse like delivery van or suchlike, and a darkly uniformed man visible only from the back making his way stealthily towards the vehicle. Just the once he looked back before climbing into the front seat. In slow motion the brake was noiselessly released and the car slowly edged its way back down the driveway, crunching over the gravel before the engine started up. As the vehicle disappeared from sight, Lorna remained deathly still in the guise of spectator to a solemn cortege. She did not hesitate further, with a violent tug she feverishly summoned her strength and drew the remaining section of the open curtain sharply closed, determined they stay that way to seal out the encroaching inclement weather and darkening sky. Once cut off from the rest of the world she recovered that all too necessary feeling of security she craved in the knowledge that this 'house of memories' rightfully belonged to her alone and no one need enter, nor, could take it from her whilst she continued to live there.

Chapter Thirteen

The Postman

Lorna found herself at the top of the stairs again. In two minds she deliberated mindlessly whether to go for her lesson. At this point another rapping sounded at the front door. This time insistent and confident. The girl shuddered and pulled her well-worn dressing gown into a shawl like affair around her bare shoulders then, remaining barefoot, she stole downstairs and tentatively waited at the foot of the staircase.

"Who is it?" she called.

"I am afraid –" a man's gruff voice replied and paused, then repeated, "I am afraid Miss it's urgent. Posty – Miss Budge. It's me, Watkins!" The voice echoed knowingly and reassuringly.

Lorna uttered a faint sigh of relief, looked down at the floor and bent over to clear a space on the inside of the door where the floor was strewn with leaves and unopened junk mail. Simultaneously on the other side of the door Watkins a Welshman bent down to speak through the brass door flap.

"I daresay you've been away, Miss. haven't seen or heard a word from you for a time. There's all manner of items here awaiting your attention I should add. I dared not leave this 'registered' without delivering it into your hands personally. It's marked 'urgent' you see."

Lorna opened the door. "Good day Miss." Mr Watkins beamed as he greeted her enthusiastically and seeing how pale Lorna appeared continued apologetically. "In your absence, being as it's marked to be personally handed to the addressee, the Hon. Miss Lorna Budge."

To Mr Watkins, Lorna could do no wrong. She being his ideal of a 'very correct young lady'. After all, she was the Hon. L Budge and as such he reserved his utmost admiration and respect for her, particularly since he'd been made aware she had been left orphaned within the period of time he had been delivering post to the house. Fondly he remembered her as a ten year old playing in the garden of Ariel Court. "Terrible thing to happen to a young lady," he repeatedly told himself every time he personally brought the post for Lorna.

"Are you out of sorts, Miss? Anything I can get you?" he enquired solicitously as he passed her several bottles of milk from the side of the entrance.

"No, Mr Watkins, but thank you. Just a slight chill, that's all. I usually catch one at least once a year. No, I'll be fine, but thanks again," Lorna said as she shivered all over holding the icy bottles, without considering how long they'd stood outside.

Mr Watkins continued acting as though he had no wish to go. "A very large package indeed," he said as he began to move a small trunk-like affair closer to the threshold. "Must be an early Christmas box – in midsummer!" he joked. "There!

Will that do? Now all I'll be needing is a signature, Miss. Ever so sorry to disturb you when you're not up to it. Here, Miss," Watkins handed Lorna a pen.

Drawing the dressing gown over the skimpy negligee, Lorna scrawled her signature onto the receipt, her hand shaking and her head pounding. The postman thanked her with a wide grin. "Nasty old day, Miss?" again putting off taking his leave, "Must watch that cold!" He kept smiling through his words, his eyes never deserting hers, "Hope you're not intending venturing out in your condition. Storm clouds a-brewing, weather forecast not very good, and it's supposed to be summer!" He looked up at the sky, "Ooh!" he gave a mock shiver, "I won't be half glad to get back to the depot and enjoy a hot mug of brew to warm me vitals. Bitterly cold, looks like the ole sun's gone on 'olidee, or taking a nose dive, one o'er the two! Strange for midsummer wouldn't you agree, Miss?" and he sang in a barely audible voice an old Welsh Air:

> How is it that the morning
>
> That used to be so bright,
>
> Is overcast with darkness
>
> With scarce a ray of light?
>
> I want to see the mountain
>
> Put on its golden crown;
>
> But O my eyes are weary
>
> And I must to lay me down."

[The Dying Boy: Professor Rowland. Victorian.]

Lorna returned his smile with a nod of affirmation. She liked the postman, always so friendly and cheerful no matter how inclement the weather. Regardless of how ill she felt, she could respond to this man who is always readily available with sound advice weather-wise or recommending her suitable clothing for cold days and hot days. "If you intend going out you'll need to button up well today if you don't want to catch your death of cold. A Sou'wester would not go amiss. Bitter cold," he repeated as he gave his nose a warming rub from a hand displaying a woollen mitten. "Never mind," he said consolingly whilst discreetly looking the other way as Lorna's dressing gown slipped a little further from her bare shoulders. By now Lorna hardly spoke, nor noticed, she just kept smiling blandly at him. Her head pounding, her mind puzzling over the other substantial trunk-like object sitting on the floor outside at his feet. Mr Watkins peered over her shoulder into the darkened interior.

"Here let me fetch this 'un in for you, Miss."

Lorna unlocked the chain and opened the door wider to permit him entry into the house.

"That's awfully kind and helpful of you, Mr Watkins, but I'm sure I'll manage."

Lorna's characteristic independence is exactly what the postman appreciated most about the young girl. Always willing to help herself, or himself if it came to it. Take the onus off another, even a menial Posty. Lorna sighed and murmured dispassionately to herself.

"I can't imagine whatever it can be".

For want of anything else to say, Watkins commented, "That's a handsome envelope awaiting your goodly perusal. Never two without three," and the well-intentioned postman smiled and generously carried the box aloft on his shoulders and placed it in the hallway.

"Here, let me get you something for your trouble, Mr Watkins," Lorna offered half-heartedly.

"No, I wouldn't hear of it, Miss Budge. You know it's always been a pleasure to come to Ariel Court. Why, I remember Mr Budge were always to be seen out in the garden in winter and rough weather." He used to call me 'the Welsh Wizard'. I once asked him why? He reckoned I could tow a half dozen mailbags all at once. Watkins laughed.

Lorna smiled. "Oh yes, he was that, my father, nature lover alright, and a sense of humour but how did you manage to get this bulky thing on your trolley?" Lorna pointed to the cumbersome boxed package, which although being marked 'Urgent' still failed to excite her curiosity. She appeared more concerned with how Mr Watkins had delivered it.

"It must have been an awful weight. Quite a chore, Mr Watkins."

"Oh no, Miss, you're mistaken. I didn't bring it. It was here already. I saw a van on my way and it must have been left here just before. I"ve only brought the 'registered' paraphernalia."

Puzzled, Lorna thanked the postman again. "Well I shan't keep you any longer, Miss," Mr Watkins said reluctantly, his eyes still sparkling. "I hope it's something nice to buck your spirits up, Miss. Don't forget it's marked 'Urgent'," and suddenly realising he'd outstayed his welcome by a good five minutes and kept Lorna out in the cold too long, he nimbly leapt off the veranda and down the few steps onto the overgrown turf.

Lorna could scarcely wait to get back inside the house again so that she failed to completely close the front door behind her. She couldn't decide whether to return to her bed or immediately open the letter. Her eyes skimmed the package. Her attention drawn to the logo imprinted with a lyre and various surrounding musical instruments on the address label. On the envelope, the same logo. Underneath in bold heraldry – 'Conservatorium of Music". At this moment those words meant nothing because her aching body refused to do her bidding and in this present state the words did not properly register. Her nose and eyes watered from the cold wind and damp air blustering over the tiles and constantly encircling her bare feet. Mr Watkins' chatter had detained her longer than she'd wished but she simply hadn't the heart to stop him and, although she'd always found him convivial and good natured, with the best intentions, he did rather tend to draw the conversation out when it came to discussing the weather! Notwithstanding today, his good nature had proved more of a burden than a help.

Chapter Fourteen

The Letter

Lorna, a vacuous expression playing over her pale features, weighed the envelope in her hand divining its contents, deferring the time when she would open it. For years she had nursed an almost congenital fear of bad news, hence the crop of unopened mail from weeks ago lying at her feet. Now with the sealed envelope and contents playing steadfastly on her mind, a pang of doubt crossed her thoughts. She surmised, far the worst thing that could happen, would be that her studies at the Conservatorium were to be suspended or worse, terminated altogether. After all Madame O had unreasonably threatened to have words with the governors. At the time Lorna did not imagine for one moment Madame O would carry out this threat, however this morning her suspicions are to be alerted by the post and already she has become less certain and less confident of where she stands 'career'-wise. Aside from which, she now regretted not having made her intention clear before to Madam O - to study the piano full time and dispense with singing altogether.

As she peered at the envelope Lorna, in a moment of lucidity, blamed her weakest characteristic – indecision. So be it. There can be no turning back once the governors are committed to her expulsion. She sighed, then cursed at the prospect of such a humiliation and dwelt upon her parents' anguish, had they been alive to witness their daughter's ultimate defeat and failure at the hands of the governors of the most prestigious music institute in the land. She sees everything for which she has striven pass by in an undercurrent of uncertainty. Abruptly she viewed Madame O in a different light. Is this woman to be held responsible for all her future problems? Impulsively Lorna read into her teacher signs of inherent evil, before she even began to consider perhaps that madness itself is not altogether far removed from evil; only to hastily banish the thought from her mind and guiltily conclude that Madame O had to be the least likely person one could remotely deem as evil. Lorna experienced pangs of remorse for even upholding such an unreasonable notion.

The wind continued to howl through the rafters and half open door. Lorna wished that her oppressively negative thoughts could be trundled aside, pitched forth piecemeal to the elements, tossed asunder, blown away, forever and forgotten. She sidled over towards the carved oak Hall chair and seated herself upon it, perversely subjecting herself to, and drawing the utmost discomfort from the chill air enveloping her body. In the hallway the grandfather clock tolled the hour of nine o'clock reminding her she had hardly slept a wink the previous night.

"I suppose this is as good a time as any to open the accursed envelope," she said, "and if its contents foretell what I anticipate then I shall never speak to Madame

O nor go near the Conservatorium again. Forget the 'star singer' as swiftly as possible. Dump my piano. Be done with music altogether," she self-threatened in a feverish, almost inaudible childlike whisper. "It ought not come as a surprise. A surprise!" she repeated endeavouring to convince herself. "I should have been prepared. This is what comes of living an out-and-out lie, an absurd day-to-day fantasy. I am no better than the Cowardly Lion in 'The Wizard of Oz."

Presently her mother"s remarks to her husband come echoing down the years. "Heaven forbid Reginald, whatever would become of Lorna should, anything happen to us?"

"Why, surely dear, I daresay Lorna and Gabriel could be trusted to look after each other. After all we have to go sometime."

"I doubt it very much, Reginald, our Lorna would be totally lost, even with Gabriel at her side. She's just too attached to us both."

"That's it! Lost!" Lorna muttered, well believing this morning that her plans for the future had been irrevocably changed overnight. A sealed envelope had become an increasing source of self-imposed misery, its undivulged contents obsessively unsettling her and filling her with that very same sense of loss that Irene Budge had knowingly predicted for her daughter.

Her breathing shallow, Lorna sank back uneasily into the chair, shivered and inclined her head to one side. When next she opened her eyes she heard the clock chiming midday. Had anyone told her she'd been unconscious or asleep for three hours she might readily disbelieve them. To Lorna it was impossible that she could have slept all that time sitting upright? She rubbed her eyes with her frozen hands, gazed around and finally looked down at her feet where the now opened envelope still lay. She raised her eyes and steadily looked through the open door, a disquieting smile gathering on her lips as she searched in her mind for the day of the week, before willing herself to proceed towards the doorway. Next with exaggerated calm she stepped out onto the porch from where she surveyed the garden, parts of which lay covered in a year old carpet of yellow and red dead leaves. Soon she waded knee deep through them on her way to the outside letterbox and mindlessly peered inside the empty space. Then retraced her steps, pacing back across the wide wooden veranda, her hair untidy and tousled in the wind. Entering her house soundlessly closed the front door, lately as usual without giving a thought to securing the lock behind her, simultaneously experiencing that same welcome sense of relief and rush of security at being enclosed within her own four walls. Inside the chilled, gloomy hallway, again she drew the curtains against "intruding prying eyes" until presently she found herself enmeshed in virtual darkness.

Passing the palm of her hand across her burning temples; next experienced her tongue fail to engage to moisten her parched lips. Her stomach writhed and contracted as she leaned with her thin arms on the sideboard. Thus she remained agitatedly monitoring herself once more in the hall mirror, scarcely recognising, nor wishing to acknowledge the wan face, which indifferently stared back at her through darkly shaded eyes. Again in profile she noted the slightly protruding stomach so alien to the rest of her wasted body, a fact due no doubt nowadays to her indifferent way of eating. She ran her hand over the unnatural protuberance and for a time tried to imagine how it would be to give birth. For a time briefly her mind cleared and it occurred to Lorna that the image that stared back at her could well have been that of her own mother, save for the fact that today this particular 'Irene Budge' had grown younger over the years! In one respect the idea consoled Lorna, except she could never recall seeing her mother with droplets of sweat, or was it rain water, coursing down over pale cheeks. Lorna recoiled at the image confronting her, causing her to move away from the mirror whilst straining to hear the soft pad of her bare feet echoing throughout her mind, somewhat both deluding and simultaneously comforting her, as she may well imagine a member of her family to be nearby.

Indeed the voice that echoed forth across the past was that of her mother, who called: "Come on Lorna dear, make us laugh. We are all here waiting. It's your birthday – remember?" "Yes, Lorna," Reginald Budge joined in affectionately, "Sing us that special song of yours you know so well and I'll play the accordion".

"Which one? I know hundreds," Lorna yelped back in a small voice tinged with exasperation and dismay.

At the time, Reg and Irene were only too aware of their dyslexic child's short memory that would only permit her to realise very few songs.

"Tell me the name of it then," the girl pretended, playing the same ritualistic game she always carried on with her parents on these specific occasions.

"The special one that goes like this," her father answered as he started up the familiar tune on his accordion.

"You must know it by now, dear."

At this stage, Lorna still pleaded mock ignorance, shaking her head repeatedly and saying in a suitably theatrical tone of voice,

"I know hundreds of songs."

"Of course you do, Lorna," her mother said encouragingly when it became her turn to egg on her daughter.

On that far off day it had not been until she heard her mother's voice sing the first word, "Goodbye", that the girl acted convinced.

"Oh, that silly old song," she replied theatrically feigning both surprise and recognition. The next moment she had scrambled up onto the table top, her makeshift stage, and arranged herself in readiness for her solo party piece so that everyone present at her eighth birthday could share in the enjoyment of her hilarious antics signalling to Irene Budge to sidle over to Auntie Meg's treasured Steck piano and act as accompanist to Reginald. As Irene Budge caught Lorna's eyes the girl made a graceful low dip in acknowledgement of her mother's appreciative audience, and then skittishly began to execute her parents' bidding and launch forthright into the jaunty little ditty of Farewell, a song that inevitably afforded all who heard her sing it such unbounded pleasure:

The ship will sail in half an hour to cross the broad Atlantic
My friends are standing on the shore with grief and sorrow frantic
My trunks are all stored down below in the great ship Dan O'Leary,
The anchor's weighed and the gangway's up and I'm leaving Tipperary.

Chorus

Good-bye Mike, Good-bye Pat, Good-bye Kate and Mary,
For the anchor's weighed and the gang-way's up and I'm leaving Tipperary,
See, there's the steamer blazing up, I can no longer stay,
For I'm bound for New York City boys, ten thousand miles away.

My portmanteau I've got packed with potatoes, greens and bacon,
If you think I won't look after that in troth you are mistaken,
And if the ship does pitch and toss for half a dozen farthings

I'll take my trunk upon my back and walk to Castle Garden.

CHORUS

Give my respects to Mrs. Mac, and likewise Mrs. Hagan,

And I'll come back to the christening when she marries Patsy Fagan,

I'm deep in love with Molly Burke as a jackass is in clover

And when I'm settled, if she'll come, I'll pay her passage over.

CHORUS

In between each rollicking verse everyone present joined in the chorus whilst

Lorna skipped and jumped an Irish reel, pulled hilarious faces and chose to grin

wickedly at a member of her intrigued audience, usually Grandma Pauline Napoleone,

who each time became convulsed with laughter and happiness. By the time the chorus

had nearly ended, Lorna had executed a chancy little turn around on the table top and

again caught the eye of Irene Budge in preparation for the next lively refrain:

See, there's the steamer blazing up, I can no longer stay,

For I'm bound for New York City boys, ten thousand miles away.

When the clapping started she called out over the heads of her audience,

"I'm not finished yet."

"Encore, encore, Lorna," and Lorna repeated the last verse again to a fresh

round of applause. Lorna then knelt down on the piano stool awaiting Auntie Meg's

prescheduled bouquet concealed behind a chair.

Throughout the last five years, Lorna had not dared sing the song again. With tears of longing welling in her eyes, she retained another flashback of her eighth birthday when she'd been inundated with greeting cards – so different from her last birthday when she'd turned twenty five years old and received just the one single plain white card with a solitary music note engraved on it sent to her by Madame O. On that other far off eighth birthday, "10,000 miles away", Lorna self-boasted. "Why, mother, father and brother, between them alone were responsible for her receiving six cards!" Of all the cards and presents she'd received down over the years, one item in particular she'd kept uppermost in her affection. It came in the form of an ingenious pop-up multi-coloured enamelled bird that perched in a cage, chinois style with a mock bejewelled golden eye. At the press of a concealed button a hidden automated spring set the bird's wings flapping and its beak opening and shutting in song upon which the cage door slowly swung open and the bird moved and tilted its exquisite body along rails to the far edge of its perch, raised its head to greet Lorna with a series of high pitched warblings. Accompanying this petite Victorian automata at its base came a gold embossed printed text in imitation of a medieval illuminated manuscript outlining the story of "The Emperor's Nightingale" by Hans Christian Anderson. Subsequently on that magical Birthday Lorna's devout intention was born to become, in her own words a living, singing, human nightingale.

But this fanciful resolution would not prove an easy task since from infancy Lorna had struggled with dyslexia and at school, also being left-handed, her teacher unwisely had attempted to make the girl right-handed with the consequence that Lorna developed a speech impediment in the form of a nervous stammer which took years of patience and fortitude to correct and control.

Today as she deliriously clambered down in her thoughts from her childhood stage, into the present to retrieve the open envelope and stray card lying at her feet. Her eyes blindly struggled to reach out across the page. Although she was looking at the words, her mind is thinking along different lines. Had the notes been there in her voice today, she would desire nothing better than to ignore everything, be seated at the piano and accompany herself in her (No. 4) set repertory standby, 'Oft in the stilly night', but those two relatively tiny vocal cords, according to Madame O, a mere half an inch each in length, had deserted her. With the result, Lorna recited, rather than sang the words of the old Thomas Moore song, conveniently superimposing the lyrics onto the surface of the card so that instead of being deciphered clearly, the true text of the letter is dizzily swimming in all directions before her eyes. Syllable after syllable she proceeds to construct and deconstruct in dogged fashion, in her quest to bury her head in the sand until she is left with little choice but to acknowledge the variegated scattered words that float piecemeal in relief to a gradual and logical surfacing, reminding her of fortune cookies spelling out their message. Against Lorna's will, soon there is no stopping the words and phrases stringing themselves together into a coherent whole. In a matter of minutes, her brain charges she shall have no choice but to accept the aforesaid announcement which at her peril she must finally deduce and comprehend. Little by little Lorna's reasoning takes a firm hold upon her capabilities. Cautiously her dyslexia begins to somehow ambiguously segment the heading announcement: -Anno – un – cement – which meaninglessly, she phonetically translates further into one – year – ce – ment. Why, why, she anguishes, do words cause so much trouble. Abnormal, absurd, irrelevant, she commiserates shaking her head from side to side. No wonder I've never got anywhere in particular if I never get to start. Words. Baffling. My undoing! My singing voice, the other stumbling block.

Lorna pauses, an ironic smile plays on her features. Briefly to mentally save face she even celebrates the odd demystifying element she is in the process of deploying. If only I could do something desperate each time I reach a stalemate, shear off all my hair, become Jean d"Arc – anything – another Sarah Bernhardt with a wooden leg! Submerge myself in an icy lake. Start anew! Lorna lambasted herself unequivocally as she set off on a concerted re-reading exercise, repeatedly once, twice, thrice going to the same words - endeavouring to make them falsely sink in below the surface of her true indwelling thoughts which invariably refused to make head nor tail of the intrinsic incoming meaning of things as Lorna succeeded to escape into her tedious mind void situations whereby little or nothing penetrates beyond or below the surface. Besides, insofar as she concerned herself, that first sentence, headed Announcement: while at the very summit of her professional powers, momentarily meant as nothing to her own mental ramblings, save for the fact earlier she questioned having read either the same thing or something similar but where and when she could not be certain. Nonetheless she is obliged to continue in yo-yo fashion with the strings of her painfully slow deciphering exercise returning backwards and forwards, upwards and downwards, to the first statement, while at the very summit of her professional powers. At this stage Lorna needs to stop to wipe away the ever encroaching hateful stinging tears that are in the habit of accompanying her in such frustrations. Meanwhile the words in small print puncturing the card's surface taunted and refused to leave her alone until Lorna found herself obliged to follow in their wake regardless of mixed feelings of anxiety and irritability, but mostly pain; developing into a gradual aggravated heightened awareness of some unacceptable unseen foe or enemy. Presently Lorna impulsively gave way and allowed her mind to ruminate on the main statement, which read thus: "To all her devoted pupils and colleagues..." At this juncture Lorna paused abruptly as though she stood on a stage re-enacting some celebrated scene – perhaps Tatiana's Letter scene from 'Eugene Onegin". Over in her mind again she perused the printed words. No longer 'stage struck". She is, after all, at her own home, both bare feet securely planted on the tiles beneath her. Both hands keenly clasping the scrap of card. Both eyes stuck to the detested print. The prolonged burning sensation in her temples now journeyed down into her chest cavity carving out a spasm of intense anxiety. Progressively word clusters clarify and change into a few meaningful menacing sentences each piled atop the other, feeding Lorna's addled mind with fresh lashings of 'incoherence'.

Despite everything that had previously occurred, Lorna's eyes clouded over and remained impaled at the same place. There simply being no reason to continue. Of course she had read it before, she persuaded herself, yet in her present state she is diverted from all sense of logic until at last she hoped to allay her uncertain misgivings by contesting, one at a time, each spelt-out word. As far as she deciphers there is no mention of any immediate plans afoot to expel her from the Conservatorium. So what then, need she worry about? There is no sense in denying the letter's existence. Proof it rested here in her hands and her name is clearly written on the front of the envelope, is it not? In any case, nothing she suggested or imagined can ease the peculiar aggressive pain gnawing away at her insides. Now she must become one of two people, the addressed, or the addressee, or lastly both but to only one of these can she subscribe to bare her soul. The other must be given over to the task of reading the enclosed announcement perhaps containing a miscellany of vague intimations, reports, invitations and the like. Frankly Lorna cared not a jot! Never mind, for the time being the practical side of Lorna Mary Budge shall wade through, word by word, if needs be, parrot fashion – as long as she applied herself with cautious, yet wholly apparent ever new found disinterest. Again with her mind on the rampage, she persevered and questioned her options, seeking out the irritable preceding statement, It is with utmost regret that we the governors... again Lorna stops short. Fresh beads of sweat gathering across her forehead reaching down over her eyelashes, "the governors!" It is true then, she jumps to conclusions, scolded and quickly changed her tactics. No one dare accuse her of cowardice. No indeed." She read on quickly determined to ruefully digest the facts crying out: "This then is a chance to show my metal!" After all had she not lost her whole family in a horrible accident? And had she not managed to pull through the whole affair? Proof of which today she still stubbornly struggles on. Although she is reminded, let it be said, not without the accompanying guilt being incurred of her own survival.

At this appointed moment, more than ever before, Lorna longed to have Gabriel at her side. But no, she alone must read on, singularly discover once and for all what 'Fate' has in store for her for, it is indeed Fate, unreasonably she repeatedly extolled, as her mind constantly disengaged, sidetracked and harked back to Janacek's disturbing opera of the same name, 'Fate', with that odd bitter-sweet opening waltz beginning the opera so admired by Madame O. There is no getting away from the facts, everything Lorna pondered or dwelt upon inevitably took her back to Madame O and music, music and Madame O. Madame O herself being music of course – one and the same thing. Everything Lorna had learned and had held to be sacred is due to the volatile woman's European background, her endless curiosity and appetite for knowledge that acted magnetically upon each one of her pupil's minds or should have, but none more so than Lorna's, which Madame O knew only too well and when the occasion merited, did not hesitate to tell the girl so.

Again Lorna"s mind harkened back, to Leos Janacek, and how Madame O believed the composer came closest to expressing the woman"s own thoughts.

"Had I been given the choice to be a composer, his is the way I should have chosen to compose. Curiously, there's hardly a proper tune and yet having said as much, throughout his music profound emotion is consistently essayed. How to put it to you, Lorna? The disembodying of life without thought of death. I like that idea," Madame O had dreamily told Lorna.

Now that cryptic sentence which at the time Lorna had noted in her diary, but failed to quite understand, fitted exactly to her present state of mind, again though without her fully realising why. Meanwhile the irascible script indelibly taunting Lorna's vision demands her urgent attention.

"Don't be duped by the governors, Lorna," she rasped as her eyes blindly wandered over the card, "They're as thick as thieves. All of them smug, without exception," she emphasised impatiently.

"Do they care or know what music truly means to the individual? For instance someone like me who stands in their indifferent shadow and strives tirelessly to achieve the utmost from herself yet finally goes unrewarded for the effort. Remains condemned, a useless draught horse whose days are numbered before being put down, out of its misery while futilely still attempting self-survival. Lorna's bitter and unreasonable invective had by now got the better of her. She rubbed at her eyes to fight back more tears of frustration whilst she agitated uncertainly over the 'report' which she self-forewarned, doubtless would soon make dire mention of her own name. But that is not to be. She is mistaken. It is another's name that finally meets her eyes as she reads on, and this time she doesn't stop. 'We, the governors, solemnly regret to announce the untimely and unexpected demise of our friend and colleague, the much esteemed Frau Prof Rosealma Oppenheimer." Lorna gasped. Rosealma – Who? Rose Alma – the girl's mind blurred into panic, strived to unscramble the 'odd data'. Alma Mater, she recalls, the name of a college, Almaviva, a count – a countess! Mozart, Rossini. Their names eddying, intertwined, whereupon Lorna smiled a secret smile and dared to contemplate how the mind plays tricks in order to react against itself, especially when least expected, but nothing she could think suggest or say anymore allowed her the desired respite from that horrible flurry of stubbornly ingrained words glaring out at her from the card face. Mater Misericordia, the hospital on the other side of town is worth a thought, followed by a surfeit of similarities, Alma Mahler, Mater, meaninglessly encroached in ever increasingly rabid printed relief. Further on she reads: 'Our most venerated and respected Professor Emeritus of Singing'. Lorna brooded, not forgetting to pause and remonstrate obstinately on how difficult it shall always remain for her to align words into a conclusive whole. Again she bemoaned and stammered irritably about the reason why people failed to write in a simple straightforward fashion! Fresh beads of sweat formed until her face resembled expressionless shiny white clay.

Caught up in a self-engaged undertow, Lorna embarked on a personal expostulation. Next she re-read on, 'announce the untimely and unexpected demise of' – whatever that is supposed to mean Lorna quipped as she pinched at the edges of the card whose "vague" message had taken on Grand Opera proportions.

Meanwhile a thread of precognition struck added alarm into Lorna. Her mind in turmoil, arrested into a permanent state of involuntarily dissembling the jumble of words chasing and toppling over each other in a mad race. Her stomach churned and contracted with the effort. Where or when she pleaded had she read something similar? Was it earlier on or just moments ago? Five years prior perhaps when that other unmentionable 'event' embedded itself for all time in her mind. Or much before, in another life altogether? Suddenly time had no value, and Lorna's mind determined that the words should possess no meaning. All she could experience now being the raw thrust of pain persistently piercing her innards, re-opening fresh wounds. Regardless however, she struggled, allowing the sickening text to convene and assault her senses, harking back for a moment in time to failed examinations. In particular her crude attempts in a set examination piece when she had been required to write an essay on Beethoven's "Consecration of the house", and how out of sheer fright she had written any absurdity that came into her mind. Similarly at this present moment; her mind depleted of objectivity remained inert, static, refusing to focus, perversely diversified, "robbing the music notes of intrinsic meaning" as Madame O would remonstrate on one of those best forgotten bad lesson days. As to the exam, Lorna had struggled on in a mad Mahlerian cortege-like March with one idea in mind; finish and escape the classroom and suffer the consequences. The outcome of that best forgotten escapade being, of course, she failed miserably. And to think it had taken years of obsessive learning exercises. And what for? To reach a not particularly impressive standard in her music which by comparison to the other students painted a bleak future and outlook for Lorna. Still she always told herself she must be grateful for small mercies, and above all for Madame O"s indomitable patience and involvement especially when she managed to console Lorna by advising her that some of the very finest professionals were poor sight readers and failed their exams. This remark had boosted Lorna's self-confidence no end. However Madame O knew only too well when it came to the important question of sight reading Lorna was most likely to stop mid-stream, come unstuck and start all over again, and sometimes altogether lose her waning powers of concentration. This learning defect, usually made worse in a particular passage when the music spoke directly to the girl, 'moved the spirit', so to speak, as Madame O so understandingly coined the phrase. Encapsulated back into the present Lorna noted the dates (given in brackets) on the card – '1878-1942' – neatly printed after Rosealma Oppenheimer's name, whilst the last sentence following the dates went on to add with utmost finality 'had passed away peacefully in her sleep.' Thereafter followed specific details of a proposed service to celebrate 'a life' to be commemorated in the gardens of the Conservatorium underneath the tree hitherto known and referred to as the Oracular Oak, and which henceforth shall be renamed the Rosealma Oppenheimer Oak. Again, with heart pounding, Lorna Budge re-read the words that now ceased to resemble a series of meaningless parables, 'Floral tributes may be placed around the base of the tree'. At the bottom of the page the announcement ended with a simple three word Latin text: 'Veni Creator Spiritus" – 'Our Souls inspire, come Holy Spirit".

Lorna now came to the final wording of the announcement, which advised that one of Madame Oppenheimer's pupils, Mr Joseph Rosenblatt, had gratefully offered to recite the 'Kaddish" in her memory. At this mention, utmost gravity and disbelief overtook Lorna. She felt an icy hand encircle and close over her heart. Again she relived that isolated ominous chill creep into her narrow chest cavity that took all the blows. The veins in her temples were ready to explode. Her whole body froze whilst she fought her utmost to remember Madame O's words. "Always follow your heart, Lorna, even if ever you should imagine it stopping. It's never too late." "But how, when it lays like a frozen lake?" Lorna pleaded and yelped in a helpless childlike murmur of a voice.

In Lorna's present harsh shocked state, she substituted in her mind the Latin text sewn into Irene Budge's tapestry, instead of what she had just read. All Lorna perceived now was a meaningless blank white empty folder that limply fluttered from her hands onto her lap and thence onto the floor to rest again at her feet. In the half light of the hallway, her cheeks ashen, her face infantile, devoid of emotion, Lorna sat upright. An immobile slight figure, the whole person caught forthwith in a state of trauma. And so she remained for an indeterminate time listening intently to the rustle of leaves eddying through the branches and brushing against the eves and the wind singing through the rafters. Finally, with a barely perceptible movement, she raised herself with an unnatural composure and made her way to the open window, gazed furtively over the garden and with no idea whatsoever of the time, or day of the week, regarded the last vestiges of the early morning frost, glistening and bestowing a silvery evanescent glow in the shadows to many of the lighter coloured shrubs now standing out in solemn relief.

Lorna turned her back on the scene and searched the interior gloom for a familiar landmark. An alien meaningless transitory smile registering over her slightly irregular soft hewn young features, her once full mouth no more than a petulant grimace, whilst a recently non-existent frown traipsed across and remained imprinted on her forehead giving birth to a faint trace of indignation which also momentarily appeared in her dulled eyes, now those belonging to a constantly lost child.

As Lorna walked into the music room, unexpectedly she experienced an almost pleasant state of 'delivery'. She hesitated in front of the brown chalk drawing hanging above the piano to allow her eyes to rest on a depiction - one of only two or so known to her - of Henry Purcell. Open on the piano lay a work composed by John Blow, his 'Lament for Adonis", which Madame O had wanted Lorna to compare with

'Dido's Lament" the idea being that Lorna would gain an even better understanding of the girls most often sung piece of music. On the keyboard, Lorna's finger managed to pick out a few notes of Blow's mystic ode with its unusual harmonies created by minor intervals. As she did so Lorna felt an unreasonable and inexplicable resentment well up from within. Why, she questioned, had her parents left her behind? Why had they taken such risks with the weather especially when her father had said the lakes posed such danger - dry in summer, flooded in winter and vice versa? Lorna stopped playing. Blindly she ran her hand over the page of music, an odd sensation playing throughout her fingertips. Her mind returned to John Blow. Just as Madame O said, she remembered how his lament had been composed some seven years before his most famous pupil, Henry Purcell, had written his more celebrated lament from 'Dido and Aeneus'. Inevitably, Lorna's thoughts returned to Madame O who had been responsible for her pupil's increasing interest in Purcell's older teacher. Madame O having made a lifetime's study of English music, would sometime intimate to the girl during lessons that the person "within yourself" needed to make a study of everything whenever possible. 'Do not limit yourself, whether it be music or life. All things are related. Look to the source. Finally one must take into account that which makes the heart beat.' There is no getting away from that last aspect. Lorna felt her heart beating heavily as never before, a great empty weight pounding away at her senses. When she had once tried to imagine aloud what the soul behind the heart looked like, Madame O had answered: "Invisible, of course. That's the mystery."

Light-headedly she had added, "But with a silent voice! Awaiting its hour to come out into the open and sing aloud for all and sundry to hear!"

Now Lorna attempted to remember more of Madame O's thoughts on the subject.

"You see, Lorna, the invisibility is a protective device behoving the souls magical nature so that one has no reason to visualise the soul or invisibility, whichever – since its only reason to exist is to make you aware of its ultimate existence." At the time, Lorna had felt quite satisfied with Madame O's explanation and ever since had upheld the notion that when this mind reaches a blank or the heart aches, it then becomes the duty of the soul to take over and decipher the hitherto diverse hidden meaning and elements, often as not previously inaccessible – that is at least how it appeared to the conscious mind! –Well- Lorna's mind that is.

At the mere thought of such a possibility and change, Lorna became unsteady and experienced that same familiar, bewildering, weakening, sensation starting up from the soles of her bare feet and journeying upwards and through her whole body before settling on her narrow shoulders so that eventually her knees and thighs became jelly-like and threatened to buckle under the weight of her slight frame. She felt her diaphragm freeze and contort, her throat go numb, so that words failed her, but without warning her mind succeeded to retrieve that odd disconnected text wherein instead of words a flood of discordant music notes split and spelt themselves out settling over her senses. Her mind seeped in the emptiness that she so wished to avoid. Yet she started singing to herself. Afterwards, Lorna drew a deep life saving breath, hypo-ventilated drastically. Her parched throat becoming increasingly dryer. Her breath at intervals refusing to escape and free itself from clamped lungs. She half chanted the words 'Veni creator spiritus'. Where, she wondered, had she heard mention of the Latin text before? She may remember shortly but now with barely a breath nor a sound, she resolutely closed shut the piano lid, turned the key in the lock and replaced it high up on a shelf where she stacked her music scores. Next she drew the curtains across the music room window leaving a chink where the curtains nearly met so that a single ray of light etched its way in a narrow strip down past her features. Lorna peered through the narrow gap to glance briefly skyward before turning away and finding her way back into the hallway.

For some ungovernable reason, the moment she closed the door behind her, her mood changed. A welcome fragment of childhood returned. One of those events caught in a time warp that had sent her parents and grandparents into stitches of laughter at the sight of Lorna dancing and generally playing the 'madcap' whilst singing that irresistible little Irish ditty with its charming chronicle of bitter-sweet words as she at this very moment pranced around in the semi-darkness in a wild danse-macabre. Scarcely able to see ahead of her, the world today her oyster as the child Lorna pretended to dust with an invisible wand and 'trip the light fantastic', play hopscotch on the tiles and just as impulsively stop at the end of the first refrain; to catch her breath, clench her bottom lip between her teeth, swallow hard forcing herself to breath normally. But all that is a throw back now she sighed deeply, and presently stood at the bottom of the stairs where she waited half-listening in the dimness, but not the merest whisper nor sound greeted her. Now she should finish the song where she left off but characteristically she'd forgotten the rest of the words.

Chapter Fifteen

Visions and Dialogues

Lorna's eyes became attuned to the semi-darkness and peered forth towards the unlit staircase. Clutching tightly on the banister to steady herself, she began to climb the stairs towards the light. Numbed with cold she stood on the landing surveying the nocturnal scene depicted in 'The Journey of the Spirit', the title Irene Budge had bestowed on her complex tapestry which she had single handedly and slavishly needled at for the best part of ten years.

Never one given over to unnecessary talk Irene had in the last decade of her life happened upon a rewarding and consuming pastime whereby, in her own words, she could concentrate all her free time and "utilize the silence to the full". Tapestry weaving suited her like a glove. Having brought up a small family, a boy and a girl, she had sought fulfilment in an entirely different area of creation which she chanced to come by when she received a book illustrated in full colour dealing with the Issenheim Altar in Colmar – a major work initially painted for the Convent of Issenheim in Alsace. Carried away by the book's contents, she'd decided to try her hand at something she had never attempted before and thus began her own very personal and highly original re-interpretation of the German masterwork, casting herself headlong into the exercise with ever increasing efficiency and enthusiasm inextricably turning the task around into one of a total 'idee fixe'.

Gradually, she divested herself of all other tasks and duties she considered menial, and over the next years made a point of embarking upon several visits to Colmar where to this day the work hangs. Each time she returned back home with a wealth of new interpretive ideas, so impressed had she been when confronted with the series of life size altar pieces. For one whose artistic skills up until then had been somewhat limited, Irene Budge surprised all who knew her when her dormant creative talents were revealed so fulminately. How did she accomplish this formidable feat? they asked. Perhaps a clue lay in her own admission that: "You never know what can be achieved until you will the spirit from its niche".

Because little had been known of the master of the redoubtable altarpiece, Irene Budge had become doubly intrigued with the mystery surrounding the work. History related how for 300 years the painter's true name had remained unknown. Irene lamented: "Can you imagine? A man paints a series of masterpieces and becomes anonymous simply because some ignominious culprit neglected to obtain the painter's correct name!" Irene could not tolerate ignorance since she based intolerance on that wholly contemptible and unacceptable universal characteristic. She noted the fact that Mathias Grünewald, the name by which he is still called today, was none other than Mathis Neithardt (1460-1528). In his time he was known as Gotthardt and was also mentioned as Mathis von Aschaffenburg, the latter, the name of the German town of his origins. At the time this information neatly tied in with Irene's already portentous sense of mystery awaiting imminent artistic release.

As Lorna begins to read one of the banners 'Lumine de Lumine' – "Light of light" sewn into a corner of the tapestry she experiences an irresistible urge to enter into that mystic world she now faces. In fact she has no option. She feels herself escaping to become an indwelling part of that other world and its occupants that Irene Budge has depicted so realistically. At a given moment Lorna's mind undergoes radical and total transformation. Her sight is drawn upwards to a single span of pale blue wings in relief skimming the heavens. The appearance of the bird brings back memories of Mozart's "Gentle Zephrs" from "Idomeneo" an aria Lorna so wanted to sing, had if not posed so many vocal difficulties. However now gazing out at the 'infinite', she contends all that shall come to pass, convinced soon she shall be empowered to sing anything she pleases!

Watching the tapestry bird slowly 'dip and soar', the girls mind and body is taken over by a pleasant floating sensation similar to the rapt state induced by her fantasy dreams, placed there to release her from the difficult constraints of an existence that tragically robbed her of family life. Presently she perceives herself in a suddenly unfamiliar yet peculiarly welcoming wilderness beckoning her adrift. The perfume of Mimosa, old fashioned Mignonette and Wood Violets fills the air as if nature is compensating for last years dead leaves, and dried twigs laying strewn underfoot. Lorna recalls past holidays spent with her family at the lakes when she had tested the meagre carrying power of her inadequate voice over the surface of the waters.

Her gaze obliquely transfixed skywards, Lorna experienced the strange illusion she is looking down from a great height as her thoughts travel back and forth to the day when Irene Budge had chosen to unveil before her family the finished tapestry of "The Journey of the Spirit". At the time, and till today, the work never failed to envelop Lorna into its mystery.

On a bank by her side a thornless crimson rose bush is in full bloom. Lorna cannot draw her eyes away from the contents of the tapestry as it 'billows in the breeze'. She marvels at the lifelike details her mother captured. The blue dove, and the angel Gabriel, who now so resembles her brother, a little older perhaps, as he attempts to lessen the shock of his sudden appearance from nowhere, until momentarily he skims back across the lake. Although he does not utter a word his eyes alone tell her what she most wishes to know, namely that shortly he will reappear with both of her parents. At the prospects Lorna's breath comes in short sharp shock waves. Now her attention is constantly drawn to the ancient Isaiah who points to the book of prophecies whereby the illuminated Latin text stands out in glittering relief.

Ecco virgo conceput et pariet filium et vocabitur nomen emes

Behold a virgin shall conceive, and bear a son,

and shall call his name Immanuel.

Butter and honey shall he eat, that he may know

To refuse the evil, and choose the good.

Isaiah, Chapter 7/14,15.

Lorna's mind is working overtime. So much is happening. Isaiah ties the book's seals together and hands it to Lorna.

"Open it" he tells her, "undo it".

The package becomes too heavy for Lorna to lift. She hesitates. Delay seems preferable to time passing. Slowly she unties the knot. Revealed before her a handsome reel to reel tape recorder, its design well in advance of its time. What is more, it is connected to twin amplifiers. A separate box reveals a carefully tethered pile of some 30 or more recording tapes. All she need do at this stage is connect the machine to the electricity to set it in motion, select a tape and play it. But before she sets the tape in motion she pauses. From far off Madame O's voice reassuringly calls to her, "Well Lorna, how long are we to wait my dear before you deign to sing?" Lorna closes her eyes, perceives she has little or no option but to carry out her teacher's bidding. Otherwise she fears that Madame O will postpone their all important next lesson when amongst other things Lorna intends to give Madame the reasons for her recent career-changing decision despite guessing Madame O will be the first person to tell her "Good! Take possession of yourself. Take the risk. Don't postpone any longer that which you are destined for. Go ahead, if needs be attempt the impossible. What have you to lose, Lorna? You only have yourself to answer to."

But Lorna need not have tried nor worried. Something within has already become unknotted and her once inert voice voluntarily emerged and effortlessly took over. Lorna's vocal cords rang out through her whole being. Never before had her voice felt so responsive, able to produce faultless sounds through and from the very core of her being. How many times had Madame O advised her?" "When the worst comes to the worst, just open your mouth like the birds do and sing. That way the voice rewardingly takes over and finds itself."

"Do you mean to let go and relax completely?" Lorna asks in an almost inaudible small voice.

"Of course not, Lorna heaven forbid if you relaxed completely you'd surely be dead."

For the first time ever, Lorna believed her voice soaring to the point where she no longer knew quite who why or what sang. Although it had a familiar ring to it, she could not identify the melody nor the lyrics. Her mind rested in between different trains of thought whereby the music remained anonymous. Until Madame O congratulated her, "Ah, at last Lorna, yes that is exactly what I mean by Bel Canto. This is indeed wonderful! Is not that the ideal spontaneity you've so desired and wished for all these years? Well, today my dear you can be more than well contented and proud. Your voice is doing precisely what it wanted to do, rather than not what it doesn't want. No longer egged on by those damaging barriers – the musician's worst enemy. The self – the ego: one and the same unwelcome twin guests, have been dispatched to oblivion where they belong, never more to return. One only wrongly imagined they were required." Madame O's voice trailed off.

"There now Lorna did you ever imagine yourself singing Paer"s Coloratura Showpiece "O Dolce Contento" "Well did you? - Comme un oiseau".

Lorna heeded. Madames" words. Everything had its rightful time and place. Presently that other wonderfully ubiquitous voice became instilled within Lorna's chest cavity, rose and fell triumphantly, surrounding the girl with its message that tripped off her tongue as next she actually heard herself, for the first time ever, sing the contralto air from Handel's 'Judas Maccabeas".

Oh thou that tellest good tidings

to Zion

Arise shine

For thy life is done...

That last sentence "For thy life is done" sank deeply into the girls thoughts. Again she recalled past times when she'd all but forgotten the words to a familiar song and Madame O had told her, "Don't let it worry you, Lorna. Everything, happiness and sadness is retained in the upper reaches of our heads where the spirit lodges throughout our lifetime. Ideally, we simply choose to leave well alone what we do not require at the time. But, when the time arrives and we truly need to resurrect that which lies dormant, our unconscious, need only signal forth and our whole past existence returns to remind us of precious events which made our past existence so fruitful and worthwhile."

Wonder of wonders, Lorna vouchsafed as she began to have visions of her whole life passing before her in brilliant illuminated fragments. The sheer overwhelming happiness of it enswathed her. It is to be the first time she 'sees|" and hears exactly what her heart desires.

After Lorna realised exactly what her teacher had meant in the past when she often intimated to her, "Lorna, sometimes all that is required of the singer for everything to fall naturally into place is to simply open the mouth till the inevitable rise and fall of the notes appears!" But on that past particular occasion, a momentary but very noticeable lapse of pitch had occurred in the girl's voice to remind her of Madame O's advice that "Old habits die slowly especially when the voice is given too much leeway. Its swoons and relaxes too much, loses height. Remember Lorna, there's a half-way house between releasing tension and letting go altogether." Afterwards 'Lorna's voice' attained to its full measure of accuracy without the merest sign or hint of faulty intonation anymore. Today Lorna's mind forever in the process of re-focussing; could be likened to a wonderful virgin spring renewed in the form of a vast tapestry of events in which both family and music are bound together wavering before her. It's true, she considered, nothing had been lost nor forgotten, just crystallised and stored. A flashback: she is at a student's performance of Janacek's opera 'The Cunning Little Vixen', and is sitting next to Madame O. She dare not turn sideways for fear of Madame O noticing how unbearably moved she has become by the work with its story of renewal and rebirth. That experience has stayed with her to this day. Another time, Madame O told her, "One need only listen and watch to discover the inherent magic in most things – even to the point of closing your eyes and shutting your ears!" Lorna had puzzled over that oddly contradictory statement.

"Well there are things I'll never understand," Lorna had despondently declared.

"Be patient."

Madame O objected. "It simply means my dear child you're not quite ready for them. By way of innate virtue each element has its redoubtable time and place. If you wish enough, these elements will discover you and finally appear with the force of a revelation. If that is, the need is great enough. However if you fight shy of them, criticize and condemn negatively, you waste and dissipate valuable time. No, Lorna, allow yourself to be overtaken, and believe me one revelation after the other will follow in your wake."

Those words vividly imprinted themselves on Lorna's permanently receptive mind. Next she foresaw herself turning pages in Madame O's book, 'Colcancas – A Singer's Creed'.

Madame O had dedicated a whole chapter to Gustav Mahler's large symphonic song – cycle in six movements "Das Lied Von Der Erde." 'The Song of the Earth' written for Contralto and Tenor soloist. Lorna comes to the section dealing with the last song. 'The Farewell' – 'Der Abschied' and carefully reads the words "All longing now turns to dreaming… I stand here waiting for my friend… where are you? You have left me alone so long.

He dismounted and gave him the parting cup,

He asked him where

He was going, and also why it must be.

He spoke, and his tones were veiled.

Er stieg vom Pferd und reichte ihm den Trunk

des Abschieds dar. Er fragte ihn, wohin

er fuhre und auch warum es mubte sein.

Er sprach, seine Stimme war umflort.

Still is my heart; it is awaiting its hours!

Everywhere

Spring

Everywhere

Still ist mein Herz und harret seiner Stunde!

At the end of the lyrics Madame O had written: "In the singing voice of an English Contralto I had found my ideal voice for the Mahler work, so that the music takes on added depth, and as such can become an unbearably moving experience." The lyrics written by Mahler himself left Lorna at her most vulnerable even though she had never heard the work performed. Looking back Lorna could only recall Madame O making brief mention of that unique English Contralto. Lorna turns the pages of the score included in the chapter and begins to disjointedly hum the words in German. Afterwards she reflects upon the text and remains deeply affected.

Chapter Sixteen

Metamorphosis

When Lorna closed the pages on the Mahler chapter it is as if time ceases to have any meaning. Indeed it is at that moment in time that she reads Mado"s shaky handwriting.

Dear Lorna,

Until now you will have been wondering why I kept 'the star singer' from you. I had no choice, my dear. He and his parents have disappeared as far as I am concerned from off the face of the earth. All I can tell you is this. By some odd stroke of fate, I believe he and his family took their holidays at the same place as you and your parents did. I have received no replies to my letters, nor have the family as much as sent me a postcard. It is for this reason I fear the worst. How I longed for you to share that miraculous voice with me in person. It was not to be, you understand. However, nothing is lost. As I told you sometime ago, because from our very first encounter to the last, I recorded every single note of his at the beginning of our first meeting, and thereafter some fifty hours of great singing, Looking back to that first encounter with him I confess I am bound to say at the first hearing of the voice, I had actually been much disappointed by the feeble colourless sound that I heard, but I swiftly realized my mistake, the outcome of which you shall bear witness to on these precious tapes. Of course, as I write these words, I bitterly lament the passing of my health which is now in utter decline and who knows if it can ever improve? Should it not then, before it is too late, I have made the decision to bequeath this extraordinary singing legacy to you, for safe keeping since I have full confidence in your integrity. A surprise awaits you on one of the tapes marked 'DIDO'. You can be proud.

Yours

R.O.

I'm afraid I can't write anymore Adieu – Till - (here the letter stopped abruptly).

Over the next days, Lorna's sadness and pain is gradually taken over by the reward of again hearing the magical 'voice'. Slowly and mechanically she sifts through the tapes. On each tape container the word 'Coloratura' is boldly spelt out followed by the contents giving the names and recorded dates of various arias and songs. She placed a tape on the machine and pressed the start button.

Immediately emerging from its 'chrysalis' there follows 'the magic voice of voices' just as Lorna vividly recalls hearing from 'Windermere' Cottage, when it illuminated everything around. In a succession of brilliant show pieces the voice increases in radiance. Night passes into day. Lorna changes one tape after the other revealing to her hitherto virtually unknown Virtuoso arias written for Farinelli. Rossini, Donizetti, Paer, Delibes, Meyerbeer and Weber arias follow. Replete with the miracle of the tapes, again Lorna begins to listen to a bewildering series of Mozart concert arias that show the 'star singer' off to perfection. Lorna as never before is overtaken and drawn into Mozart's vocal music. Next she finds a tape that Mado has not labelled Coloratura but Contralto. The girl places this reel on the turntable and switches on the machine, and this time listens to another revelation – the boy is singing the contralto parts to the St John Passion and St Mathew Passion, the 'Agnus

Dei' from the B Minor Mass and various other sacred pieces after which there is a pause before Mado begins to play on the piano Mahler's last song of Farewell. Mado is accompanying throughout, painting colour harmonies and transparencies on the piano as only she knows how, so that Lorna is able to imagine a whole orchestra accompanying the voice rather than a single instrument.

Several times throughout that last song, the marvellous voice falters on the words 'Er stieg vom Pferd und reichte ihm den Trunk' and again 'Still ist mein Herz und harret seiner Stunde!' and almost omits the final 'Ewig' as it disappears into the distance. Lorna, deathly still, catches her breath as she whispers into the all pervasive silence the words – 'Anew! Forever Ewig Ewig. Forever forever,' gently, ringing forth imprinted upon the ether ushering from the depths of her whole being. Everything is born anew. Lorna lifts the tape from the turntable and places it safely back in its container. One last tape remains to be played, the one with 'Dido' spelt out on its cover. The moment Lorna sets it in motion she is greeted by Mado's voice announcing, "the voice you are about to hear is that of a twenty year old pupil, Lorna Rosemary Budge." So many times I have listened to this particular recording made in 1939, and I state unreservedly, from beginning to end there is nothing here in the singing to default.

The piano began and Lorna"s voice of five years ago entered: There follow Lorna's four most sung pieces ending with 'Didos Lament" that Mado had attached such importance to.

Darkness shades me

On thy bosom let me rest.

More I would but Death invades me;

Death is now a welcome guest.

When I am laid in earth, may my wrongs create

No trouble in my breast

Remember me! But ah, forget my fate.

Given to further reflection Lorna's mind fights to deal with Mado's Laudatory comments which have the effect of redeeming and elating the girl, but before she is further given to reflection a violet shadow skims overhead. At close range Lorna catches a glimpse of a bird, its blue and silver feathers glinting with unearthly tints from tip to tail, its eyes the colour of sapphires. Tingling cadenzas, flawless extended trills and cascading couplets accompanying its unerring instinct for the flight of the music that determined it keep climbing further till it reached its warbling's zenith. Now Lorna fully realised what Mado had meant when she had described "an endless coloratura tapestry of sublime sounds gathered together in an eternal panoply of sung notes.

The bird, lark-like continues to soar and reach beyond itself. Each renewed set of scales growing increasingly disembodied and softer than the previous ones, until exhausted, caught in the rays of the dying sun the wings barely visible, flap lifelessly, gently disengage as it floats earthwards. Its distant song accompanying the fast fading colours of the sun sinking behind a dark cloud. Lorna feels a strangely weightless tingling sensation throughout her body and reflects upon how so small a creature could contain such a wealth of height and depth in its spectacular song. Her eyes remain on the bird. In the meantime a remarkably soothing sigh, becoming increasingly sweeter and clearer settles upon her ears before she realises it surges from within, to escape upwards through her, finally hovering overhead. Encircling her in a cloud of diamond bright echoes. Each rendered sound in turn becoming more velvety and resonant, softer and deeper as the blue vision finally descends back to earth.

As Lorna's eyes stray from the bird, her thoughts return to the time when Irene Budge chose to unveil her finished tapestry with the Latin parable sewn to one side spelling: "Illum aportet crescere me autem minui", "He must grow while I diminish". Soon Lorna felt herself gazing down from an immense height. All at once she surveyed everything she has previously known as though borrowed from a previous life, whilst the tapestry, self accordingly billowed and increased magically in size until it filled the sky. Repeatedly reading those haunting words, "He must grow while I diminish," Lorna slowly began to realize their true portent, unlike when they had been first explained to her all those years ago.

She recalled how Irene Budge's idea had been to add stars that were not in the original Grünewald masterpiece, and now as evening approached, Lorna realized why; because her mother's vision had been nocturnal working late into the night to finish the tapestry. So it seemed perfectly natural and befitting that the "blessed candles of the night" should eventually fill the woman's particular version of the sky.

With her ears still ringing from the trail of spellbinding vocal roulades, cadenzas and embellishments Lorna allowed her exhausted body to sink back down into the cool tall grass by the riverbank.

When next she opened her eyes a new day had begun. But the moment she attempted to utter a sound not even the merest hint of a whisper or breath issued forth. She lay unable to move. Everything within having deserted her as her mind is virtually turning in on itself, drained. At best she can mutely mouth her brother's name through her parched throat. Effortfully she coaxes her body into doing her bidding and finally raises herself as one guided and directed by some great unknown all-seeing force. Next she perceived herself to be kneeling forward. Her hair loose, her dress faded. Her pale face reflected in the silent mirror surface of the lake. Throughout these moments a mere whisper of the ubiquitous voice is enough to wholly embrace her mind, body and soul, assuage her thoughts, and caress her slight form back into motion. The ever-changing sky now charged with violet and indigo glinted and glowed over the water. The air has become moist with dew and nectar. Gradually throughout that long last day spasmodically Lorna's strength returns and with it at last her voice.

In the afterglow Lorna scarcely need open her mouth for the notes in her voice to slowly rise mist like from the furthermost point of her toes; to climb and settle forth upon the crown of her head, the voice's final all powerful launching pad for pouring forth in song. Gleaming and resonating across the lake.

"Exactly Lorna! Just perfect"

Mado's voice beckons to her student "again – again Lorna".

The girl obeys, stutters out the lyrics of the blessed Virgin's expostulation. "Tell me, tell me some – some pit-ying angel... Quickly, quickly – little footsteps press unregarded through the wilderness. I call, I call. Gabriel, Gabriel. He comes not"....

"Such a difficult piece Lorna and you've conquered it! But what of the new pieces you promised me?"

For a moment Lorna registers bewilderment.

"Again a 'voice of voices' launches into a spectacular vocal display – a true virtuoso aria from Graun's "Montezuma", interspersed with another section of

Purcell's jubilant stuttering Expostulation – was it a Waking Dream that did fore-tell thy Wondrous birth? Thy Wondrous, Wondrous, Wondrous vision…"

Now as she'd promised, Lorna believes herself capable of all sorts of fresh vocal feats. Albeit she has only to think upon the 'voice of voices' for it to take over her whole being, and shelve her faulty intonation forever as a thing of the past.

Likewise her limited range. When Mado asks her how she managed the difficult tessitura so easily Lorna answers simply. "My head is spinning, I felt as if I were flying."

"And when you took the unbelievable A in Alt?"

"Yes, it is true Madame, I was a cage bird in flight liberated at last from its shackles".

"Wonderful Lorna, that explains everything.", "But that is enough for one day, you are tired and you must rest".

Lorna nods in affirmation listening as never before. She sits under a wide tapestry of stars in the midnight blue sky. Watches the flowers turn pale in the moonlight. The word 'coloratura' indelibly glistens imprinted in her mind and on the tape reels laying at her feet. Everywhere. She gazes towards the far shore. Any moment now she can expect Gabriel to return with her parents and everything will be born anew. She repeats to herself 'Anew!' Forever – Ewig. Ewig!. The words spell out fulfilment of a kind she has never known. Her body airborne weightless relaxes slowly. She rests her head upon a cushion of soft earth – closes her eyes, - relaxes, a wide smile beams across her face.

Relaxes completely, as one by one the last stars fade to shine anew upon another shore.

Epilogue

Some time later Joseph Rosenblatt is disturbed that he cannot contact the girl. He decides to visit her at home. When he arrives at the house, the front door is ajar. He calls her name. There is no answer. He climbs the stairs and enters her bedroom. Lorna is not there. At her bedside a page from her diary is open at the last entry. Joseph notes the handwriting bears a strong resemblance to that of their teacher. It reads: a tale of the spirit ever moving forward, proving that within each and everyone of us reclines the artist, if only, that is we choose, or wish it so.

Joseph slowly leaves the house and wanders outside into what has become a veritable wilderness. He falters in his tracks. Some distance from the house, at the water's edge almost hidden in the tall grass he finds his friend Lorna. Her head rests gently upon the damp earth. On all sides she is surrounded by tape reels, neatly tucked in their cardboard sleeves. As he, silently bends down over her, he can take comfort in the knowledge that the serene radiant smile on her face tells him she has died peacefully, accompanied by wondrous dreams and visions.

Made in the USA
Charleston, SC
08 September 2016